The Salukis in My Life

Here, there and everywhere from the Arab World to China

The Salukis in My Life

Here, there and everywhere from the Arab World to China

Published by

Medina Publishing Ltd
310 Ewell Road
Surbiton
Surrey KT6 7AL
medinapublishing.com

© Sir Terence Clark 2018

ISBN: 978-1-911487-03-6

Designed by Kitty Carruthers
Calligraphy by Taha al-Hiti, Mustafa Ja'afar & Sir Terence Clark
Printed and bound by Interak Printing Company, Poland

All photographs from Sir Terence Clark collection, except the following:
Gertrude Bell Archive, Newcastle University p42; Lord Lichfield p62; Professor Joan Oates p86; Peers Carter p140; Margret Tamp p152; Brian Duggan p316.

CIP Data: A catalogue record for this book is available from the British Library.

The Salukis in My Life

Here, there and everywhere from the Arab World to China

Terence Clark

Medina Publishing

As-Salūqī by Mustafa Ja'far

For all my Iraqi and Syrian friends and their hounds whose way of life
in recent years has been destroyed in local conflicts.

Contents

Acknowledgements

This series of adventures with my elegant companions of the chase would not have come about without the advice, encouragement and support of so many people that I could not possibly thank them all here by name, though I have mentioned most of them in the text. I am, however, particularly grateful to two of my outstanding mentors in the Middle East – Subhi Yasin Agha in Iraq and Badr Khan al-Barazi in Syria – who gave so generously of their vast knowledge of the desert-bred Saluki in my early days in the breed. I am also grateful to Adrian Phillips, the late Paul Sagar, the late Rosie Lewis and her husband Chris from the Saluki or Gazelle Hound Club for guiding me throught the formalities of coursing in this country on my return here.

My Salukis have been celebrated in various art forms but I am most grateful to Gillian Heywood for the watercolour from the time when we lived in Oman that decorates the cover of this book and for the portrait of Tayra on page 137. I am also deeply indebted to my friend and master calligrapher, Taha al-Hiti, not only for the masterpiece on the back cover but for his beautifully executed chapter headings from the *Tardiyat*, or hunting poems, of the great Abbasid poet Abu Nuwas and Abu al-Fadl Ahmad bin Abi Tahir, with their translations by Rex Smith and M.A.S. Abdel Haleem (1978), the complete texts of which may be found in the Annex. My former calligraphy tutor, Mustafa Ja'far, was also kind enough to give me two other calligraphic illustrations. My former diplomatic colleague Sir Alan Munro kindly gave me permission to reproduce the portrait of one of his Salukis by Patrick Lichfield as well as some of his Saluki anecdotes, as did another former colleague, Gordon Pirie. Yet another former colleague, the late Peers Carter, had previously given me permission to publish the story of his most unusual Afghan hound. The Gertrude Bell Archive at Newcastle University also gave me their kind permission to reproduce the photograph of Gertrude Bell's father and her two Salukis in Baghdad. Kitty Carruthers of Medina Publishing deserves my warm thanks for bringing the book together so effectively, and Martin Rickerd, who copy-edited the text so meticulously. I also thank Brian Duggan for his constant encouragement and support.

My deepest gratitude goes to Liese for her patience with our often demanding companions, particularly during times of my absence, and for putting up with my hours on the computer getting these words down.

Foreword

'Is that your girlfriend, Mister?'

The cheeky jibe came from the young driver of a car that had pulled up beside me at a red traffic light on a hot London summer afternoon. His eye had been caught by the silky head of our Saluki, *Sabah*, sitting upright on the passenger seat beside me. And no surprise, for these most elegant of hounds invariably attract the attention.

This ancient breed, recorded from early times in monumental art and known by a variety of names from the steppes of Central Asia and throughout Iran, Turkey and Arabia's sands to the Atlas ranges of North Africa, has become an all-absorbing passion for Terence Clark and his wife Liese. For them the Saluki has been not only a firm family friend but also an opportunity for active sport through hunting, coursing and the show ring in Britain and abroad.

Like the Clarks, my own involvement with these handsome and affectionate, if wilful, sighthounds began in the Middle East on a visit to a desert encampment of Al Mutair bedouin during a spell at the British Embassy in Kuwait in the early 1960s. Having understood that dogs in general are proscribed as unclean animals within Islamic culture, it came as a surprise to see several of these hounds around the dark goat's-hair tents. I was soon reassured that a convenient dispensation was made for the fastidiously clean Saluki, so invaluable to the tribe as a provider, along with the hawk, of game in the sparse desert environment, be it gazelle, hare or fox. I came away with a lively black and tan feathered puppy, *Sabah*, who was to become a part of our close family, in Lebanon and Libya as well as in London. Indeed he found himself much in demand for siring purposes as his arrival coincided with a crisis among the breed in Britain through the spread of progressive retinal disease as a result of inbreeding and an absence of fresh Arabian gene stock.

Sabah and his successors were to give us years of companionship, as well as plenty of exercise. Here is an animal with a stamina that can well outrun its greyhound cousins over a distance, and that likes nothing better than the sensation of loose sand between its webbed toes, be it on desert or seaside beach. Here too is great character that would afford us memorable adventures over the years, some of which are recounted in this book. Never underestimate Salukis for getting into a scrape and then, with native intelligence, getting themselves out of it. Among episodes that come to mind are a visit in the middle of the night by a young police constable in Notting Hill to check out an allegation by some busybody that we owned a half-starved dog; an impressive feat of canine memory navigation through a network of London streets back to the doorstep of a newly occupied house after running off in the park; a close-finish win in a race on a greyhound track in rural Bedfordshire; and, best of all, the causing by our splendid cream Saluki, *Mancha*, of two runway closures and one aborted take-off from Heathrow following his serial escapes from aircraft cargo holds en route to Algiers.

Hunting ranged from rabbits on the Sussex Downs to feral cats in Algeria, and, less benign, a couple of chases after a doe in Richmond Park and a flock of sheep, both fortunately unsuccessful. There was one merciful instance in Libya of the Saluki's instinctive and singular hunting style, coupled with its strong sense of loyalty to its human family, when my wife found herself menaced on the shore outside Benghazi by a pack of the pi-dogs that infested the town. Without hesitation, *Sabah* charged the pack leader and, inserting his long nose between the brute's forelegs, flipped him into the air to land heavily on his back. The pack fled while *Sabah* returned well content. We were subsequently told by Arab friends that it was a traditional Saluki hunting technique to overtake its gazelle prey and halt it with a flick of its strong neck muscles. *Sabah* did try it once again, more rashly, on a cantering horse I was riding.

Terence Clark's travels in pursuit of Salukis and their cousins have taken him far and wide, from China to Morocco, through conflict – the first Gulf War – and, in more peaceful times, on hospitable hunting expeditions in remote communities and as participant and judge in more splendid arenas. His commitment to the study, enjoyment and preservation of the breed is total. It is encouraging to read how the Saluki is now recovering its popularity in ancestral regions, and especially within Arabia. I had been discouraged on my return to Saudi Arabia in the early 1990s to find how the Salukis that were so often to be seen ten years earlier had almost disappeared – into the cooking pots of Korean construction workers, it was alleged. The few that were to be found had mostly been imported from English kennels. Today sees a welcome change, with the advent of nationally sponsored breeding centres and public race meetings. This is despite the imposition of hunting bans in several countries, including England, where this has brought an end to the sport of hare coursing. The Clarks have played a significant part in this revival. Their story, recounted in lively detail, deserves its place in the canon of canine literature.

Alan Munro

Were it not for the chase, there would be no pleasure – Anon

Introduction

I was born into a family with no connections with animals, least of all Salukis, or the countryside and lived the first years of my life in a flat in London. As for so many people of my generation, the Second World War changed everything. My father was called up to the army and served mainly abroad throughout the war. My mother, older sister and I were evacuated from London after our flat was bombed and we went to live on a farm on the Norfolk–Suffolk border in the fen country of eastern England.

Life on the farm was totally different from anything I had experienced before and I loved it from the beginning. The fens are by their very nature flat and as a result you could see for miles in all directions, which may be why I have always felt happiest in the freedom of wide, open spaces. In winter, the fens would freeze and we would have such fun sliding and skating about among the frozen reeds. In summer, we would help with making the hay and bringing it into the barns for the animals. There were all kinds of animals to look after and play with, but I remember most the Rhode Island Red hens, especially collecting their eggs still warm from the nest, and the rabbits, which were kept for their meat and not as pets. The nearest village was a couple of kilometres away and we walked to school and back no matter the weather, learning at an early age to look after ourselves and not complain. This idyll came to an end after only about 18 months. The farm lay under the flight path of our bombers flying on missions over the Continent. One night a returning aircraft crashed in flames near the farm. My mother thought that was too close a call and decided that we should move to somewhere safer.

We went to live in a village in Buckinghamshire, surrounded by woods and fields, with the River Thames nearby. Here I spent so many happy hours out of school exploring the countryside and learning its ways. I can still recall the thrill of the first hare I had ever seen as it lay motionless in its seat before leaping away from under my feet. I could identify all the birds, insects and the life in the chalk streams that fed into the Thames, in which I learnt to swim among the watering cows without a care for health and safety. We kept a black Persian cat and I wept when he came home one day trailing his rear legs from an injury to his back, which had been caught in a snare. He had to be put down and I was given my first pet of my own, an albino rabbit – or so I thought. But this was wartime, and food rationing meant that it, too, would end up in the pot; it proved a hard lesson not to become too sentimental about animals that were there to sustain us.

Moving back to London after the war was a shock. Fortunately, we now lived close to a vast park and I was allowed to have my first dog. *Rikki* (named after Rikki-Tikki-Tavi, the mongoose in Rudyard Kipling's *The Jungle Book*) was a black Labrador–Terrier cross and became my constant companion; however, on grounds of hygiene I never allowed him or any subsequent dogs to sleep in the same room with me. *Rikki* was eventually struck down by distemper, a prevalent canine disease in those days. He was replaced by *Rikki II*, a similar crossbred who, like his predecessor, accompanied me on my training runs through the park for my favourite sport of cross-country running. He too was claimed by disease but, in any case, I had moved on to higher education, compulsory military service for two years and entry into the British Diplomatic Service, where, at least initially, there was no scope for dogs.

Having already qualified as a Russian interpreter in the Royal Air Force, I had imagined that on entry to the Diplomatic Service I would deal principally with the Soviet Union and its satellites in Eastern Europe. However, things turned out rather differently. It was thought that as I had already shown the ability to handle one hard language, I could probably take on another, e.g. Arabic. So it was that, after a full semester at the School of Oriental and African Studies at the University of London, I embarked for Beirut in Lebanon to attend for the following 15 months a total immersion course at the Middle East Centre for Arab Studies in the village of

Shemlan in the Shuf mountains high above the capital. It was a challenging experience in such a completely different environment, but it was also increasingly rewarding as my developing confidence in the language opened up unimagined vistas. I was able to travel extensively in Lebanon and Syria, establishing with the latter a relationship that was to prove central to my life with Salukis later.

My service over the next period took me to Bahrain, Jordan and Morocco, but my acquaintance with the breed was at most subliminal. I had begun to study in Bahrain the poetry of the period in Arabic history called the *Jahiliyya* or 'Ignorance', before the coming of Islam to Arabia in the 7th century. The pre-Islamic poets wrote evocatively of the life of the desert nomads, including hunting with hawk and hound. I remember in particular a poem by Labid ibn Rabia al-Amiri in which he describes graphically a female oryx being hunted by a pair of hounds, who turn her at bay but are then skewered on her spear-like horns. At the time I was concentrating more on the difficult vocabulary than the type of hounds involved and, in any case, neither then nor for years afterwards had I so much as glimpsed a Saluki anywhere in the Middle East. Considering that the Saluki is an indigenous hound, that may sound strange but, in fact, it is the common experience of most travellers in the region. As I discovered much later, Salukis were regarded as such precious possessions that they were generally kept out of sight for fear they might be stolen or simply admired by someone to whom the owners might feel obliged to gift them in accordance with Arab custom.

Meanwhile, I had married Liese in Amman and our first son was born in Morocco, where we acquired a Japanese Chin, called *Li Chang*, as a companion for him, though sadly only for a year or so. I had a horse-riding accident and broke my leg badly, so that I had to be flown back to England for a long period of treatment and recuperation, followed by a period of duty at the Foreign Office. With our then tough quarantine regulations and Liese's other preoccupations, we felt obliged to leave *Li Chang* in Morocco in a more settled environment with friends.

After I was literally back on my feet, I returned to the Gulf with my family and spent more than three happy years in Dubai, where two more children were born. My work took me all over the area we now call the United Arab Emirates. We also explored and camped at weekends in the desert and along the coast. I even went out with some of the young shaikhs hunting for houbara bustard with their falcons. But still I did not see a single Saluki. They were undoubtedly there, as I discovered much later; and this was, after all, only a mere 15 years or so after the great British explorer

Wilfred Thesiger had hunted with Salukis in that area, as he described so vividly in his masterpiece *Arabian Sands*. So, consciously or unconsciously, I had been bitten by the desert bug and had experienced in real life some of the romance described by the Arab poets. As time went by, I became even more immersed in the Middle East and its traditions.

But first I had a break from the region in what was then Yugoslavia, to where we took another dog as a companion for our three children. She was a Shih Tzu called *Popsy*, who proved to be a really feisty little terrier and gave us much pleasure. Sadly, we had to leave her with friends when we were transferred back to London, rather than put her through quarantine for six months.

In 1973 I returned to the Middle East with a posting to Muscat in Oman, where at last I saw my first Saluki. He was a cream feathered dog called *Pasha*, originally from Jordan, and belonged to some expatriate British people who were about to return to England and were unsure what to do about him. He was already 11 years old and it was thought that he would not survive the journey and quarantine. We loved the look of him and offered to take him in, but it was decided that the change would be too traumatic, so he was put down. Nevertheless, I resolved there and then that when our circumstances permitted we would have such a Saluki, though I did not realise that it would take more than a decade of service in Europe before an opportunity arose.

In the interval and later, people would ask me what was so special about having a Saluki. I had done some research and one of the aspects that most impressed me was the breed's antiquity. Most breeds are creations of the last century or two, whereas the origins of the Saluki are lost in the mists of time, though there is some archaeological evidence to suggest that a similar hunting hound evolved in the area of Ancient Mesopotamia at least 6,000 years ago. Indeed, recent research into Saluki DNA has confirmed its ancient lineage and its uniqueness to the region of South-West Asia (Ahrens, 2016). Saluki-type hounds were also vividly represented in the art of Ancient Egypt (Houlihan, 1996), perhaps most evocatively on the so-called Painted Box found among the grave goods of Tutankhamun. It is also clear from the literary record that in the period before Islam the Saluki was important for the very existence of the bedouin in the Arabian Peninsula (Smith and Abdel Haleem, 1978) as a meat provider, a role that earned for it an elevated place in bedouin society as evidenced by being given a name and genealogies. As the conquering Arabs fanned out from the

Arabian Peninsula under the banner of Islam to Spain in the west and Central Asia in the east, they took their hounds with them (Clark, 1999). Hunting in all its forms probably reached its peak in the full flowering of the Abbasid Caliphate in Baghdad in the 8th to 11th centuries, when the nobility maintained huge establishments of beasts and birds of prey (Ahsan, 1979), but it remained a popular pastime throughout the later Ottoman Caliphate and with independent rulers in other parts of the region. Although most of the beasts of prey are no longer used, the Saluki has managed to continue in its hunting role into modern times, though on a much-reduced scale as lifestyles have changed and the abundance of its prey has diminished. Nevertheless, to retain its identity for so long suggested to me that it had to be something really special.

The desert-bred Saluki has been kept true to type over millennia largely because it has shown itself to have evolved in a form so ideally suited to its purpose in the conditions in which it lives that no other breed can improve on it. Moreover, in earlier days there were no other comparable breeds with which to cross it. It is only in more recent times that some of the richer shaikhs have experimented with other sighthounds, such as Greyhounds, but generally such crosses have not been successful. However, as I shall show, across the region as a whole Salukis can still be found today performing their traditional role in much the same way as they did over a century ago when the first Westerners discovered the joy of hunting with them and brought some back with them to start the breed at home (Duggan, 2009).

Once I had my own Salukis, I became even more impressed by their exceptional role in Arab and Muslim society and culture. Throughout the Islamic world, dogs are regarded as *najis* (unclean) and Muslims avoid coming into contact with them; but I soon found that Salukis were different. It was often stressed to me that they were not dogs but Salukis. By way of illustration, I was told the story of a man in Tehran at the time of the revolution there in 1979, who had a Tazi (Persian for Saluki) that escaped from the house one hot day, ran next door to a house that had been taken over by some Shia zealots and jumped into the pool of water that they used for their ritual ablutions. This caused great consternation and the Tazi was condemned to be shot. However, the owner appeared and successfully reclaimed the hound merely by declaring that it was not a dog but a Tazi!

My Salukis opened doors for me in my professional life and introduced me to some extraordinary people and places. With their elegant shape and graceful movements, these 'Companions of Kings', as Vera Watkins called them (1974), also gave my family and me so much pleasure along the way. This is their story.

Although I have made the case (e.g. on my website, www.saluqi.net) for the name of the breed to be written 'Saluqi', as that is how it should be transliterated from the Arabic language from which the name derives, I decided to use the conventional spelling of Saluki here as it is more easily recognised by the general public.

Some readers may also find confusing the different spellings of 'Tazi' and 'Tazy'. To be clear, they are specifically written differently because they are the names of what some regard as two different breeds and may also have different linguistic origins. As mentioned above, تازى = Tazi (pronounced 'Taa-zee') is Persian for Saluki and means either 'Arabian' or possibly 'swift' or 'fast' from the verb taazeedan = to gallop. In Ottoman Turkish, which used Arabic letters, the word was written similarly and also had the meaning of 'Arabian', as well as designating a coursing hound. 'Tazy', however, is the transliterated form of the Russian word Тазы, the last letter of which has no direct equivalent in English but is pronounced something like 'uh', thus 'Taa-zuh', and is used for the hunting hound of Central Asia. Interestingly, the word sounds like the modern Turkish word Tazı (NB no dot on the 'i'), which is also pronounced 'Taa-zuh' and may have the meaning of 'pure' or 'clean'. Indeed, both in Russian and in the languages of Central Asia, the hound is sometimes referred to as Taza, which has the meaning of 'pure' or 'clean' in the Turkic languages spoken there.

Terence Clark
London, September 2017

I will sing the praises of a hound whose owners' ...

Chapter One

My First Saluki

In late 1984, I was given the good news that I had been appointed as British Ambassador to the Republic of Iraq. This opened up the probability of a long period of service overseas, when we could contemplate having a dog again. We had already been to Crufts to see the Salukis on show there and had decided that it would make an interesting basis for comparison to take a puppy with us to Baghdad – back, arguably, to the breed's historic origins in Mesopotamia. We made some enquiries of Mrs Zola Rawson of the Mumtaz kennel, near to us in Surrey, and visited her to see a litter of puppies, from which we selected a black-fringed fawn bitch that we called *Amira*. We were going to drive to Baghdad, and arranged that *Amira* would be flown out to join us after we arrived in March 1985. Our daughter Sonja would be flying out at about the same time to spend the Easter holidays with us. Or, at least, that is what we planned; but fate determined otherwise.

At that time, Iraq had been locked in an exhausting war with Iran for five years and, as we were driving across Turkey on our way to Baghdad, we heard on our radio that for the first time Iranian aircraft had succeeded in attacking Baghdad International Airport. We tried to increase our speed to reach Baghdad as quickly as possible to take stock of this new situation, but heavy rain and an unmade road choked with juggernauts churning up the mud thwarted our efforts to reach the Iraqi frontier. When at last we reached Baghdad, I learned the devastating news that British Airways had ceased flying to Baghdad because of the Iranian threat. The immediate question was: what to do about Sonja and *Amira*? Together with a group of other parents with children coming out for Easter, we arranged for Sonja to fly to Kuwait and for Liese and some of the group to drive down there in convoy to bring them to Baghdad. Sadly, we could not include *Amira* in this arrangement and, as there was no other way we could bring her to Baghdad, Mrs Rawson kindly took her back. So that was the end of that dream; but it was also an incentive to explore the possibilities of finding a Saluki in Iraq.

My early days in Baghdad were very busy, managing the usual process of taking charge of a large embassy and settling into a new residence but also establishing relations with a regime waging a war with Iran. So, Salukis were not uppermost in my thoughts, and in any case a surprise was in store for us. One day as we came home, we found a small whimpering bundle by our front door. A puppy had somehow wandered past the Iraqi security guard at the gate and settled in. It was a pretty little fawn bitch with a black muzzle and she responded eagerly to some food and attention. She took up residence with us and we called her *Amina*. However, as she grew older her street breeding began to tell and she became very naughty and incorrigibly destructive, so much so that we decided we could not keep her in the official residence. Our Indian cook took her off to a camp on the other side of Baghdad, where some of his fellow countrymen were working on a building site, and she settled in happily with the camp cook there.

This period was at the height of the Iran–Iraq war, when the two sides were exchanging long-range missile attacks and we were under constant threat of evacuation. This tended to keep us tied to Baghdad and for the next 18 months or so I had little opportunity of exploring more widely in Iraq. When I asked Baghdad acquaintances about Salukis, they often professed ignorance of them and thought they did not exist anymore. They were, however, mostly professional townspeople and had little idea about life in the desert or the village. However, one day my Iraqi Kurdish driver, Qadir, told me that there were many Salukis in his village and he could help me to acquire one from his family. I was sceptical, as he was a comfortably built town Kurd and prone to exaggeration. I needed to see the situation for myself.

The problem was that, because of the war and persistent Iranian shelling, his family and many others had been displaced from Khanaqin on the border with

Iran to the small town of Kalar, still in Iraqi Kurdistan but set further back from the border. The displaced Kurds had built their own small courtyard houses in an enclave on the outskirts of the town and his wife's sister and her husband were living there. Qadir claimed that his brother-in-law was a renowned hunter and could easily find a Saluki for me. But the movement of foreign diplomats was severely restricted in wartime Iraq and to travel anywhere outside Baghdad required a special permit, requested two weeks in advance of the proposed journey. Such permits were rarely given for journeys near the border with Iran. I applied for a permit several times and was always refused. Nevertheless, I applied again for one weekend and, as luck would have it, this was granted. I encouraged my American and Swiss colleagues to join us for the ride into what was generally inaccessible territory.

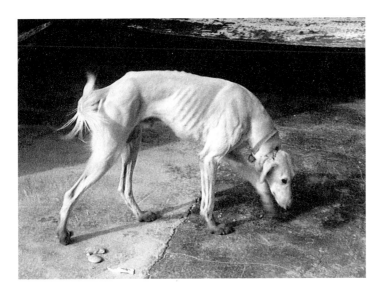

Qaysar with hennaed feet in Kalar.

When the day came, we set off early in two vehicles for the three-hour drive to Kalar via the heavily war-damaged town of Khanaqin within sight of the Zagros Mountains of Iran. As we approached the enclave where Ali, Qadir's brother-in-law, lived, I was amazed to see some beautiful feathered Salukis wandering about the surrounding wasteland, evidently foraging. Some of them were wearing padded coats, as the weather had already turned cold. In some cases the coats were nothing more than sacks stuffed with straw, which provided warmth but made the hounds look more like ungainly sheep. We made our way to one of the single-storey breeze-block houses, where Ali welcomed us and showed us into the small courtyard, where we were met by a most majestic cream Saluki with a flowing silky tail but no feathering on the ears. He was superbly built, with the prominent muscles and sinews of the coursing Saluki, and his feet were reddened with henna, which it is believed hardens the pads against damage over rough terrain. He was, appropriately, called *Qaysar* or Caesar.

Peeping shyly out of the kennel behind him was his smooth-haired daughter, a sandy puppy of about five months called *Tayra*. She was the product of a liaison with an almost white smooth bitch from another village, which, as I discovered later, had been mated with two different Salukis. *Qaysar* had sired *Tayra* and an almost identical dog, but they also had a quite different-looking feathered tricolour half-sister by another sire. While this practice might be frowned upon in the West, where written pedigrees are all-important, the Eastern breeder, as Ali explained, is more concerned with making the best use of the bitch's season, if he has two dogs of high coursing merit. Ali also made a point of correcting me gently in my use of the Arabic word *kalb* (dog) when speaking of a Saluki. He said I should never use any other word than *Salūqī*: a Saluki was not a mere dog!

All the Salukis in this Sorani-speaking Kurdish area had intact ears, as is also the custom across the border in much of Iranian Kurdistan. However, further west towards Turkey in the Kurmanji-speaking Kurdish area, the ears were usually cropped. I discovered much later that it is done on Sloughis in Tunisia and it is also practised in Algeria. I asked many times for an explanation of this practice and nearly always had a different answer. Some said that it was for speed or alertness, others for protection against damage from fights with other dogs or predators or from thorn bushes. Still others said that it was for beauty or for identification, according to the proportion of the ear that was cropped. Sometimes the ears are carefully shaped to stand erect, but often the cropping is crude and uneven. Often, only one ear of bitches was cropped, giving them a curious, lopsided look, for which there was no good reason at all. I concluded in the end that it was simply an old custom, the reason for which, if there ever had been one, had long been forgotten. I heard more recently that, even in the Gulf, where many of the crop-eared Kurdish hounds are sold for racing, local breeders have started to crop their own hounds' ears in the hope of emulating the imports' success on the track.

Meanwhile, Ali and his family in Kalar had made us very welcome and pressed us to stay to eat the hare baked in pastry that *Qaysar* had caught, but I needed to get down to the serious business of negotiating for *Tayra*, who had instantly taken our fancy. She was a fine, well-proportioned hound of whose impeccable hunting lineage Ali left me in no doubt as he regaled us with stories of his hunting exploits. However, Ali was very reluctant to let me have *Tayra*, as he was raising her for his own use; but he sent his sons out to scour the community to try to find another puppy for me. After about half an hour they returned empty-handed. No one was even prepared to discuss the matter. Salukis at that time were not traded but only given away in the expectation of a puppy in return at a later date or for some other favour. I was very disappointed, but cheered up when, under pressure from Qadir – who explained to Ali that he would not be the loser for it – Ali very generously said I could have *Tayra*. This was the start of a long and adventurous relationship.

Tayra as a puppy.

Tayra in her prime..

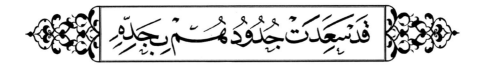

Chapter Two

Early Adventures in Iraq

The journey home from Kalar was itself an adventure. While we had been enjoying Ali's hospitality, we had not noticed that *Tayra* had slipped out of the courtyard and had gone foraging. She had found somewhere four chicken legs and had swallowed them whole, feet, claws and all. She had never been in a car before and was very nervous, so much so that, one by one, she vomited up the chicken legs. Hence, we had to keep stopping to clean out the car. This was not a problem at first, but on the way we were stopped at a military checkpoint and told we had to make a long detour as there had been a shooting incident on the road ahead. We were provided with a temporary military escort of a pickup with a machine gun mounted on the roof and taken to the area military headquarters, where Qadir was interrogated for about half an hour about what we were doing in the area. It seemed the army found it hard to believe that no fewer than three ambassadors were there just for a dog. However, just when we began to think we would be detained there overnight, we were suddenly told we could go and the escort was doubled by the addition of an armoured car.

Trying to persuade the jittery escort to stop because *Tayra* was being sick was no easy matter, but eventually we were out of the danger zone and could travel on our own for the rest of the journey. We were all shattered by the time we reached home, and *Tayra* collapsed into a basket in an outhouse without a murmur. The next morning, we found her in exactly the same position, as if she had not moved all night.

However, once she was up and had explored her new surroundings, she made it clear that her place was inside the house with us and not in a kennel. Right from the start she expressed a strong will of her own that was characteristic of her for the rest of her life. I took her back to Kalar a couple of months later, mainly to return Ali's generosity with a gift, and to my surprise *Tayra* seemed to show no pleasure at being with her sire again in her former home; on the contrary, she was nervous and anxious to get away. Maybe she did not want to be reminded of her earlier, much harder way of life?

Over the next few months she developed well, with plenty of exercise in the embassy's extensive grounds by the Tigris. Sometimes at the weekend we would take her to an historic archaeological site just outside Baghdad that holds a special significance for Salukis. It has been argued by the great Arabist Professor Rex Smith, in a study on the origin of the Arabic word for the breed – *Salūqī* (Smith, 1980) – that it may have been derived from Seleucia, the Empire founded by Ipsus Seleucus, one of Alexander the Great's generals, in a large swathe of territory in Western Asia, which lasted from 311 BC to 126 AD. Seleucia is written in Arabic as سلوقية (*Salūqiyya*) and a person or a thing from there is a سلوقي (*Salūqi*), which today, in accordance with the precedents of Iraq and Iraqi, should be transcribed as 'Saluqi' rather than 'Saluki', but that was the fashion in the 1920s, when the Saluki or Gazelle Hound Club's constitution was drawn up in Britain. Several cities across the Seleucid Empire were called Saluqiyya after Seleucus, but probably the greatest was by the Tigris just south of Baghdad in ideal hunting territory for coursing hounds. The site has been excavated to reveal the layout of the city and, whenever I walked there with my 'Saluqi', I always thought of her possible connection to Saluqiyya going back two thousand years or more.

The connection to this ancient land was, of course, much older. One of my more agreeable duties as British Ambassador was to act as Vice-President of the British

Tayra at Saluqiyya.

School of Archaeology, founded in Iraq by the distinguished British explorer and diplomat Gertrude Bell after the First World War. The school had built up over the years a large library of books on the history and archaeology of the region. In quieter moments, I would dip into the collection and often found references to indigenous hunting hounds. I discovered among the reports of archaeological excavations evidence for the existence of a Saluki-like hunting hound in ancient Mesopotamia going back to the fifth millennium BC. For example, a seal impression in sun-dried clay from the Chalcolithic period (c. 5000 BC) found at Tell Arpachiya in Mosul was described by the British archaeologists Max Mallowan and J Cruikshank Rose as 'some kind of coursing dog, perhaps a greyhound'. British and American excavators at Tepe Gawra, also in the Mosul area, found hundreds of seals and seal impressions going back to c. 4000 BC and commented in their report: 'The animals depicted are rarely of any domesticated variety, except for the commonly represented Saluki'.

On one of my periodic visits to Mosul, I happened to pass one day the site of Tepe Gawra. Indeed, it was hard to miss it, as it is a huge mound that rises up starkly against the flat skyline of the surrounding countryside. I climbed up it and on the way found the stone-lined shaft of the ancient well where the archaeologists had found a skull of a Saluki from the pre-Sumerian period (c. 4400–3800 BC), on which they commented: 'this breed of hunting dog is frequently depicted on contemporary seals and impressions'. Standing on the top of the mound, I could easily imagine such a popular hound coursing in the surrounding area, once rich in game of all kinds. I was curious to see whether such hounds might still exist there, as the basic conditions for coursing had not changed significantly, though game was scarcer, and an enquiry of an off-duty policeman waiting at the roadside for a lift led me into the nearby village of Fadhliya, inhabited by one of Iraq's rarer minorities called Shabaks, Kurdish-speaking Shia. The policeman had assured me there were Salukis there, but at first the people who gathered in the village square denied all knowledge of them, possibly fearing that the policeman would force them to give me one. However, after I had assured them of my good intentions and showed them photographs of other Salukis, they started to bring out their hounds for me to photograph – and what a variety they were! One puppy was spotted with black on white, almost like a Dalmatian. Another puppy was brindle and different in colour from both its siblings and its dam. All the Salukis there had their ears cropped in the Kurmanji Kurdish fashion, except for the puppies' handsome smooth tricolour dam, indicating she had probably come from somewhere else, such as Mosul, where the Arabs tended not to crop the ears.

Further evidence of the continuity of Salukis in that area was provided by another British archaeologist, Seton Lloyd, whom I met later in England and who kindly gave me photographs of the Salukis he and his wife, Hydie, had kept in Iraq in the 1930s. He had worked on the nearby site of the palace of the Assyrian ruler Sargon II (c. 700 BC) at Khorsabad, or Dur-Sharrukin as it was once known. Some amazing sculpted wall panels were found there; but, according to press reports, anything left on the site was pulverised as idolatrous by the so-called Islamic State in 2015. Seton Lloyd described in his autobiography *The Interval* (1986) how, in more peaceful times, he had seen Salukis streaming down the hill towards him and his party as they approached the site. Indeed, during my own travels, I was to find many such localised populations of Salukis, especially across the Kurdish areas of northern Iraq.

For example, one day I was being guided round the vast Assyrian mound at Tell Hoshi in the Sinjar area west of Mosul by the British archaeologist David Stronach, then working at Berkeley in the United States, when I spied on the plain below a couple of hunters returning to their village with a pair of Salukis criss-crossing around them. When I approached them, they were proud to show me the rather suspicious feathered black and tan bitch and the more approachable feathered red dog. The dog was standing protectively over a hare the black and tan had just killed, which the men were taking home for their families' supper. The hares in this area are of the size of the European brown hare and provide a good amount of meat. Looking back now, I am saddened to think that the name Sinjar has acquired a grim significance since 2014, when members of the so-called Islamic State overran the mainly Yazidi villages there, forcing the adherents of this ancient religion either to convert to Islam or be killed and abducting the women and girls to serve them as sex slaves.

About four months after acquiring *Tayra* in Kalar, I thought I should try and find a companion for her. My work often required my absence from Baghdad and I thought it would be comforting for *Tayra* to have a playmate. So, one day in the New Year I returned to Kalar to see her breeder, Ali, with my visiting daughter, Sonja, and Sue Aldridge, the wife of my Defence Attaché, who had had Salukis in England before and was interested in acquiring an Iraqi hound. *Tayra* stayed at home with Liese this time as she had been so unhappy in Kalar on the previous occasion.

As I now knew, acquiring a Saluki was a serious business that could not be rushed. We had first to sit down in Ali's courtyard and drink sweet, milkless tea from small glasses, while he related stories about hunting on the plains around Kalar. He claimed that his hounds were trained not to kill the hare immediately but either to hold it until he could come or to retrieve the hare alive to him to despatch by slitting the throat ritually. I heard similar stories later in the Gulf but I rarely saw it happen in practice. Most often the Saluki killed on the spot and the problem was always to reach the hare before any other hounds arrived to dispute it. Only occasionally an inexperienced hound might not kill immediately and might retrieve the hare alive. Some hunters believe it is lawful to eat the hare only if it has been ritually despatched but, according to the *Hadith* (the Sayings of the Prophet Muhammad), it is sufficient if the hunter says '*Bismillah*' (in the name of Allah) before slipping the hound for the meat of the caught prey to be eaten lawfully.

Ali had an almost white feathered male puppy in his yard, which I liked the look of, but Ali's wife kept saying that it was no good, clearly trying to put me off as they did not want to give this one up. So Ali took us around the community and introduced us to another hunter with a feathered grizzle bitch called *Ziwa*, with six puppies almost a month old. There were two black and tans, a male and a female, two cream females and two red and white particoloureds. The sire was also there, a feathered red and white particoloured called *Qais*. The puppies were all in excellent condition, but the owner was keen for us to take two of them to reduce the burden of raising them. We were doubtful about taking them at such a tender age but the owner assured us that they were on the point of lapping milk and would not be a problem to feed. Sue Aldridge, who was experienced in raising Saluki puppies, agreed. She selected the black and tan female and called her *Laila*; I took one of the creams and called her *Ziwa* after her dam.

We stopped on the way home to buy a baby's bottle to feed the puppies, just in case they were not quite ready to start lapping, and this proved to be a wise precaution.

Ziwa and Laila in Baghdad.

When we reached home, Liese was delighted with our choice but was also pleased when Sue volunteered to take both puppies home for the first couple of weeks, as they would be more comfortable together. She found that after only two days they were indeed lapping and by the time we brought *Ziwa* home she was eating solid food and sleeping through the night. She was more fortunate than we were, as the exchange of long-range ballistic missiles with Iran, which came to be known as the 'War of the Cities', often meant that our sleep was disturbed by the thunderous crash as they struck seemingly at random around Baghdad, known ironically in Arab history as '*Madinat as-Salaam*' (City of Peace). More than once, we were on the point of evacuating our citizens – which would have posed a dilemma for us and our hounds, since we would have been allowed to take only what we could carry – but fortunately the period of heightened danger passed.

In any case, I had formed a contingency plan at the back of my mind as a result of a chance encounter. I was taking my hounds for a walk one day along the very long avenue on which we lived in Baghdad. The local inhabitants never walked their dogs, which were mostly of the guarding variety and spent all day chained to a kennel to be released only at night to wander round the garden as a deterrent. Hence, I presented an unusual sight and my hounds always attracted attention, serving unconsciously as a means of getting to know my neighbours. On this occasion I was approached by a man from inside his front garden to ask me about my hounds. He spoke impeccable English and admitted that he had an English mother and had lived in England. Apparently satisfied that I knew what I was talking about, he asked me in to see his Salukis in pens at the back of the house. He was an airline pilot but loved to go hunting with his hounds whenever he could. One was a somewhat stocky feathered grizzle dog with cropped ears, from Kurdistan. The other was a beautiful feathered grizzle bitch, which he had found tied up to a tree, apparently abandoned. They were later to have some very nice puppies. It occurred to me that, if we had to leave Iraq in a hurry, it might be possible to park our hounds there until we could make other arrangements for them. Fortunately, we never had to implement this plan, as I learnt sometime later that, when the pilot had been away, the grizzle dog had accidently hanged himself on his own leash, which had become entangled as he tried to jump over the wire round his pen.

All the good things they have come from him;

Chapter Three

More Adventures in Iraq

We took some home leave that summer to escape for a while the ferocious heat of Baghdad, when the thermometer could hit 50° C. *Ziwa* had gone to stay with her sibling, *Laila*, while *Tayra* had gone into the kennels run by our vet. We had to keep our two apart as together they could make trouble.

Tayra had shown from the beginning that she was exceptional. Just as she had done on her very first day with us, she always asserted her strong personality, whatever the surroundings. We had to lay down some firm lines and teach her that that was as far as she could go, otherwise she would have dominated the household. Even so, she could be a challenge. When fully grown, she measured 63.5 cm square, weighed 20 kg and was sturdily but elegantly built. She was a natural hunter and needed no training in that regard. Some Arab hunters told me that they liked to start puppies on jerboas or tame rabbits and work up to coursing hare from there, but *Tayra* hunted instinctively. Wherever we went, the moment I unclipped her lead she would sprint ahead as if coming out of slips on a hare. She would always seek the high ground or some vantage point from where she could survey the scene below for anything she could chase. This natural talent had its downside, however, as she would chase anything that moved. She once pursued a light aeroplane as it taxied down an airfield for takeoff! Nothing was immune from her attention, including joggers and bikers! On the other hand, when we went coursing, she was fearless in pursuit of jackals, foxes, hares and even low-flying birds. She terrorised the feral cats in our neighbourhood, but met her match one day in the desert when she came face to face with a ferocious wildcat.

In the house, she guaranteed our security. When she was young she would sleep outside the door to our bedroom. She would bark at and threaten anyone who came unannounced to our house. Once when I was out hunting with her alone in the desert, a probable deserter from the army suddenly appeared out of a wadi and attempted to rob me. I called her to me and she flew at the attacker. She bit him in the leg and brought him to his knees, whereupon I told him to make off while I restrained her or else; he fled! Yet, in our company, especially with our children or with visitors, she was as gentle as a lamb and never destroyed any of our possessions when left alone. She knew her place was on the floor and never climbed onto chairs, sofas or beds. She could be so expressive that she almost talked. She would come and bang on our bedroom door in the morning when it was time to go out. She would stare at you or growl and nudge you into the kitchen when she was hungry and wanted food. She would rest her head lovingly on your lap in the evening when she wanted a little attention. She could open doors by standing on her hind legs and depressing the handle with a front paw. She was, in short, an alpha female, which is probably why we never succeeded in mating her – she would see off any of the suitors we brought to her.

This dominant side of her almost inevitably spelt trouble for little *Ziwa*. They were introduced when *Ziwa* was only six weeks old, and from the start *Tayra* made it clear that she did not like this interloper. We always had to keep a close eye on them together as, if unsupervised, *Tayra* would pounce on *Ziwa*. This antipathy may have led to later psychological problems with *Ziwa*. Even when she grew bigger and could defend herself, she was always being pursued by *Tayra* as if she were a prey object. Once, when chased, *Ziwa* ran straight into a glass door with such force that it brought up a huge swelling on her head. Thereafter she became even more nervous and she even changed physically. Her ears, which had hitherto hung down at the side of her head, began to stick out sideways – aeroplane ears.

Consequently, when Liese and I were invited for the weekend by some of the British archaeologists in the area of the Sinjar Mountains in north-western Iraq to see their work, I decided to take only *Tayra*, while *Ziwa* went to stay with her sister. Our first objective was the mainly Turkoman town of Tel Afar. The Turkomans form an ethnic enclave in an area which is largely Arab and, although I was not aware of this at the time, were nominally divided between Sunni and Shia. This religious divide only became apparent after the overthrow of Saddam Hussein's regime in 2003, when bitter fighting broke out between them, leading eventually to the departure of the Shia community. In 2014, the town was overrun by the so-called Islamic State and the Turkoman Shia would probably have had to leave then anyway or face death as not being true Muslims.

The town is dominated by an Ottoman fort on a hill and our archaeologists had established their dig house there. The roof of the fort provided a vantage point from which to survey the endless Jazira plain below and as the sun went down it was possible to make out over a hundred archaeological mounds by the shadows they cast. Each mound would have represented an inhabited site in antiquity, but only a few had been excavated, leaving the onlooker to dream about what might lie beneath them. The weather turned stormy overnight and, while *Tayra* slept peacefully through the gale and rain that buffeted our caravan, I feared we would take off at any moment and go flying down the hill.

The weather was so bad the next morning that we had to abandon our plan to see the dig at a vast Assyrian mound called Tell al-Hawa towards the Syrian border. Instead we went with Professor David Oates, one of the British archaeologists, and the local Director of Antiquities to Sinjar to see the site of Singara, a Roman fort excavated by the British some 30 years previously, part of which had been turned into a house with a family living in it. I also called on the local *Qaimakam* (a government official), who by chance came from *Tayra's* hometown of Kalar, so I could ask him naturally about Salukis in the area. He knew of none; but as we walked back to our car, our Iraqi guide said that he recalled seeing some in a village near Tel Afar a couple of years before and thought he knew the way. We eventually turned off the asphalt and proceeded on a slippery dirt track towards a small hamlet, where we were directed to the house of Subhi, a larger-than-life character who was to become my friend and Saluki mentor. A tall, spare man in his forties, he was the grandson of a former Ottoman Turkish *Agha* (a military officer) and had inherited from him and his father an unbroken line of Salukis, of which he was very proud.

Subhi was a great breeder in general. He had four wives, two in the hamlet to look after the smallholding there and two in Mosul, where he ran a stone-crushing business, and innumerable children. He bred livestock and Arabian horses, which he used

Subhi's pack near Tel Afar.

for hunting with his pack of Salukis. He had seven at that time, all smooth with ears cropped 'for beauty', he said, and – most unusually – all branded on the thigh with his mark of a half-circle. He hunted in the immediately surrounding area, part arable land and part scrub, and he showed me in an outhouse a collection of wolf and fox pelts, which his wives would use for making winter clothing for the children. He maintained that feathered hounds were impure and he would cull any of his hounds that developed feathering as a result of outcrossing. He would sometimes outcross to Salukis from across the border in Turkey. As the brindle pattern is said in the West not to exist in Salukis, I was surprised to see a red brindle puppy in his pack. He said it was one of eight brindles born to a brindle bitch from Turkey and his top dog. The other puppies had been given away, though I saw one of them on a subsequent visit in a nearby village.

He selected his breeding hounds very carefully and when any of them died he would carry out an autopsy himself to ensure there were no congenital defects that might have been carried on. To avoid accidental mating, he covered bitches in season with a kind of leather apron over their hindquarters. He fed them once a day in the evening with a meal of bread, dates and cracked wheat, and only occasionally meat. They looked good on it. When he suggested we went out to give them all a run, I went along gladly. We drove into some low hills cut by a flowing wadi and the hounds raced about. *Tayra* was a bit unsure of herself in this pack of strange dogs but she was soon charging around with them and gave a good account of herself. We parted on the best of terms, with an invitation from Subhi to return the next day for some real hunting. Sadly, the inclement weather persisted the next morning and we had to retreat back to Baghdad, with a promise to return.

At the New Year, I paid another visit to Kalar to bring Ali's family some sweets and pastries for the children. *Tayra* had cut her leg badly coursing a hare at Christmas, so she stayed home this time. We were met by a distraught Ali, who told us that his beloved *Qaysar* had been run over by a truck, along with the puppy he was bringing on. With tears in his eyes, he said: 'Hunting is life'. Without his hounds there was no hunting, and his world had collapsed. Such road accidents were all too common because of the practice of letting the hounds out to forage free in the morning and evening, and I felt glad that we had averted such a possible fate for *Tayra* and *Ziwa*. We walked around the local community but it was not the season for puppies and most of the hounds, including *Ziwa*'s siblings, were away hunting, so I could only admire the few mature hounds that were left, muffled up in their padded coats.

We stopped at several villages on the way back to Baghdad and chatted with people about local affairs, their Salukis and hunting. As I found throughout my travels then and later, a Saluki in my car invariably acted as a key for opening the door to local society. Indeed, I used to refer to them as a kind of Trojan horse. In wartime Iraq, the people were officially discouraged from talking to foreigners, especially diplomats, but on seeing the Salukis they used to forget all about the ban and welcomed me, often into their homes, almost as one of them. I had added an Iraqi accent to my Arabic and that helped to strengthen the natural bond between hunters with Salukis. As a result, I was offered many puppies, and only once was a price mentioned. This was, of course, in the days before the rich Gulf Arabs started to scour the northern region for mature hounds for racing back home, for which they would pay ridiculous prices. It was no wonder that people in these poor villages abandoned their old practice of treasuring their Salukis for themselves and joined the age of the free market economy. They quickly learnt to exploit the market, keeping their best hounds for themselves for hunting and breeding and selling off the rest to the highest bidder. All this was a far cry from my drive back from Kalar that day, when in one village I was offered a pathetic feathered cream bitch with her two crossbred puppies that had been expelled to fend for herself for defiling herself with a guard dog.

One of my chance meetings with Iraqis was different in that it established a link of friendship that has lasted ever since. At a diplomatic reception in Baghdad, I happened to be talking with an Iraqi doctor, who told me that his family came from a small town on the Euphrates called Hit (pronounced 'Heet'), which was famous since Babylonian times for the bitumen that bubbles up naturally from wells in the ground. I had heard that this was also a good area for Salukis and that it was near one of a series of fortified staging posts along the old camel mail route that ran for centuries from Beirut via Damascus to Baghdad. Gertrude Bell had described the fort, called Qasr al-Khubbaz, in her great work *Amurath to Amurath* (1911) on her travels in Iraq in the early 20th century, and it sounded like an interesting place to explore one day and to give the hounds a run in the desert. In typical Arab fashion, as soon as I expressed my interest in visiting the area, the doctor immediately invited me to use his house in Hit as a base from which to explore. This was too good an offer to refuse, because one of the problems about travelling round Iraq was the lack of accommodation and, although we sometimes camped, it was more comfortable and safer to stay somewhere privately, especially if we had the Salukis with us. So, as a public holiday was approaching, I arranged that Liese and I and a couple of friends would visit Hit.

It was still winter and black clouds threatened as we drove along the Euphrates to Hit, where we were guided to the doctor's newly built house in a date garden by the river. We were expected by the doctor's brother and everything had been prepared for us, including a huge dinner, from which *Tayra* also benefited. (*Ziwa* had had to stay behind as she was in her first season.) The next morning was bright and clear of rain. After a good breakfast, we set off with our host to drive first to Kubaisa, a small town set in an oasis a few kilometres to the west, where we picked up a delightful old bedouin called Obaid to guide us some 30 km further west across the desert to Qasr al-Khubbaz. Obaid related that, in the old days, the post route was known as 'the road of death', because it took eight days to reach Damascus and if the water skins leaked or the camel went lame, the postman died. The stone-built fort still stood there, breached only on one side by a vaulted doorway, leading into a hollow square with the remains of vaulted rooms around, where travellers would have stayed, much as in a caravanserai or khan. Soldiers were stationed there to protect the postmen from attack by the bedouin.

Obaid then showed us, in an adjacent wadi, the remains of a water tank fed by a dam that provided water for the fort. In the mud I spotted some large paw prints, which Obaid identified as those of a wolf. He said a wolf had recently killed 50 sheep sheltering there, which made us look around somewhat apprehensively. He took us back into Kubaisa, where he showed us some beautiful feathered Saluki puppies, including a black and tan that we found very tempting. However, it was held by a little boy, who was not going to let his puppy go for anything. Still, it was clear that Kubaisa and the surrounding area had much to offer and we resolved to come back another time to explore further.

Hit and Kubaisa were occupied by forces of the so-called Islamic State in 2014 and my doctor friend, like so many in the professional classes in Iraq, was forced to flee for safety after he received death threats. He turned up as a refugee in England and we were able to renew our friendship after more than 20 years. As he remains in touch with his homeland, I continue to hear stories of the grim life of the less fortunate who have had to remain behind. Life in Iraq was not easy for anyone during the war with Iran, but at least people in the rural communities enjoyed comparative safety; now no one was safe there.

The danger to us living in Baghdad in 1988 flared up again in the spring, the seventh year of war with Iran. The missile attacks on the two capitals intensified and once again we had to review our plans for evacuation. Then, to general relief, a temporary ceasefire was brokered by the Turkish government to cover the period of a visit by their president to Tehran. As it was Easter and our daughter was visiting us, we arranged to take a short break in Amman, Jordan, by road. The route took us via Rutba on the border with Jordan, where we could break our journey at a comfortable guesthouse run by a German construction company. Rutba has been historically important as a staging post for caravans between Damascus and Baghdad, not least because of its still-functioning Roman wells of fresh water. Carrying on that tradition, it became after the First World War a halfway house for the Nairn Transport Company, founded by two former soldiers from New Zealand, who exploited a need for a fast means of transportation initially between Beirut and Baghdad, which they later extended to Tehran. They ran a fleet of specially built Buick and Cadillac cars for passengers and mail, which took a mere 16 hours to do the journey, and later added a fleet of articulated buses, which maintained a regular service into the 1950s. I thought we might see whether any signs of the Nairn bus station still remained.

We did not have much time to spend in Rutba but saw enough to whet the appetite for a return visit. I easily found the Nairn bus station as it was built like a fort, with crenellated walls around a large square. It had become the police headquarters, so I doubted whether we would be allowed in. However, as soon as I announced myself to a policeman on the massive gates, we were ushered in to see the commandant, who was delighted to take us on a tour. He showed us the former rooms for travellers, which had become cells for detaining prisoners, and the former offices, on the wall of one of which I saw a yellowed advertisement in English for haircuts for travellers, with the prices in sterling! I asked the commandant about Salukis and he detailed a policeman to take us on a tour of Rutba, where we saw not only some handsome feathered Salukis, but also some Saker falcons. We were also shown a vast enclosure outside the town where herds of gazelle roamed in safety. Clearly we would have to come back.

We continued on to Amman via the oasis of Azraq, whose black basalt-built fort featured prominently in T.E. Lawrence's great work *Seven Pillars of Wisdom* (1935). The journey then became a trip down Memory Lane, as Liese and I were married in Amman, when I was at the British Embassy there, and this was the first time we had been back in nearly 30 years. It was the first visit for our daughter. But after a delightful few days seeing the magnificent Roman sites at Jerash and Umm Qais as well as the unparalleled Nabatean 'rose-red' city of Petra and having a swim in the Dead Sea, we were brought back rudely to earth by news from Baghdad that we had to return immediately because of a sudden intensification of missile strikes and the prospect again of evacuation. So we headed for home, stopping briefly at Qusayr ʿAmra, a former Umayyad hunting palace of the early 8th century, which is remarkable for its beautifully painted frescoes of Salukis hunting wild ass (onager) and gazelle. We felt somewhat let down on reaching Baghdad to be greeted by the news that Iraq had suddenly declared a unilateral ceasefire during the elections in Iran, so all was quiet again. But the lull did not last long and, after one or two missiles landed uncomfortably close, I was obliged to evacuate all my non-essential staff to prepared accommodation at a British construction camp outside town and to advise the British community to do likewise. For the next couple of weeks, we were on high alert, a period punctuated by air raid warnings at odd hours, which used to set *Tayra* off howling in unison with the siren, but then things quietened down again and we could relax.

A major Muslim festival fell in the middle of May and we decided to revisit Rutba while Iraq and Iran were on holiday. The initial round of the places where we had seen Salukis before proved disappointing, as everyone was away hunting with their falcons

Dalli in Rutba equipped for the chase.

and hounds. This was a constant difficulty for me as I could get away only on some weekends or public holidays but it was precisely at such times that the hunters were most likely not to be at home. However, the next day we saw a pile of camping gear outside one of the houses and guessed the owner was back. He turned out to be yet another extraordinary character, called Dalli. He was in his 60s but had the sprightliness of a much younger man. He cut a fine figure, with a bandolier of bullets around his waist, an old Lee–Enfield .303 rifle in one hand, a falcon on the other and two superb Salukis at his feet. He had just returned from a month's hunting in the desert and showed us some of his trophies. He had used his hounds to chase gazelle to the point of exhaustion, whereupon he would capture them alive to stock the gazelle reservation that we had seen on the previous occasion. In his backyard he produced a young gazelle that had unfortunately broken a leg in the chase. He had had to amputate part of the foreleg but had fixed it so that the pretty creature could hop around quite well. He then produced a basket in which he had four falcon eyasses that he had taken from their nests. They were no more than balls of down and feathers, but he would train them for falconry and probably sell one or two for a very high price to falconers in the Gulf.

His stories were interrupted by a shout that one of his falcons had broken loose and was flying away. We all piled out of his house and set off across the desert, where the falcon had been spotted sitting on the ground. It had just eaten and was heavy with food. So, with the aid of a live pigeon on a string as a lure, Dalli was able to recapture the falcon in triumph.

Although the art of falconry was popular under the Abbasid Caliphs when they ruled over the Arab world from their capital in Baghdad in 786–902 AD, it had few practitioners in Iraq in my time, so this was a golden opportunity to seek confirmation of what the literature said on the subject of flying falcons in tandem with Salukis. In *Social Life Under the Abbasids* (1979), which draws heavily on medieval Arab sources, M M Ahsan describes how falcons were trained to take meat from between the horns of first a stuffed gazelle and then a live animal. The falcon became thus habituated to stooping on the head of the gazelle, which had the effect of slowing it down and giving time to the pursuing Salukis to catch it. Dalli did not resort to this form of hunting. He certainly used his Salukis to hunt in tandem with a falcon, but only for hare, reversing their roles so that the hounds kept the hare moving and the falcon made the final swoop.

The growing heat of summer reduced our weekend hunting expeditions but there was no let-up in the war with Iran. Although the missile strikes had ceased, the ground fighting continued with a series of Iraqi attacks in which they recaptured most of the territory previously lost to Iran. Suddenly, in mid-July 1988, Iran announced unconditional acceptance of a United Nations Security Council Resolution that would pave the way for an end to the war. There was euphoria in Baghdad, as if the war had ended; but it had not, and dragged on intermittently for another month until a permanent ceasefire took effect on 20 August 1988. Now it really was all over and we could get back to a more normal way of life.

his master is always his slave.

Chapter Four

Further Adventures in Iraq

In August 1988, the end of the exhausting war of attrition between Iraq and Iran – in which there were over a million military and civilian fatalities and countless casualties and not an inch of territory was gained by either side – was received with universal relief. The change in the population was palpable. People were smiling again and keen to start rebuilding their lives after eight years of austerity and insecurity. Travel within the country became more relaxed.

After the weather cooled down in the autumn, I took to the north and passed through Kalar on my way to see the effects of the war on eastern Kurdistan. Ali and his family gave us a warm welcome in Kalar, which was full of wonderful Salukis. They seemed to be everywhere and the more I photographed them, the more were brought out of houses for me to see. It was as if the end of the war had lifted a lid and the hunters and their hounds felt released from all constraints. Among them was *Tayra's* almost identical brother – he was just a bit bigger. What I liked to see was the way the children handled the hounds without any sign of fear. This is so unlike children elsewhere in the Muslim world, who are generally afraid of dogs and would rather throw stones at them than handle them. These children in Kalar related naturally to the hounds and represented the next generation of breeders and hunters to continue the traditions of their forebears. I noted how they called the hounds '*Tanji*' in their Sorani Kurdish dialect rather than '*Tazhi*', which is used in the Kurmanji Kurdish dialect

Sami in Kubaisa with Bora and Howa.

of western Kurdistan and southern Turkey. However, they all spoke Arabic too and in talking to me invariably said '*Saluqi*', pronounced like '*Slougui*' in Iraqi dialect.

I later went back to Kubaisa on the edge of the great Syrian Desert to have another look at the Salukis there. While taking some photographs, some boys said I must go and see 'the Kurds' and indicated where to find them. 'The Kurds' turned out to be some Turkoman refugees from a village near the oil town of Kirkuk, towards the border with Iran. One of them, called Sami, had two Salukis: a powerfully built smooth black and tan dog, called *Hawa*, and a flashy feathered black and white particoloured dog called *Bora*. He immediately proposed we should go hunting and put his two dogs in the back of my car with *Tayra* and *Ziwa*, and off we went to a nearby wide wadi between some low limestone hills. It had rained heavily the night before and the going was very muddy and slippery. The young lads who had followed us simply kicked off their sandals and ran barefoot. I slithered along, struggling with three cameras and *Tayra* on the leash. After she had nearly pulled me over in her excitement to be free, I let her go and she and *Ziwa* had a great time racing around with *Bora* and a crossbred Saluki, called a Luqi, which was quite fast but was employed for its nose, since it was better at scenting hares in the undergrowth and driving them out for the Salukis to course. *Hawa* remained on a simple rope poacher's type of slip lead (a single length of rope tied around the handler's wrist, while the free end is passed through a ring on the hound's collar and back to be held in the hand; when the hound is slipped, the handler simply lets go of the free end) waiting for a hare to get up but, though we walked for an hour and a half, we saw none. We saw tracks, scrapes and droppings but the wet weather must have forced the hares to take to higher and drier ground. I promised Sami I would come back.

I found an opportunity about a month later and drove straight to Sami's house early one frosty morning in January. Sami offered breakfast of freshly baked bread and yoghurt and then we set off with his father and brother and the same two hounds, all squeezed into my Range Rover. We drove to the same wadi as before but this time the going was easy, though an icy wind blew. Again we found lots of signs of hare but nothing for the hounds to chase. After a couple of hours, when we had almost given up, Sami spotted a hare sitting under a clump of weeds. It got up and the chase was on. Although *Tayra* had been running free all the time, while Sami's hounds had been held on slip leads, she quickly showed her power and pace and overtook the Turkoman hounds on the straight run up. At one point the hare suddenly stopped and all four hounds went right over the top of it. It then turned to the side of the wadi and disappeared down some holes. It was, as I had already discovered, a feature of these hares that they would go to ground anywhere they found a hole, almost like rabbits. I suppose they had learnt to use such an evasive tactic in the general absence of ground cover. Sami was so impressed with *Tayra* that he proposed a mating with his *Hawa* when she was next in season. He invited me in for a huge lunch that seemed to

Kubaisa.

materialise instantly on the floor of his sitting room. We had not quite done, however, as he still wanted to show me some puppies nearby, but to my disappointment they had all gone to new homes.

Foxes, too, would deploy the disappearing tactic, as we found one glorious spring day when we were driving across the desert from Karbala to see a medieval Abbasid hunting palace called Khan al-Atshan. The gravelly desert was a sea of grass and wild flowers after the rains, and the smell of crushed herbs as we drove along was almost intoxicating. Suddenly a fox got up in front of us and I decided to give our hounds a run. By the time I had stopped to let them out, the fox was almost out of sight but the hounds soon locked onto it and raced in pursuit. We followed over the firm, flat gravel and saw *Tayra* grab the fox and throw it in the air. It lay still on the ground as I went over to photograph it, but as I approached it suddenly jumped up, having only feigned death, ran a short distance away and, before the hounds were onto it again, disappeared down a hole.

We continued our route to visit the well-preserved 8th-century Abbasid fortress at Ukhaidhir, which Gertrude Bell had excavated in 1911. Arriving late and in the dark, we made camp nearby and found the next morning that we were among the ruins of two churches of the 5th century, evocative reminders of Iraq's Christian heritage but just a little spooky. From there it was a short drive to Lake Razazah, a huge expanse of water collected in a depression as a measure of control for flood water from the Euphrates. In the small oasis of Ain Tamar by the lake, I had hoped to find Shaikh Bandar ibn Hadhdhal of the Amarat branch of the great 'Anaizah tribe. It was from the then shaikh of the tribe, Fahad Beg ibn Hadhdhal, that in 1919 Gertrude Bell, who had become Oriental Adviser to the British High Commissioner in Baghdad, received the gift of two feathered grizzle Salukis. She wrote in a letter home on 30 November 1919:

… two most beautiful Arab greyhounds … had walked ten days down the Euphrates with two tribesmen to conduct them, and came in half-starved. They are sitting beside me as I write, after wandering about the room for half an hour whining. They are very gentle and friendly and I hope they will soon get accustomed to living in a garden instead of a tent. They are perfectly lovely and of course of the finest Arab breed. We have named them Rishan and Najmah – the feathered (that's because of his feathered tail) and the star. (Bell, 1927)

I wanted to see whether the tribe still kept Salukis. Sadly, the elderly shaikh was ill and had been taken to Kuwait for treatment, but some men in the village said there were no longer any Salukis there. They thought I might still find some among the 'Anaizah at al-Nukhaib, a small town further west towards Saudi Arabia. I did pass through there at a later date and was astonished to find a red feathered Saluki bitch tied up at the only petrol station, at which I stopped to make enquiries. However, it turned out to be the only Saluki there and she involved me in an altercation with the attendant, who accused me of taking photographs of a vital installation and could not believe I was only interested in the hound!

Gertrude Bell was instrumental in acquiring a Saluki for another grande dame of English society, Vita Sackville-West. She made her mark as a poet, novelist, biographer, travel writer, journalist and broadcaster. She was also one of the most influential gardeners of the 20th century, creating with her husband, Harold Nicolson, one of England's most famous gardens at Sissinghurst Castle in Kent. In March 1926, she was passing through Baghdad on her way to join her husband, who was at the British Legation in Tehran. In *A Passenger to Tehran* (1926), her fascinating account of her journey, which took her via Egypt and India as well as Iraq and back via Russia, she describes how she was greeted on her arrival at Gertrude Bell's house in Baghdad by a 'tall grey saluki'. She said that she wanted one like that to take with her to Tehran the next day. In no time at all, Gertrude Bell was on the telephone to explain what was needed. While Gertrude was away at the office, Salukis began to arrive.

> They slouched in, led on strings by Arabs in white woollen robes, sheepishly smiling. … I had them all tied up to the posts of the verandah till Gertrude should return, an army of desert dogs, yellow, white, grey, elegant, but black with fleas and lumpy with ticks.

She chose a smooth female that Gertrude said must be called *Zurcha*, meaning 'yellow one'. This was a curious name to give a hound and Vita must have misunderstood what Gertrude said. *Zurcha* is not an Arabic word and does not resemble the word for yellow (*Sufra*). It is more likely that the word was *Zurqa*, meaning blue, which is the colour used by the Arabs for describing a grizzle. Anyway, *Zurcha* she became and the next day Vita set off with her in a car of the Trans-Desert Mail for Tehran. She wrote:

Gertrude Bell's father and her Salukis Rishan and Najmah.

I got into the front seat ... with Zurcha, who although as leggy as a colt, folded up into a surprisingly small space and immediately went to sleep. I was glad to see this, as I had not looked forward to restraining a struggling dog over five hundred miles of country, and had not been at all at ease in my mind as to what salukis straight from the desert would make of a motor. The yellow nomad, however, accepted whatever life sent her with perfect and even slightly irritating philosophy. Warmth and food she insisted on; shared my luncheon and crawled under my sheepskin, but otherwise gave no trouble. I was relieved, but felt it a little ungrateful of her not to notice that she was being taken into Persia.

Zurcha was, however, not a great success. Vita described her in *Faces: Profiles of Dogs* (1962) as

... without exception the dullest dog I have ever owned. Salukis are reputed to be very gentle and faithful: this one ... was gentle enough, because she was completely spriritless, and as for fidelity she was faithful only to the best armchair ... nothing would induce her to come out for a walk – perhaps because I omitted to provide a gazelle. In the end I followed the historical tradition and gave her to a Persian Prince, who subsequently lost her somewhere in Moscow. I was unlucky, of course, in the only saluki I ever owned, and these remarks must not be taken as an aspersion upon an incomparably elegant race.

She was indeed very unlucky.

On another free weekend, I tried to follow up a lead given to me by a man I chanced to meet in Baghdad, who happened to have a smooth white Saluki in his garden as I passed by. I stopped and asked him where the hound came from, as it had a distinctly short tail. He said it was from Saudi Arabia originally but that he had acquired it in Fallujah, a small town to the west of Baghdad on the Euphrates. He described the place and I resolved to look in there when I had a chance. So, following his directions, I drove with Liese one day to a smart villa set in a beautiful garden backing onto the Euphrates in Fallujah. I went up the drive to ask some children if the owner was at home and one of them went into the house and reappeared with a tall, handsome young man with a falcon on his wrist. I told him of my interest in Salukis and he warmly welcomed us in to what proved to be an extraordinary house. Inside the large entrance hall and an even larger reception room, the walls were decorated with an array of stuffed game birds, such as houbara bustard, francolin and various species of duck, and the skins of animals such as wolf, hyena and fox. He read my astonishment and explained that he was a passionate hunter, mostly with falcon and gun, though he had had Salukis too. He then showed us round the extensive garden at the rear, where gazelle and Nubian ibex ran about in large pens. He said we should come back when his father was at home and we could go hunting together.

Another opportunity did not occur for many months and, when we did go back one weekend morning, I could hardly believe that it was the same young man who greeted us. He had grown a long beard and declined to shake hands with Liese, always the sign of someone who was an ultra-orthodox Muslim. When I asked him about his falcons, he said he did not hunt any more. His father was there and immediately invited us to lunch. I felt I had to ask him about the change in his son. He said simply and, I thought, with a hint of regret that he had abandoned his old way of life and turned to religion. However, he himself had some new falcons, which he proceeded to show us. He said he no longer kept Salukis as they took up too much time and he was too busy. He believed the smooth hounds, for which he used the word *Saqlawiya* ('polished' or 'burnished'), were better for hunting, as the feathered became too heavy in the wet and the mud. After lunch, he took us across to a huge hangar, which we were amazed to see was alive with rabbits. There were hundreds of them, so that the floor appeared to be moving. They were being bred for their skins, he said, which were in demand in Egypt for manufacture into fur-lined gloves for sale in Europe.

Today, whenever I hear Fallujah mentioned in the news about the so-called Islamic State in Iraq, I wonder what became of those people we had got to know. The father, as a wealthy merchant, would no doubt have become a target for extortion. The son, however, would have adapted quickly to the imposition of Sharia law and might even have become an active *Mujahid* (religious fighter). In 2016 the town came under siege from Iraqi government forces and the remaining civilians there suffered terrible privations.

It was Easter time again and some friends proposed to drive out from England to spend it with us. Liese and I agreed to meet them in Diyarbakir, across the border in Turkey, and guide them to Baghdad. Diyarbakir is a fascinating city with a mixed population predominantly of Kurds but also Turks, Arabs, Armenians and other Christians. It has a rather forbidding appearance as it is concentrated within several kilometres of massive walls of black volcanic basalt rock. Once inside the walls in the warren of narrow streets, you are no longer aware that it stands besides the River Tigris, which flows from there into and right across the length of Iraq to the Gulf.

Because of local disturbances involving dissident Kurds and the armed forces, the local police thought fit to assign to us two minders for our protection. I wanted to show our visitors a ruined Assyrian fortress at Egil, about 50 km into the Taurus Mountains behind Diyarbakir, but the minders had to come too and thoroughly alarmed everyone by driving in front of us with their automatic rifles poking out of the windows. On the way, we stopped at a stone-built tea house in the picturesque Kurdish village of Kalkan, where I asked if they had any Tazis there. The owner said he would bring one for us to see on our way back down from the mountain. Our tour of the castle was made hilarious by our minders, who acted as if there was a terrorist lurking behind every bush. But it was cold and damp there and we were glad to go back to the warmth of the tea house, outside which stood waiting for us a jolly-looking Kurd with a mouthful of gold teeth. He held a rather stocky silver and grey grizzle female Tazi with cropped ears. He said she was five years old and a regular hunter, and explained the cropped ears by saying that it was to keep them out of her eyes when running. He joined us in the tea house, where he produced a wooden flute and someone else a drum and together they played some stirring Kurdish tunes, which brought all the other male tea drinkers to their feet in a wild circular dance, into which my friend and I were inevitably dragged. Our Turkish minders became thoroughly anxious, so we had to leave this merry band and drive in the rain back to town.

In 2016, Diyarbakir was the scene of violent demonstrations and clashes between resident Kurds and the armed forces and became unsafe for foreign visitors.

We guided our friends around some of the impressively fortified Syrian Orthodox monasteries in the vicinity, which remain as testament to this once Christian area, before crossing back into Iraq to show them more of the similar monasteries north of Mosul. The latter escaped the destructive attentions of the so-called Islamic State, as they stand in an area resolutely defended by Iraqi Kurds; whereas churches in Mosul itself, which was captured in 2014, have been damaged or destroyed. As we were so close, I thought we had to pay a visit to my friend Subhi and his Salukis near Tel Afar, west of Mosul. When we arrived, we found Subhi at home but, apart from a heavily pregnant bitch, all the Salukis were out hunting with some young lads. He quickly saddled up a horse and took off to find them, while we drank tea provided by one of his wives. In no time at all he reappeared over the horizon at the gallop, making a wonderful sight with his three hounds running beside him and a hare they had caught dangling from his pommel. Subhi invited us in for lunch, during which he offered me a puppy in due course from the pregnant bitch, called *Moda*. She had been mated twice: first by a smooth black and tan and then by a smooth cream, so it would be interesting to see what resulted.

Subhi back from the hunt near Telafar.

All this time, the relationship between *Tayra* and *Ziwa* was proving difficult. They just could not get on together and *Ziwa* seemed to be suffering psychologically from the strain of being constantly bullied. So, when some German acquaintances told us that their dog had died and they were looking for another, we offered them *Ziwa* in the hope that the separation might be good for her. It was a dismal failure. She simply sat by the gate of her new home and pined. We had to take her back but, although she was pleased to be reunited with us in her old home, the relationship with *Tayra* did not improve. Then I was faced with an awkward dilemma.

Just 120 km north of Baghdad on the east bank of the Tigris stand the ruins of Samarra, briefly (836–940) but gloriously the capital of the Abbasid Caliphs. The site has been well excavated, not least by a team of British Museum archaeologists while I was there, and there was a lot to see and admire. I derived particular pleasure from visiting there because Samarra is believed to derive from the Arabic *'surra man ra'a'* ('happy was he who saw it!') – and I saw it many times! I sometimes used to go there to give the hounds a good run in the area that was once a walled park, in which the Caliphs and their entourage used to hunt gazelle and onager, possibly with Salukis, as this reconstruction by Herzfeld (1927) in watercolour of a wall-painting from the Caliphal palace there, known as al-Jawsaq al-Khaqani, suggests.

By chance one day, I saw three Salukis lying near a track as if in wait. A lad on a passing motorcycle told me they belonged to a farmer called Hatim, who lived on a smallholding by the Tigris, and they were waiting for him to return home. I later visited him at his home on a number of occasions and we became good friends. He had four male Salukis – an unusual feathered deer grizzle patterned like a brindle, a feathered cream, a feathered red and a smooth red – and a beautiful smooth grizzle bitch from his long-established line going back to the early 1940s, when, he said, all the Salukis were smooth. He showed me photographs of his father coursing gazelle on horseback in the area with a pack of similar smooth hounds. His bitch was mated twice in the early part of 1989 with his grizzle and cream dogs. She produced five puppies, of which two were smooth cream, two were feathered silver grizzles and the other a feathered black and tan. They looked sturdy and I went away thinking over whether I should take one of them as a potential mate for *Tayra*.

Soon after, I was asked by an archaeologist friend whether I could find her a Saluki puppy. She set me a tall order. She wanted a cream feathered bitch not more than three months old and she had to have it within a week as she was leaving Iraq for her home in California. I told her about Hatim's puppies in Samarra and that Liese and I would see them again that weekend, when he had invited us to lunch there. I agreed to ask him if he would let her have one.

Our route to Samarra took us past the Baghdad pet market where, in a small square outside the Abbasid Mosque of the Caliphs, at the weekend there was always an amazing collection of hawks, eagles, pigeons, songbirds, ducks, hens and dogs for sale. As we drove by, I spotted out of the corner of my eye a Saluki in the dog section. I stopped to photograph it and as I chatted to its owner – a blond Kurdish boy who had brought it down from a farm near Sulaimaniya in Iraqi Kurdistan – I suddenly noticed a forlorn bundle curled up on the pavement nearby. In a flash, I could see it was a cream feathered bitch, not more than a couple of months old – just what my friend wanted! I picked her up, gave her a quick examination and decided to take the chance that she would be acceptable. After a little bargaining with the boy with her, I made a mutually satisfactory deal and she was mine.

We took her straight home and when we put her on the lawn we realised that she could hardly walk, and feared we had been sold a pup methaphorically as well

Ataliya.

as literally! An inspection of her feet revealed the problem: her pads were worn raw from walking or being dragged to market on the hot road surface. We soon sorted that out, and in a few days she was fine. My archaeologist friend was delighted and immediately named her *Ataliya*, after an Assyrian queen whose stupendously beautiful gold jewellery had been discovered a few months earlier during excavations at Nimrud near Mosul (a site that was more recently devastated by so-called Islamic State occupiers). *Ataliya* went off to San Francisco and developed into a fine hound.

The same day that we found *Ataliya*, we continued our planned journey to have lunch with Hatim in Samarra and to see his puppies. Our arrival at his house was inauspicious: no one was at home! A farm worker told us everyone was at another farmhouse nearby. Here we found a great gathering of Hatim's family – uncles, cousins and hordes of children – but no Hatim. For what seemed like ages, we sat around and chatted with no sign of Hatim or lunch. In the end, we said we had to get back to Baghdad, whereupon a huge spread of local delicacies appeared and so did Hatim, who merely excused himself by saying he had gone fishing in the Tigris – with dynamite! Anyway, he took us on to see the puppies but, to my regret, they were all already promised to others.

However, I did not quite give up acquiring one of them, and on returning to Samarra some months later I went to see the two smooth cream dogs on a neighbouring farm. They had grown into very solid young hounds and one of them struck me as particularly strong. I asked the new owner whether he might be prepared to let me have him and, after a long discussion, he agreed to do so, but on one condition: he needed a bitch and asked for *Ziwa* in exchange. I said I would think it over and would meanwhile borrow the dog to see how he was at home. So, *Sami of Samarra*, as we called him, came home and settled down very quickly. He and *Tayra* hit it off immediately and they would have made a good couple, but *Ziwa* took a dislike to him, possibly sensing that her own future was in question. So that was our dilemma. We agonised over what to do, what was best for *Ziwa*, but in the end we decided we could not make the swap and I returned *Sami* to his owner. I was quite touched when I saw the small son of the farmer pick up *Sami* and give him a hug, obviously very happy to have his puppy back.

Most of my enquiries after Salukis that bore fruit were in the northern half of Iraq in respect to Baghdad, but that is not to say that I did not explore the southern half too. In fact, my official duties often took me there, not least to inspect the large

British and Commonwealth war graves from the First World War at Kut and Basra. I was also spurred on to look there by the archaeological record, especially in the areas around the great Sumerian city of Eridu, or Tell Abu Shahrain as it is now known, where the skeleton of a Saluki-type dog was excavated in 1947 in the grave of a young boy from the fourth millennium BC. A small meat bone was placed near its mouth as sustenance for the afterworld. A cylinder seal from Babylon from around 1900 BC also shows a Saluki-type hound. Evidence of their existence into modern times is also to be found. It is reported, for example, that after the First World War every British military establishment between Basra and Baghdad kept a 'Bobbery' pack of 'Persian Greyhounds' for hunting hare, fox, jackal and occasionally the odd pariah dog, if one got in the way. So there were at least some Salukis in the south in the last century, albeit in the hands of the British. It may have been in any case a less than propitious area for them because the tribes of the south are largely Shia and, unlike Sunnis, the Shia do not generally eat the meat of hare on religious grounds, so the main point of keeping Salukis would have no attraction for them. I was, however, told an interesting story that casts some doubt on this abstinence.

One of the great tribes of the south is the Bani Lam, who came originally from Nejd in Arabia and converted from Sunni to Shia Islam in the late 19th century. They seem, however, to have retained some of their centuries-old customs and, notably, their Salukis, as related to me by the late Mrs Henderson, widow of the late Colonel Victor Henderson. They lived in Iraq in 1954–7 during the monarchy and befriended some of the feudal shaikhs of the Bani Lam living around Amarah, a large town on the Tigris south-east of Baghdad, close to the border with Iran. One of the shaikhs gave them a smooth red bitch called *Dhiba*, and another shaikh later gave them a lightly feathered brown and white particoloured dog, called *Rihan*. They came with a long pedigree, which, according to Colonel Henderson, was recited …

> … by a very old tribesman accompanied by his sons: the sheik telling me he was the record-keeper of the tribe, handed down through generations. The colours and hunting abilities of both sexes were given at great length. I could only wait for five generations, but I feel I could have listened for hours. I had some pedigree forms with me, so we put the particulars on paper.

The Hendersons took the two hounds back to England, registered them with the

Kennel Club and bred them twice under the 'Kumasi' affix. Some of the offspring went on to become both coursing and show champions.

After the overthrow of the Hashemite monarchy in a bloody revolution in 1958, successive regimes sought to destroy the power of the feudal shaikhs. The Bani Lam tribe was not spared. Moreover, Amarah, because of its proximity to the Iranian border and its location on the edge of the marshes between the Tigris and Euphrates, was frequently attacked during the Iran–Iraq war. So it was perhaps unsurprising that, over the course of nearly five years, I never saw a single Saluki there or anywhere else in the south and all my enquiries in the area drew a total blank.

By now the summer was approaching and, before it got too hot, I wanted to spend one last weekend exploring the old camel mail route from Hit to Rutba across the desert. With a small group of friends in three vehicles and camping equipment, we set off from Baghdad for the old stage post at Qasr al-Khubbaz, where we intended to camp that night. We dropped in on my Turkoman friend Sami in Kubaisa on the way to see whether his hound *Hawa* might be interested in mating *Tayra*, as she was in season. He seemed very interested, but *Tayra* was definitely not having him, so we moved on to our camp site. The hounds had a great time in the freedom of the desert but did not put up any game. They also ran free for an hour the next morning before we set out to try to find the next stage post called 'Amij, about 55 km away to the west. As we went along, we were stopped by a bedouin pasturing camels. He said he knew the way, so he rode with us to guide us. He claimed to have a smooth white Saluki from Saudi Arabia, but when, after following a long, twisting track, we reached his tent, he reported that it had gone out with his flock of sheep. So we made a short stop for coffee and to meet his wives, who were making lengths of coarse black goat's-hair cloth on a primitive loom for the side panels of their tents. He then escorted us the short distance to some disappointing piles of stones outlining the once substantial foundations of the fort, all that was left of 'Amij. It was no place to stop, so we pressed on westwards towards the next stage post at Muhaiwir, but were misdirected by another bedouin en route and found ourselves suddenly on the asphalt road into Rutba. To make the best of it, I took our friends to see the gazelle reservation outside the town, where the scent of them drove our hounds frantic.

We had to see my friend Dalli, too, and found him in his garden with two peregrine falcons. His hounds were away hunting with one of his sons but, on the open ground opposite his home, I saw two Salukis with a young shepherd boy and a flock of sheep. One was a striking lightly feathered red dog with a black mask and black fringes, who picked up *Tayra's* interesting scent immediately and followed us around everywhere, but she was still not ready. Another lovely feathered grizzle then appeared from behind a second flock of sheep. This was the frequent practice in rural communities, where the young children would take small flocks of sheep or goats out to pasture in the morning and again in the evening with a Saluki or two to hunt whatever they came across and a guard dog for protection. Before leaving Rutba, another young lad came up and told me that his Saluki, which I had admired on my previous visit, had gone to a Saudi prince after it had been timed running at 80 kmh behind a vehicle. Such measurements are, of course, wildly inaccurate but it was enough to impress the Saudi and was indicative of the traditional movement of Salukis between the countries of the region.

It was during the summer that I had confirmation of my transfer from Baghdad at the end of the year and my appointment as ambassador to the Sultanate of Oman. This gave us plenty to think about, not least the future of our Salukis. I deliberated on acquiring a male puppy to take with us with a view to breeding from *Tayra* at some stage, and on my various trips around the country I kept this possibility in mind.

Elections were being held in the Kurdistan region in September and I drove up there as an observer. My driver, Qadir, took me via Kalar to see his family and I also had a quick look around for puppies. Asleep outside a neighbour's house was a smooth solid black Saluki, the first I had ever seen in Iraq. As I was taking some pictures, the owner came out and said he had some month-old puppies sired by a rather strange-looking dog I had seen once before. He was a smooth white speckled with brown, and rather chunkily built with a strong jaw almost like a Foxhound's. The owner said he killed and retrieved. One of the pups was just like him, but they were too young for me to consider and I had to press on to the elections.

After making my official calls in the main town of Sulaimaniya, we drove for about an hour to the west to the Kurdish town of Chamchamal, where I spent some time visiting the polling stations and observing the conduct of the elections. I asked a man outside one of the polling stations about Salukis and he said I should see Shaikh Jamal, who lived in Sharash, a new town added onto the back of Chamchamal to accommodate Kurds who had been cleared from the border with Iran during the war. We found him easily enough, because I quickly spotted a Saluki tied to a kennel outside one of the new breeze-block houses. It was a pretty feathered grizzle bitch of about five months. As I was photographing her, a neighbour appeared with a mean-looking cream slightly feathered crop-eared dog and a lovely feathered brindle, the black stripes just showing on a grizzle background. She was the sister of the bitch in the kennel and would have been just right, if she had been male. She was also further evidence that brindle is a Saluki colour, contrary to the popular belief in the West.

We were on the road back and passing by the oil town of Kirkuk, when I remembered that my friend Sami in Kubaisa had said that his Salukis came from his cousin, Shakou, who lived in Mulla Abdulla, a small village outside the town. We found the village and were directed to Shakou's house, where a surprise lay in store for us, for we were greeted by Sami himself, visiting from Kubaisa to help his cousin with the sheep shearing. So we had a jolly reunion and an introduction to sheep shearing. No machinery was used, just a pair of wickedly sharp long shears. I suspected that they had also been used on one of Shakou's three Salukis. The ears of the feathered cream male were cropped back so severely that virtually nothing remained, giving it an oddly aerodynamic effect, which was apparently the object. There was also a black and tan pregnant bitch, a sister of Sami's *Hawa*, and a nice black and tan puppy, but another female.

Meanwhile, my friend Subhi in Tel Afar had telephoned me to say his bitch *Moda* had had eight puppies and he was reserving four of them for me to look at. One of them was of an interesting colour, which he described as 'like an elephant'; two were cream, like one of the sires, and one was tricolour, like the dam. Knowing my aversion to cropped ears, he said he had left the ears intact on these four. By the time I had a chance to visit him, the pups were already five months old and some had left for their new homes, including the 'elephant', so I never did discover what colour he really was. The tricolour had also gone, and I was left with a choice between the two cream pups. One was nicely built and promised well, but it was another female; whereas the other was a male but seemed rather undersized. I had to decline both. Subhi did not mind, as he always had lots of requests for his Salukis and would have no trouble in finding a home for any he did not wish to keep.

When I was passing his house in Mosul some time later, I dropped in and found the two puppies were still there. By now they had been branded on the thigh with a crude half-circle. He was the only breeder I came across in Iraq who put brand marks on his hounds; and this was a clear indication that he intended to keep the two puppies for himself. I bade Subhi a tearful farewell, as my time in Iraq was running out. He had been a good mentor and I would have liked to stay in touch, but in the circumstances I doubted whether our paths would cross again. However, I had an unexpected surprise over 20 years later, as I shall relate in due course.

One of the things I enjoyed most in Iraq was to meet Salukis in their natural habitat when I least expected it. In the last few weeks before leaving the country, a prominent landowner and politician invited Liese and me with a few friends to a farewell lunch on his family farm east of Baghdad. Before lunch we were taken on a tour in the area to see if we might put up something for our hounds to chase. We did not find any game, but we were suddenly confronted by the idyllic sight of a shepherd leading his donkey followed by a small flock of sheep tended by the most beautiful feathered tricolour Saluki and a sheepdog. Further on we saw a blip on the flat horizon which, on inspection, proved to be a hide, with a falcon trapper inside. A domed roof of branches covered a pit deep enough for him to stand in. From the pit ran strings that were tied to a live crow and a spring-operated net. When the trapper spotted a falcon aloft during the migrating season, he would agitate the crow and if the falcon stooped on it he would release the net to trap it. Such wild falcons would then be trained and sold to Gulf falconers for large sums.

After an enormous lunch of a whole roasted sheep and rice, we were heading along a country road for home, when I spotted a gorgeous red feathered Saluki standing like a statue at the roadside. I stopped and asked a man walking along if he knew whose it was. He said that it did not belong to anyone and I should take it, if I wanted it. In other circumstances I would have been very tempted, but we could not risk taking on an unknown mature hound at that stage. Pity, as it looked so sad.

Before our departure I had to squeeze in farewell visits to my friends in Rutba and Kubaisa and to present them with blown-up photographs of themselves and their hounds. Sadly, when we reached Rutba Dalli was away hunting in the desert. However, his wife invited us in and showed his two new acquisitions: a beautiful red and white particoloured bitch wearing a padded coat against the cold, and a really lovely smooth red male puppy of just two months – just what I had been looking for. But his wife would not dare to give me the puppy without Dalli's permission and, in any case, it was now too late for me to take on such a young puppy.

A young boy, whom I had photographed before, was also pestering me to come and see his Salukis and hawks. He had quite a collection of birds, including a buzzard, a kestrel and a couple of young saker falcons, and two Salukis – a black-fringed red bitch and a feathered red and white particoloured dog. He was keen for me to take him out to where other members of his family and friends were camping in the desert with their falcons and Salukis, but it was some 65 km away and we still had to have lunch in Fallujah on the way home. We arrived late to a warm welcome and an enormous spread of food to which it was impossible to do justice, but we did not feel guilty as we knew that what was left would go out through the back door to feed many hungry mouths and nothing would be wasted. (People in Fallujah later could only dream of such food, when they had been reduced by the fighting to eating boiled weeds.) Before leaving, our genial host insisted we saw his new acquisitions – two peregrine falcons, a young mountain goat and some gazelle. We had some Australian friends with us, who were absolutely mesmerised by this display of Arab hospitality and tradition.

Shepherd boys and their Salukis near Kubaisa.

Christmas was approaching and we had time for one last visit to Kubaisa to say goodbye to Sami and his family. It was a brilliant, cold morning as we drove into the oasis and we were met almost immediately by a boy with a feathered three-month-old red puppy with a white bib and her identical brother. The temptation was hard to resist but …

The boy said the other hounds were out hunting nearby and showed us the way. As we drove he asked shyly whether we ate fox. He admitted that the locals did and the meat was very good. Meat of any kind was something of a luxury in these small rural communities and even a fox was better than nothing. We found a group of young lads with their sheep and about half a dozen Salukis and Luqis. I recognised the group from the time I had seen them as puppies. The feathered tricolour dam had been mated twice, once with a Saluki and once accidently with a shepherd dog. She had produced two puppies like her, which had grown into very nice Salukis, and two crossbreds, which had also grown into useful hunting dogs. Together with the other hounds there they would have been a formidable hunting pack, but there was nothing to chase. So we went on to Sami's house, only to find that he was in his date plantation. But as soon as we arrived, he dropped everything and said, 'Let's go!' So, for one last time, we drove to the wadi where we had coursed before, and we were in luck. We had not walked far when I spotted the shape of a reclining hare. It got up, I slipped our two hounds and they engaged in a thrilling chase. The hare twisted and turned but could not lose them until it finally shot up a dry wadi and disappeared, probably down a hole. It was with such happy memories that we flew home for Christmas.

At night the master brings him nearest to his bed;

Chapter Five

Salukis in Arabia

We flew back to Baghdad in the middle of January 1990 to a joyful reunion with our hounds. We packed our remaining personal belongings into our estate car and armed ourselves with all the necessary visas and documentation to enable us to drive right the way down the Gulf to Muscat. The hounds had more documentation than us, as we were advised to take multiple copies of health certificates from the Iraqi Ministry of Agriculture's Veterinary Service to the effect that they were free from rabies. The veterinary inspector merely patted *Tayra* on the head and did not even notice *Ziwa* asleep in the car, before issuing the necessary papers. We then trundled around to the Saudi embassy, where every copy had to be stamped again.

After fond farewells to all our many colleagues and friends, we set off one crisp morning on the first stage of our long journey and reached Kuwait without incident just as it was getting dark. We had stopped at intervals on the way to let the hounds run and they were very good about jumping back into the car when it was time to move on, clearly not wanting to be left behind in the featureless desert on either side of the road. We stayed overnight at the British Embassy, where the hounds could run free in the garden and chase all the cats, and continued our journey the next morning. We crossed easily from Kuwait into Saudi Arabia and from there into Bahrain and felt slightly cheated that, after all that trouble to obtain the hounds' documents, we were never once asked to show them.

Once again we stayed at the British Embassy, where friends had laid on a wonderful welcome for us. We were whisked off immediately to see Shaikha Danah Al Khalifa on her farm, where she keeps her famous stud of Arabians and her pack of Salukis. The latter had been shut away as they did not take kindly to strange hounds on their territory and they howled in protest in the background. Shaikha Danah was enchanted by our hounds and kindly agreed to register them with the Bahrain Kennel Club, founded in 1973, a measure that was to prove very helpful later on when I sought registration with the Kennel Club in the UK. We had a lovely time with her as she showed us around and told us her story of falling for Salukis when she first arrived in Bahrain in 1967 and keeping them ever since. Salukis were then fairly uncommon and exclusively with the Ruler and his family, which partly explains why I did not see any when I served there in 1957–8 on my first diplomatic posting, even though I met the then Ruler Shaikh Salman bin Hamad Al Khalifa at his palace on a number of occasions.

Shaikha Danah had done a lot to preserve the Bahraini type of hound, which is quite tall and feathery by comparison with the generality of hounds in Arabia. Indeed, Colonel HRP Dickson goes so far as to opine on the Bahraini hounds in the 1930s in his encyclopaedic work *The Arab of the Desert* (1949):

> Personally I am inclined to believe that Shaikh Hamad's salūqis have Persian greyhound blood in them, or possibly were originally imported from the Persian shore of the Gulf. I have certainly never seen such big animals as his on the Arabian littoral.

The breed has become more popular since, with imports from elsewhere in the Gulf and further afield. It was hard to drag ourselves away from such an interesting and hospitable hostess, but our time was limited and I knew we would remain in touch.

The next morning, as we crossed back into Saudi Arabia we encountered a particularly obtuse official who ignored all our diplomatic documentation and insisted on searching our baggage. He then disappeared into an office and reappeared brandishing an envelope, which he ordered that on no account should we fail to hand over to the Immigration Office on exiting Saudi Arabia. In pouring rain, we continued our route, crossing at one stage a narrow finger of Saudi territory between Qatar and the United Arab Emirates. Here, by the Qatar Customs post, I saw the rare sight in the Middle East of a pretty cream feathered Saluki wandering about loose. She

Shaikha Danah Al Khalifa's farm.

was pregnant and looked abandoned, poor thing. But we could not help her and had to move on to the Saudi border, which was a desolate place marked only by two large huts and a boom across the road. When I presented the letter I had been given earlier at the Immigration Office, the effect on the previously rather sleepy official was electrifying. He ran out of his office round to my car and indicated with his forefinger that he was counting the hounds – one, two! Satisfied that there were no more nor fewer than before, he waved us through. We reached the British Embassy in Abu Dhabi late and the hounds, who had been so good in the car, were able to run free at last in the grounds.

We still had a long way to go, and set off early the next morning for the border at Hatta in the United Arab Emirates, stopping only to let the hounds have a good run in the sand dunes before making the crossing into Oman. Here our documentation for the hounds was scrutinised and found in order, and we were through the formalities to be met by some of my new staff to guide us the rest of the way down the Batinah coast to the embassy in Muscat, which was to be our home for the next four and a half years.

The embassy was set in a large compound, surrounded on the landward side by a high wall, access through which was by massive teak doors, and by a lower, pierced wall on the seaward side facing Muscat Bay. It looked dog-proof, even for such remarkable escape artistes as Salukis. The embassy and residence were combined in a single building redolent with history. Britain has had trading relations with Oman since 1645, but it was not until 1800 that it signed with the then Sultan a treaty, which said: 'an English gentleman of respectability should always reside at the port of Muscat' and 'the friendship of the two States may remain unshook till the end of time, and the sun and moon have finished their revolving career'. I felt honoured to be that English gentleman. The original building was replaced in 1890 with another in the Arab style around a square courtyard, with massive walls and deep shaded verandas all round to keep out the oppressive heat of summer.

The offices were on the ground floor and the residence above. This arrangement was less than ideal for our hounds. Access to the small garden at the back was via highly polished tiled verandas and a narrow metal fire escape stairway, but they quickly learnt not to take the corners and stairway at speed and lose their footing. Free space within the compound was limited, and outside lay the old walled town of Muscat, encircled by craggy mountains of volcanic rock; so we would clearly have to find space elsewhere where they could run free. Fortunately, there were kilometres of empty golden beaches a short drive away where the hounds quickly adapted to the novelty of the sea and liked nothing more than racing through the shallows sending up clouds of silver fish. We also found wadis running through the mountains, but the problem there was that the hounds would often cut their feet on the sharp rocks in pursuit of foxes.

Sometimes there was no alternative to walking them through the streets within the walls of Old Muscat, and here one day I was pursued by an old man who, clearly having no idea of my identity, attempted to thrust an Omani banknote into my hand, equivalent to about £10, with the muttered comment in Arabic that it was to feed my skinny dog! It seemed that, even in an Arab country where the Saluki's lean characteristics might have been more easily recognised, the sight of a dog with its ribs showing was cause enough to attract sympathy or, indeed, criticism.

This reminded me of an incident a couple of years previously that had made quite a splash in the press. A colleague of mine, Gordon Pirie, had a Saluki in London, who was particularly picky with his food and therefore looked even leaner than usual. Gordon and his wife, Maria, had acquired the hound they called *Tazi* as a puppy while they were serving at the embassy in Beirut, Lebanon in 1981 and had taken him around with them on postings to Milan and Rome and eventually back to London on a home posting. They had already served twice before at the embassy in Tehran, and in 1988 were asked to go back to reopen the embassy there after a break in diplomatic relations following an incident when the British Chargé d'Affaires had been beaten up and expelled from the country. Gordon and Maria decided they would travel there with *Tazi* by car to take a holiday en route and spare him the trauma of flying.

The resumption of relations had attracted a lot of media interest and on 19 November 1988, the day of their departure, a scrum of reporters and photographers awaited them outside their house. Naturally enough in a dog-loving nation, *Tazi* was the centre of attention and his picture, showing his prominent ribs, appeared all over the press and on television. The Foreign & Commonwealth Office then had to field a stream of protests about the shameful starvation of the dog, whose owners were apparently not paid enough to feed him properly! Eventually the FCO found a Saluki breeder to publish an article in the *Daily Telegraph* to confirm that Salukis were indeed meant to be thin and that *Tazi* was just a bit thinner than usual. *The Times*, however, took another angle, criticising the FCO and the Piries for not hurrying to Tehran. Gordon and Maria were blissfully unaware of all this as they crossed Europe before boarding a ferry in Greece and landing in Istanbul for the final drive through Turkey, where the Turks at once recognised their hound as a Tazi. *Tazi* behaved impeccably throughout this long car journey, oblivious to his celebrity status, and settled down for a couple of months in Tehran, closer to his country of origin. Sadly, another sudden break in diplomatic relations with Iran ended this idyll and *Tazi* was bundled onto a plane for Rome and a return to Italy, where he died a few months later.

Another of my Diplomatic Service colleagues, Sir Alan Munro, had also had a spot of bother in London with his lean Saluki, as he relates in his memoir *Keep the Flag Flying* (2012). Alan had acquired in Kuwait in 1961 a handsome feathered black and tan puppy from some of the Mutair tribe camped near the town. Colonel Dickson opines in *The Arab of the Desert* that the Mutair are among the best breeders and trainers of Salukis in Eastern Arabia after the 'Ajman tribe and their cousins the Murrah. Alan and his wife Grania moved to London in 1963 with *Sabah* and spent the first night in a rented flat in Notting Hill. Suddenly, well after midnight, there was a loud knock at the door: it was a policeman wanting to know if they had a thin dog. *Sabah* then appeared and the policeman remarked: 'Ah, it's a Saluki'. It seemed that some busybody had reported seeing Grania walking with a 'half-starved Gordon Setter'. By happy coincidence, the policeman had lived as a boy on a Royal Air Force base in Libya and was familiar with Salukis. So no further action was taken and he departed content. *Sabah* was a very handsome hound and, Alan told me, was even photographed by the society photographer of the day, Patrick Lichfield. He was successfully registered with the Kennel Club and his services were much in demand by breeders as a fresh source of genes. He died of pneumonia five years later when the Munros were serving in Tripoli, Libya.

'Sabah' by Patrick Lichfield.

Settling into my busy new job kept me confined to Muscat for the first couple of months, but I always seized on any of my frequent contacts with Omanis to ask if they knew about Salukis in Oman. Time and time again I would be told that there were none. I found this hard to believe, since they were known to exist there historically. After all, the Honourable Florence Amherst, in her chapter on Oriental

Greyhounds in *Cassell's New Book of the Dog* (1907), had thought fit to designate the Omani Saluki as one of only four distinct types – the others being the Shami (Syrian), Yamani (Yemeni) and the Nejdi (Saudi). She described the Omani and Yemeni types as having 'not much feathering on ears and tail'. It would therefore seem that, at that time at least, there were sufficient Salukis of a distinct type in Oman to merit recognition. Forty years later, the renowned British explorer Wilfred Thesiger had hunted with Salukis and falcons in the Liwa desert on the border between Abu Dhabi and Oman and his magnificent photographs include one that exactly met the Amherst description of an Omani type of Saluki (Clark, 1995). Could they all have disappeared from Oman in the interval? That was the question that I asked over and over again, and eventually I learnt from some bedouin that all forms of hunting, including with Salukis, had been banned since 1976 to preserve wildlife and that the ban was so rigorously enforced that it was no longer worth their while to keep Salukis. That was a blow, but I did not give up.

A major public holiday was coming up and some knowledgeable friends suggested a camping expedition into the Empty Quarter, where they said the views of the mighty dunes were spectacular. They mentioned the area around a borehole that produced water for the bedouin at an oasis called Fasad. The name rang a bell and I remembered that someone had told me that he had seen a Saluki at the end of a train of camels coming in from Saudi Arabia to water at the borehole some years before. So it seemed a doubly interesting place to explore, though I could not possibly know that it would nearly cost the lives of my own Salukis.

Our route cut through Thesiger country, taking in the well at Shisur, which the explorer visited during his epic crossing of the Empty Quarter by camel in 1947 described in *Arabian Sands*. Now there was a graded track to it and a modern housing estate for the bedouin, quite different from when Thesiger had had to dig out the saline well to water his camels. I was amazed to find, when talking to a young bedouin lad about Thesiger's visit, that he knew all the details, including the names of Thesiger's companions, as if the event had happened recently instead of some 40 years before. Oral tradition remains strong among the bedouin and he must have heard the story of Thesiger's visit many times over.

From Shisur we drove on towards Fasad on a graded track across the flat gravel plain, where our vehicles threw up great plumes of dust, fortunately carried away by the strong cross-wind. Suddenly our leader, who was very experienced in desert travel, pulled up and began running after a large *dhub*, or spiny-tailed lizard. I loosed the hounds to join in the chase and they quickly stopped it. They had never seen one before and were not sure what to make of it. The bedouin regard it as a delicacy, but we let it go.

On reaching Fasad, we reported our presence to the Frontier Police that patrolled the border with Saudi Arabia there and went to see the borehole, where clear but sulphurous water gushed out to supply the emerald-green oasis. Some bedouin were camped nearby and I thought I would see what they made of my hounds. However, *Tayra* decided to chase one of their camels and the irate owner asked what I thought I was doing with Salukis (which he at least recognised as such) when hunting with them was banned. That was not a good beginning and it was clear that further conversation would be fruitless. So we left the ease of the graded track and turned off into the dunes, looking for a spot already reconnoitred by our leader, lying at the base of one of the highest dunes in that area. We arrived towards sunset and I went up the steep slope to photograph the breathtaking display of colours made by the setting sun. The hounds came too, and promptly disappeared to explore. *Tayra* returned about two hours later in the dark and *Ziwa* sometime after her, apparently none the worse apart from a huge thirst. I was unconcerned by their absence as I was used to them going off on their own for long periods during our camping trips in Iraq. So I was not at all worried when we climbed the dune again at dawn to see the colours of the sunrise and the hounds disappeared again. They had not eaten or drunk since the night before and I expected that they would return with their tongues lolling out by the time we had had breakfast and broke camp; but they did not.

I shall never know exactly what happened but, the longer we waited, the more the terrible thought began to grow in my mind that their hitherto infallible homing instinct had failed and they might be lost in that barren, pitiless desert. Some of our friends had to leave, but a few others stayed with us, sheltering from the blistering heat of the midday sun under a makeshift awning. As it grew cooler towards evening, I decided to go back to the police post in Fasad to ask if they had any news of the hounds and if they would pass a message back to the embassy by their radio telephone that our return would be delayed by a day. The police asked immediately why I had not tracked the hounds, as if that was the most natural thing to do. I had to explain that I had only the vaguest idea in which direction they had gone some ten hours earlier and that I was not skilled in tracking. Two policemen promptly volunteered to track them down and zoomed off in a pickup with balloon tyres that enabled

Lost and found.

them to ride easily over the soft sand. Less than an hour later, we saw the lights of the pickup coming back. Nonchalantly the policemen said that they had found the hounds but they were some way off and we should come quickly. They roared off again and I jumped into my vehicle to follow them, but it promptly sank into the soft sand. Fortunately, our leader had a better-equipped vehicle and we went on a crazy, hair-raising drive across the dunes in the dark, trying to find the policemen's pickup. Eventually we located them as they flicked their lights to guide us. As we approached I could see, to my great relief, both hounds standing in the lights of the pickup. They were alive but visibly exhausted. They drank all the water we had with us, with both muzzles squeezed into a small bowl. They wanted more but we had to get them back to camp. Once there, they drank copiously, ate a little and settled down to sleep. *Tayra* seemed fine but the more delicate *Ziwa*, who, with her thicker fur, always suffered more from the heat, breathed irregularly in distress and I was concerned whether she would survive. The next day, however, both hounds seemed in remarkably good form, though I kept them on the leash – no more running away in the dunes!

I called at the police post in Fasad on the way back to thank the trackers, whom I rewarded later, and I was able to piece together from them some details of their extraordinary feat. They said they had circled round in the general area I had indicated until they picked up the tracks. They had followed them as best they could in the dark, sometimes losing them but then picking them up again. They had covered some eight kilometres in this way until they found the hounds. They had then let them smell a small bottle of water and headed back to our camp with the hounds trotting behind. Part-way, they noticed that the hounds were distressed, so they raced ahead to fetch us – they did not like to pick the hounds up and put them in their vehicle. So, when we caught up with the hounds they had been going from before dawn to well after sunset without food or water, in high temperatures most of the time, while covering anywhere from 15 to 25 kilometres across the desert. They may have sheltered in whatever shade they could find during the heat of the day, perhaps even digging down into the cooler sand, and fortunately they had stayed together. They might even have been on their way back to camp when they were found. The trackers' skill was remarkable, but so was the ability of these Salukis to survive in these unaccustomed surroundings.

The experience reminded me of an episode described by the British explorer Abdullah Philby in his epic work *The Empty Quarter* (1933), when his Saluki bitch, called *al-Aqfa*, went missing on a trek in the early 1930s:

> A single incident had caused a slight commotion during the march. Al-Aqfa was suddenly discovered to be missing. She had missed her good friend the cook in our company, and had apparently gone back to Naifa in search of him. We resigned ourselves philosophically to the sad loss, but our joy was great indeed when the familiar shape was seen sidling into camp soon after we arrived. She had drawn a blank at our abandoned dwelling place and returned following our tracks. The intelligence of the desert Saluqi is almost human.

Wherever I encountered bedouin in Oman thereafter, they always seemed to know about my hounds' adventure, as the bush telegraph had spread the story far and wide, but they loved to hear it again from me so that they could embellish it when retelling it around the campfire later. However, none of them ever gave me any encouragement to think I might find Salukis anywhere in Oman, until one day my hopes were raised.

I was accompanying a British minister on various calls in Muscat when we were suddenly invited to join his counterpart to see what was described as democracy at work, Omani style. We flew to a landing strip near one of the oilfields deep in the interior where, in the shade of some trees, there was a gathering of the local tribes. Here a couple of Omani ministers held a kind of court at which anyone could pose a question and receive an answer. The bedouin are not at all shy and the debate was quite robust, mostly about matters that touched their lives directly such as employment, housing, roads, etc. I found myself squatting next to Shaikh Saif from the Duru' tribe, who once led a nomadic existence pasturing their camels and returning to their date plantations for the annual harvest. They are now settled and many of the men have moved to employment in the oilfields. Shaikh Saif knew all about Salukis and invited me to visit him at his home near the small town of Tan'am.

A public holiday was coming up and we decided to go and visit the Duru' in the Wadi Aswad. Everyone knows everyone in those parts and I had only to stop a passing vehicle to be guided towards Shaikh Saif's home. I then stopped another vehicle and the driver happened to be one of the shaikh's sons. He guided us the remainder of the way to a warm welcome from the shaikh outside his small house set among palm trees. Carpets were spread on the sand and, as we sat taking refreshments, a succession of well-wishers dropped in for a chat. One told me he knew of a Saluki nearby and volunteered to take me there. Although it was getting dark, we raced over to another house where there was indeed an elderly Saluki, called *Saddah*, who had clearly seen better days a long time before. It was a smooth silver grizzle with a white band across its neck and rather small, turned-back ears; and, most unusually, it was castrated, apparently to stop it straying in search of a mate. So it was definitely the end of the line for him.

Back at Shaikh Saif's, we were entertained to a huge dinner, the centrepiece of which was a whole roast goat, eaten on the carpets outside under the stars, where any number of relatives and friends joined us. As we chatted, they described rather wistfully how their nomadic way of life had changed forever. They were finding it hard to adapt to the discipline of regular employment, when they were so used to the freedom of the past. Sadly, there was no longer a place for the Salukis and falcons that once played an important role as providers of meat. The law banned their use and, in any case, people could so easily drive to a supermarket for their needs. I heard the same story from some other shaikhs of the Bani Qitab and Bani Ghafir tribes, on whom we called on our drive back to Muscat. So, although we had had a stimulating introduction to the traditional side of Omani society, it left us also just a little disappointed that so much had changed in recent times. My disappointment was compounded on arriving home in Muscat.

I took the hounds for a little walk to stretch their legs and, as we re-entered the compound via the little wicket gate set in the main doors, I heard a growl and a yelp behind me. I turned and saw *Tayra*, ever watchful and protective, standing over our watchman who was squatting on the ground holding his wrist. He always carried a heavy stick and, after opening the gate for me to come in, had followed behind me. *Tayra* must have thought a man with a stick behind me was not good for my safety and she had gone for the hand holding the stick. I grabbed her by the collar and gave her a whack on her bottom – whereupon she twisted around so fast she dislocated the middle finger of my left hand! Somewhat shamefacedly, I was obliged to go to the hospital with the watchman and explain how we both needed treatment on our hands. I really should not have blamed *Tayra*, as she was only doing what she saw as her duty.

That first summer proved hot in more ways than one. The hounds were not used to the combination of ferocious heat and high humidity, and developed different kinds of skin infections, caused by bacteria that thrived in those atmospheric conditions. We were constantly taking them to the vet for treatment with anti-bacterial shampoos and antibiotics, despite the fact that they were in the salty sea almost every day. *Ziwa*, with her thicker coat, seemed to suffer more. Then, on 1 August 1990, came the devastating news that Iraq had invaded Kuwait, and we were heavily involved in engaging with the Oman government over the international response, including the stationing of Royal Air Force aircraft in Oman. This high level of activity continued for much of the next six months as preparations were made by the international coalition to expel Iraq from Kuwait in January 1991. Fortunately, the so-called First Gulf War was all over in a matter of weeks but the heightened, at times frenetic, diplomatic and military activity meant that my field trips were largely put on hold during this period until the situation reverted to something like normal.

However, in my many discussions with Omanis the name of one tribe kept coming up as the only one likely to still have Salukis. This was the Al bu Shamis tribe, grouped around the major oasis town of Buraimi, which faces the equally important oasis town of al-Ain in Abu Dhabi. I knew that al-Ain had a zoo that included, oddly enough, a pack of Salukis, so I thought that, even if I drew a blank with the Al bu Shamis, I could at least see the zoo collection. So, one holiday weekend, we drove to Buraimi and I called on one of the shaikhs of the tribe. He advised me to see his relatives at Sunaina, a village some way back on our road home. We were, however, so close to the al-Ain Zoo that we thought we would first drop in there. I met the Director, who took me to a compound where, to my surprise, there were about 30 Salukis of all ages, including a couple of bitches with litters. The hounds were a complete mixture of types, ranging from rather showy feathered to somewhat chunky smooths, which served to confirm their varied origins from within the region and further afield. They lived in a series of cage-like kennels with access to a large open sandy space for exercise and, it was said, some of them would be used on a new racetrack then nearing completion, which was due to be opened early in 1991. The track did indeed operate for several years, with both Salukis and imported Greyhounds competing in separate events. However, it proved not to be a success and eventually closed down, with the consequent difficult disposal of the hounds.

I also heard at the zoo that one of the litters there had been sired by a Saluki from the large kennels nearby at al-Khazna, belonging to the then Ruler of Abu Dhabi and President of the United Arab Emirates, Shaikh Zayed bin Sultan Al Nahyan, and on another occasion I paid a visit there with my family and our Salukis. I never expected to see so many hounds in one place! I stopped counting when I reached 70, but there must have been many more. Most were Salukis, but there were also some other sighthounds, such as Greyhounds and Afghans, and some crossbreds. One powerful smooth red Saluki of Saudi origin, which had allegedly pulled down a dozen gazelle on a hunting trip in East Africa, looked particularly good and, as *Tayra* was in season, we introduced them to each other, but sadly it was not love at first sight. However, my daughter Sonja kept falling for the puppies that, with typical Arab generosity, were offered to her as we went around the kennels.

On our way home from Buraimi I succeeded in tracking down in Sunaina the Al bu Shamis shaikhs to whom I had been referred. As it was a holiday, they were sitting together greeting well-wishers in a reception room in one of a small group of modest houses. Over dates and coffee, they showed that they knew all about hunting with Salukis and falcons, but related the now familiar story that since the hunting ban no one kept Salukis or falcons any more – or almost no one! After some discussion among themselves, one of the shaikhs told his son to take me to a *Fareeq* (farmstead) some distance away, where there were two Salukis. Off we went across the desert and after about half an hour came to the *Fareeq*. Even as we approached, I could see a familiar shape lying in the shade under a parked truck. It was a small black and white Saluki bitch, probably no more than 58 cm at the shoulder and about a year old. She too had rather small, folded-back ears, like the one I had seen previously. The owner confirmed he had had another male but had given it away to someone in Buraimi as it had started chasing livestock. He seemed rather reticent about his hound, as if he were concerned about the legality of owning one and may have suspected my motives in asking questions about her. He maintained that she was merely a guard dog for his flocks and I did not press him on the point. At least I had found one representative of the breed and this led me to wonder whether there were not more on similar isolated farmsteads in the area.

I was reinforced in this view when, a couple of years later, I happened to be talking one day to a bedouin in Oman's other great desert, the Wahiba Sands (now also known as the Sharqiya Sands). He said that he had seen a Saluki just like *Tayra* in a small town on the edge of the Sands and gave me directions to the place. These were not difficult to follow, and I was in luck: I found the man with not one but two Salukis! One was a beautiful tall feathered cream dog called *Shahin* and the other was his sister, called *Fitna*, a smaller smooth cream bitch. They had been brought into Oman from Saudi Arabia as small puppies. Their owner said with a twinkle in his eye that he kept them only as pets because of the hunting ban; but then he and another man who joined us proceeded to relate stories of hunting in the Wahiba Sands! One of them said that he had had a Saluki that was a real 'artist' when it came to coursing gazelle. It could pick up the tracks in the early morning dew and follow the gazelle until they came into view, when it would hunt them down by sight. It would then return to fetch the owner. The fame of the hound was such that he had been persuaded to sell it for a large sum to a shaikh from Abu Dhabi.

Shahin.

Shahin looked as if he would make a very good mate for *Tayra* and I said I would be back when she was next in season.

In the meantime, I had had an invitation to visit a wildlife reservation in a remote part of Oman called the Jiddat al-Harasis, where the fabled Arabian white oryx (*Oryx leucoryx*) was making a comeback from extinction. I had never seen one before and was curious to know how it matched up to the description of an oryx hunt with Salukis that I had once read, which was written in the 7th century by one of the great pre-Islamic poets called Labid ibn Rabia al-Amiri, quoted here in the translation by Lady Anne and Wilfrid Scawen Blunt:

> *She, the white cow, shone there through the dark night luminous*
> *like a pearl of deep seas, freed from the string of it. …*
> *And they failed, the archers. Loosed they then to deal with her*
> *Fine-trained hounds, the lop-eared, slender the sides of them.*
> *These outran her lightly. Turned she swift her horns on them,*
> *Like twin spears of Samhar, sharp-set the points of them.*
> *Well she knew her danger, knew if her fence failed with them*
> *Hers must be the red death. Hence her wrath's strategy.*
> *And she slew Kasabi, foremost hound of all of them,*
> *Stretched the brach in blood there, ay, and Sakham of them.*

The Arabian white oryx is an antelope that, due to its bovine tail, shoulder hump and other features, is often called a wild cow in Arabic. About the size of a donkey, it is certainly a large animal by comparison with a Saluki. It is not known for its speed; indeed, it lumbers rather clumsily on its out-sized hoofs when it is put to flight. It relies for its defence more on its ability to live in areas remote from water, as it needs to drink only rarely and derives much of its moisture from the vegetation it grazes, and on its long straight horns. It certainly does nothing to hide its presence; on the contrary, its brilliant white coat reflects the sun and the moon and can be seen from kilometres away. Its natural defences were no match for hunters with rifles and cross-country vehicles, and by the late 1950s there were probably only 50–60 oryx left in the wild in all Arabia. The last known herd was actually on the Jiddat al-Harasis and this was slaughtered in October 1972 by a hunting party from outside Oman. Fortunately, ten years earlier a project had already been launched, with financial help from the World Wildlife Fund and encouragement from other conservation groups by the Fauna Preservation Society of London, to save the oryx from extinction. With a combination of three wild oryx caught in the Hadhramaut in Yemen and six more donated from zoos in London, Kuwait and Saudi Arabia, a nucleus herd was established in Phoenix Zoo, Arizona, where the climate is similar to that of Arabia. A breeding programme was started with a view to reintroduce the oryx one day into its native habitat. In October 1974, the Sultan of Oman decided that the oryx should be returned to where it had last existed in the wild and, after careful research and planning, the first batch of five animals was delivered in March 1980 to Yalooni in the Jiddat al-Harasis. Over the next ten years other oryx were received from Phoenix Zoo and, together with those born in the wild since 1984, the numbers increased to several hundred so that they could be allowed to range freely, until poaching started again in recent years and preservation measures had to be reintroduced.

Against that background, I was curious to see whether the ancient Arabian poet could really have been describing an oryx hunt with Salukis. I could not take mine with me to put them to the test because of the hunting ban, but I could observe, listen and imagine and I came to several conclusions. First, the poet's description of the oryx as white like a pearl shining luminously at night is wholly true. The oryx is dazzlingly white when the sun or moon shines directly on its flanks. However, when it turns head on, its black face and leg markings render it almost invisible against the light and shadows of the trees under which it often shelters for shade. Second, it is a very large animal, a bull standing about 1.20 metres at the shoulder and weighing about 80 kg, and both the bull and the cow carry a pair of long, sharply-pointed horns. One of the local Harsusi rangers taking me round said that he had once seen how an oryx had skewered a wolf on its horns in the same way as the poet said the cow oryx had slain the two Salukis. I found it hard to imagine a much smaller and lighter animal like a Saluki taking on an oryx; in a pack, it would clearly be a different matter. Some would distract the oryx from the front, while others would harry it from the rear (I have seen my own Salukis use such tactics on other prey) until the animal was exhausted and could be killed. Hunters in Algeria and Morocco employ packs of hounds to hunt wolf and jackal in this way. However, it seems to me more probable that in earlier times the Arabs used Salukis more often in pairs (the poem speaks of only two hounds) and their role would have been to harry and turn the oryx at bay until such time as the hunters, whether mounted or on foot, could come near to despatch it with lances or arrows or ritually with the knife.

The Jiddat al-Harasis is also home to the Nubian ibex (*Capra ibex nubiana*) and various types of gazelle. An adult male ibex is also a large animal weighing upwards of 60 kg and is crowned with a pair of massive scimitar-shaped horns. It is essentially a mountain goat and its narrow hooves allow it to adapt to life on rocky outcrops, crags and ledges of the sort found on the eastern edge of the Jiddat al-Harasis. A seal impression from Tepe Gawra near Mosul in Iraq and a decorated beaker from Susa in Iran from the fourth millennium BC show Saluki-type dogs hunting ibex. Once again, I could imagine Salukis being used only to harry and turn the prey at bay for the hunter as they are not built for pursuit on steep escarpments, where the sharp rocks would lacerate their feet. So many times did my Salukis return with torn and bloody feet from pursuing foxes among jagged rocks.

The ranger with me told the amazing story of how he earned his appointment at the Research Centre at Yalooni. He had caught a male ibex with his bare hands when it came to drink at a waterhole, wrestled it to the ground, tied it up and carried it in alive to be fitted with a tracking collar. Such exceptional ability was recognised with a job as a ranger.

I saw a lot of gazelle on the Jiddat al-Harasis, mostly in small groups rather than the great herds of 50 or more that once existed in the area. They were of two species: the small Arabian gazelle (*Gazella gazella cora* or *Gazella gazella Arabica*) and the larger rhim or goitered gazelle (*Gazella subgutturosa marica*). The different species are, however, notoriously difficult to classify and to add to the confusion experts in Oman believe that there is interbreeding between them, producing further variations. All these species would be well within the capability of Salukis to catch, as they weigh from about 11 to 20 kg, but once again I suspect that in the heyday of hunting with horse or camel, hawk and hound, Salukis were used more to run down gazelle to the point of exhaustion for capture alive or for immediate ritual despatch with the knife, just as my friend Dalli in Rutba, Iraq used to do.

After all the hullabaloo following the expulsion of the Iraqi armed forces from Kuwait in February 1991, I was faced with a heart-searching dilemma of a different sort with regard to *Ziwa*. Her relations with *Tayra* had not improved and she started running away when we went on walks at the beach, to escape being chased by *Tayra*. Once when she ran off and refused to come back I had to abandon her as I had to get to a meeting. I found her again some hours later, quite unconcerned about being left alone. Her skin infection had become chronic and we were constantly seeking veterinary help. One day the vet told me that he could do no more for her. I asked whether her skin problems might be psychosomatic. He agreed that it was entirely possible that she was becoming increasingly neurotic under *Tayra*'s domination. Reluctantly we came to the conclusion that, as we could not separate them by rehoming her, we had to put her out of her misery; and the deed was done.

By strange coincidence, *Tayra* came into season that night and our gloomy spirits were uplifted by the thought that we might be able to breed a companion from her. The Royal Oman Police had two male Salukis, which they thought might have derived from England, but they could not find the pedigree papers. When we thought *Tayra* was ready, they sent round a feathered grizzle and we introduced them in our small garden. The male seemed rather old and tired, and after two days together it was clear he was not up to the job. So the police took him away and brought their other male, a younger version of the first. He was certainly interested but *Tayra* seemed to have passed her peak and refused him. So that was the end of that idea until she came into season next time.

Meanwhile we had been over to Dubai, where I made contact with some resident Swiss breeders, Susi Leimbacher and Jim Oechslin, and their houseful of Salukis. They had a litter of ten puppies out of a Saudi bitch, but I decided I would prefer to breed from *Tayra* if I could. I thought I had a possible future match for her when I met a Swedish physiotherapist working in Oman who had previously worked in Dhahran, Saudi Arabia, where he had had Salukis. He had brought with him a handsome young feathered cream male, called *La'iq*. At the end of the year, when she was in season again, *La'iq* came to stay with us for a few days. They got on very well together but never succeeded in reaching a tie; and then *Tayra* indicated that that was it and *La'iq* had to go home again. It was beginning to look as if we would never succeed in mating her, so I turned my mind to other possibilities.

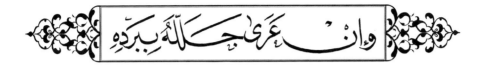

If he is uncovered, his master puts on him his own coat.

Chapter Six

Fate Takes a Hand

At Easter 1992, we decided to take some local leave and formed an ambitious plan to drive to Syria. Liese and I thought it might be fun to revisit some of the places where we had spent our honeymoon; and I also had the ulterior motive of finding a possible companion there for *Tayra*. After all, was it not in Syria that Brigadier General Frederick Lance had acquired his first Salukis in 1919? – and if there were top-quality Salukis there then, might they still be there a mere 75 years later?

It was at the end of the First World War that the then Major Frederick Lance was serving in the 19th Bengal Lancers in Syria. He was already an experienced horseman and huntsman, since his early days in the Indian Army. So it was perfectly natural for him, once hostilities were over, to indulge once again in his favourite recreation – coursing on horseback. For this purpose he acquired a small grizzle bitch from a local official in Baalbek – hence the name he gave her, though she was called *Becky* for short. He also acquired from a Syrian shaikh near Damascus a rangy white dog with black and tan markings, called, rather unimaginatively, *Seleughi*. He bred them twice and kept a couple of the puppies for hunting in Palestine, where he was to spend the last two years of his army service. He retired back to England in 1921, taking with him two of his Salukis. He added the affix *Sarona* to their names *Kelb* and *Tor*, from the town of that name in Palestine where he had served. *Sarona Kelb* (an odd choice of name again, since *Kelb* means 'dog' in Arabic, though it is also the name of a once

*I am offered
Saddah.*

major Syrian tribe – the Banu Kelb) became 'arguably the most significant sire of Salukis in the West' (Duggan, 2009).

With thoughts of Lance's hounds in mind, we set off with the somewhat daunting task before us of driving the long, circuitous route from Muscat around Saudi Arabia. We did it in stages, which were complicated from the start by exceptionally cold and wet weather all along the Gulf, making driving conditions tricky at times. After an overnight stop with friends in Abu Dhabi, we continued up the Gulf until I spotted the signpost pointing to Anbak, a small oasis on the edge of the Empty Quarter, where a friend had told me there were always lots of Salukis of the Al Murrah tribe, who are known as the *Bedu al-Bedu* or 'nomads of the nomads', famed for their camels, falcons and Salukis (Cole, 1975). It was only 15 km away, so we made the detour and were so glad we did. The oasis really was full of Salukis.

My friend had given me the name of the headman there, Faisal, who produced a guide to show us around. The traditional Al Murrah hounds are smooth and light-coloured and we certainly saw some magnificent specimens. I was offered a year-old smooth dog called *Saddah*, but we could not possibly travel onwards with him in our car and we had to decline. There were also some feathered hounds in among the tents where the camels were tethered, and Faisal explained that sometimes hunters from

Saluki emerging from a tent of the Shammar tribe.

the north would leave some of their hounds as gifts to the Al Murrah trackers who had helped them hunt in the Empty Quarter. We could have stayed for ages, but it was raining and so cold and we still had some way to go to our next stop in Bahrain.

The journey was broken briefly in Hofuf, where I found myself driving behind a vehicle in the back of which I could see the heads of three smooth red Salukis bobbing up and down. After a chase, I managed to wave the driver down and found they were from the Dawsari tribe. The hounds were in tip-top condition at the end of the hunting season and we wished we could have accepted the driver's invitation to visit his home; but friends in Bahrain awaited us. Shaikha Danah Al Khalifa came over to join us for dinner and we spent hours catching up with her.

Ahead of us the next morning lay hundreds of kilometres across Saudi Arabia and the omens were not good. We left Bahrain under a lowering sky and pouring rain to pick up the old oil company route known as the Tapline. The rain stopped eventually and the sun shone on the amazingly verdant desert. Here and there were scattered the black goat's-hair tents of bedouin profiting from the grass for pasturing their flocks and camels. At one point I needed a break from driving, so I went over to some tents and was about to ask an old man if they had any Salukis, when out popped a familiar-looking head: it was a very friendly big smooth cream male Saluki. The man said there was another one in the next tent. Sure enough, as we approached, a superb smooth cream male Saluki emerged. The owner said he was of the great Shammar tribe but we could not continue the conversation as the weather suddenly changed dramatically. A menacing yellow cloud could be seen racing towards us – clearly a sandstorm was on the way. We thought it prudent to get back onto the asphalt before the storm hit us, and drove off into the approaching gloom. The wind was whipping up the sand all around us and we could hardly see where we were going. Then, just as suddenly, the air turned from yellow to black as a torrential downpour hit us, but at least it cleared the air of dust and we were able to reach thankfully the oil company guest house where we were to spend the night.

We were away early the next morning for the long drive to Sakaka, where I had an introduction to the emir. He was kind enough to receive us, although he was resting in the fasting month of Ramadan, and directed one of his retainers, called Agail, to show us some of the local Salukis. Agail was a knowledgeable hunter and told us how he would go off every winter to spend up to a month hunting in the desert with his falcons and Salukis. He knew my friend Dalli in Rutba, Iraq and had also met one of my diplomatic colleagues, Sir Mark Allen, who is also well-known as a falconer and the author of *Falconry in Arabia* (1980). Agail took us first to one of the Sharari tribe, where we found a beautiful young smooth cream dog called *Saddah*, who was apparently a proficient solo hare courser, and a rather nervous young smooth grizzle bitch called *Fahda*. We also saw *Saddah's* dam, a seven-year-old feathered red, the oldest Saluki I had ever seen in a region where Salukis do not usually last long beyond their best coursing age. She had been mated with a smooth cream dog – hence her offspring's coat and colour. We were interrupted by a little boy who wanted us to see his puppy – a three-month-old, cream-and-white particoloured bitch. Unusually it wore a belt around its waist, which Agail said she would wear for the first five months to ensure a good tuck. The boy held on firmly to his puppy and said very seriously that it was not for sale. Agail wanted to show us others, but not until the afternoon when their owners returned from work. Sadly, we had to move on as we had some 560 km to go to Amman, where friends expected us, stopping only briefly on the way to photograph again some of the superb murals depicting Salukis hunting onager at the early 8th-century Umayyad hunting palace at Qusayr ʿAmra.

Liese and I were married in Amman over 30 years before and we had quite an emotional reunion with some Jordanian friends whom we had known then. At the

Qusayr 'Amra mural.

British Embassy we met Mark Allen, who was managing to find enough time off from his duties to fly occasionally his English peregrine. He said that Salukis were so rare in Jordan that he had seen only one, near the Saudi border. I did find a small population some years later in Wadi Rum near Aqaba in the south of the country, but generally I heard the old story that since a ban on hunting had been introduced people no longer bred Salukis. We spent the next day in appalling weather looking at some of the magnificent Roman mosaic floors in the 4th-to-6th-century churches at Syagha, where Moses is allegedly buried, Madaba, and Makhaiyat, where one of the hunting scenes depicts a black Saluki coursing a hare.

On the following day the rain still hung around and accompanied us all the way to the Syrian border but then, as we turned eastwards towards the great Nabatean and, later, Roman city of Bosra, the sun came out and our spirits rose again. Bosra is the most important Roman site in Syria after Palmyra – some of whose monuments were destroyed in 2016 by the so-called Islamic State – and was particularly noted for its exceptionally intact 15,000-seat theatre from the early 2nd century AD, built of massive blocks of black volcanic rock, which give it a rather forbidding aspect when seen from a distance. But it was so cold there that, after a brief look round, we were about to leave, when a little old man came up to us and asked if we had seen the mosaic displayed on the roof. We had not, so we returned and there on the roof was a huge mosaic devoted entirely to Salukis coursing hare!

Roman mosaic of hare coursing at Bosra.

It was from the Bosra area that the intrepid traveller Lady Anne Blunt acquired a Saluki as a gift from a friendly bedouin in 1875. In her account of her tour of Central Arabia, *A Pilgrimage to Nejd* (1881), she wrote that 'the pretty little fawn greyhound' was called *Shiekhah* after a plant of that name and was 'very docile and well-behaved. She is a real desert dog and likes dates better than anything else.' She was adept at coursing and, together with another Saluki acquired in Jordan, helped to provide Lady Anne and her party with food for the pot.

I asked the old man if there were still any Salukis in Bosra and he said that there were some. He called over a young man named Abdulrahman, an engineering student in the morning and a guide in the afternoon, to show us the way. We were out of luck at the first house as the owner was away hunting with his Saluki. At the next there was a hunting dog, but of the retriever type. At the third house we were in luck, and found a smooth cream male Saluki, called *Farhud*. The owner said he was a superb hunter of hare and fox and took us inside his house to see some stuffed specimens. There was also a little black and white terrier, called a '*Booji*', the same word used in Iraq for such dogs, which are employed in driving out prey from thickets. By then it was getting late and we needed to get to our hotel and warm up, though our guide pressed us to join his family for dinner in a typically Arab gesture of hospitality. At least we had established that Salukis were still to be found in Syria.

The next morning, before leaving Bosra we went to see some of the other Roman sites in the town and what a thrill it was to be driving along a Roman road made of white flagstones laid down originally some 1,800 years before between still-standing Roman houses of two and three storeys. From there we took a round-about route towards Damascus so that we could visit the fortress at Salkhad, built at the beginning of the 13th century by the Arabs as a defence against the Crusaders, and the so-called Jebel Druze, a mountainous area inhabited largely by the Druze, followers of a small monotheistic religious sect that originated in Egypt as an offshoot of Ismaili Shia Islam – though they are not regarded as Muslims and have been often persecuted for their unorthodox beliefs. We climbed above the snowline to reach the principal town of Suwaida to see the remains of an early Nabatean temple, but were waylaid by a hospitable Druze family as we were photographing the improbably snowy scene around us. Over tea and coffee, they confirmed what I suspected, that this was not Saluki country.

We moved on as I was keen to explore an area called Abu Shamat, where the late Dorothy Lees, a stalwart of the Saluki or Gazelle Hound Club, had seen lots of Salukis when she was living in Syria in the 1950s. In the meantime it had become a military zone, and some hunters with guns by the roadside assured me that there were no Salukis there but that we would find them at Safita, near the Crusader castle of Krak des Chevaliers, where we intended to go anyway. We still had time for one more stop before Damascus at the small town of Rahaiba, where I had an introduction from Mark Allen to a falconer friend of his called Hussain. We were directed to his house by the first person I asked and were soon sitting with him and his friends discussing the business they did in trapped falcons with the Gulf, but they knew nothing of Salukis in the area. And so we continued to Damascus, where as newly-weds we had lived for three months, and looked forward to staying with friends and seeing the sights of the old town again.

After a couple of days sampling the delights of Damascus guided by an old

English lady called Fatie Darwish, who was so long resident there that she knew every nook and cranny, we intended to set out on the road north towards Aleppo but encountered an unexpected last-minute hitch. The British Embassy had submitted our passports to the Syrian authorities to have our visas extended but they had not yet been returned. After some telephoning, I was told they were ready for collection at the embassy. On the way there, we passed near the president's palace, where we were suddenly stopped by a plain-clothes man who aimed a Kalashnikov menacingly at me. He was suspicious of the Omani registration plates on my car and was reluctant to let me pass. When I explained that we would not be able to leave Syria if we did not collect our passports, he agreed to let me by, but only on condition that Liese stayed in the car while I went inside the embassy as a guarantee that I would not detonate it! Safe with our passports again, we could continue north on the road towards Aleppo.

It was a clear day and we could see to our left the snow-capped mountains of Lebanon as we made our way first to Homs, from where we turned west towards Tartous looking for the 11th-century Crusader castle of Krak des Chevaliers. It came into sight on a hilltop up a winding road through orchards carpeted with wild flowers – but it was closed! However, a guide appeared and opened the massive gates for us so that we had the castle to ourselves. Here had been quartered some 2,000 knights of the Order of Saint John in what was regarded as an impregnable fortress. Indeed it was never conquered, but the knights were tricked into surrendering it by the Mameluke Sultan Baybars in 1271. The views all around were breathtaking but its very ruggedness did not suggest to me that this was Saluki country. So it proved to be for, when I enquired in the nearby small towns of Tell Kalakh and Safita, where various hunters along the way had assured me there were lots of Salukis, we found only Pointers and Retrievers for the main sport of shooting quail and partridge. It would seem my informants had not understood the difference between a hunting dog and a Saluki!

From Safita we took the road towards Hama, pausing only at the ancient city of Apamea, founded by Seleucus I Nicator in the 3rd century BC. The site was chosen by the Seleucids not least for its setting in rich pastureland for the army's cavalry horses; and I could see immediately that this looked more like Saluki country. I felt confirmed in this view by some of the depictions of identifiable Salukis in hunting scenes in the collection of fine Roman mosaics of the third and fourth centuries AD that we saw displayed in the restored Ottoman caravanserai on the site.

Without knowing it, we then took a fateful decision, the outcome of which was to have a profound influence on my later life with Salukis. We decided not to stop in the next town, Hama, but to continue eastwards to see the great 6th-century Byzantine complex of palace, church and military barracks at Qasr ibn Wardan on the edge of the Syrian Desert, which has been described as among the most impressive collection of ruins in the whole of northern Syria. We drove through fields of winter wheat and stopped for a moment in a small village, Rabbah, where I asked an old man by the roadside if there were any Salukis there. He said I should speak to the *Mukhtar* or headman, called Ali Jukhedar, whose house was up the road. In front of the house on a patch of grass was a small flock of sheep watched over by the *Mukhtar* himself. His face lit up when I asked about Salukis and he confessed that he was a passionate hunter, going out with his hound almost every day. He would show him to us with pleasure and brought out *Khattaf*, a slightly feathered, well-made cream dog about two years old, bundled up in a padded coat against the cold wind. Kennelled nearby in one of the strange beehive-shaped mud-brick buildings that are typical of northern Syria was another similar Saluki, *Saida*, *Khattaf*'s litter sister. Both hounds had cropped ears in the Kurdish fashion, and the village was indeed inhabited mainly by Kurds who had been settled there long ago in Ottoman times. Ali said that these were the only two there, but as we soon discovered this was not true. His hounds came originally from the next man we chanced upon, who turned out to be the leading breeder in the area.

We were enjoying the route onwards to our goal of the desert palace when I suddenly realised that the shape I could see standing in the back of the old Opel station wagon in front of us was that of a Saluki. It was a stroke of pure luck! I overtook and waved the driver down. The car was crammed with five men and five Salukis.

A stroke of pure luck!

The driver, called Badr Khan al-Barazi, was delighted by my interest in his Salukis and immediately invited us to join them in the hunt. So we abandoned our goal and followed the party a few kilometres before we turned off onto a dirt track that ran between the winter wheat fields. We stopped on the edge between the desert and the sown land and Badr let the five hounds out. He had bred them all: a smooth two-year-old black and tan dog called *Guru*, which he described as his ideal hound; a four-year-old feathered silver grizzle dog called *Jinah*; a two-year-old smooth grizzle dog called *Mirya'*; and two smooth eight-month-old puppies, one cream, called *Jinah*, and the other grizzle, called *Radih*, out on their first hunt. I noted that he used the word *Azraq*, meaning 'blue', for the grizzles.

As we walked, Badr talked continuously about his life with Salukis. His family had come originally from Ain al-Arab on the border with Turkey, a town better known today as Kobane for its heroic resistance to the so-called Islamic State. They had been settled by the Ottomans in the area east of Hama, where they had become big landowners. They had more or less forgotten their Kurdish, though interestingly they still gave some of their Salukis Kurdish names and their type remained very similar to the Salukis from the Urfa area in southern Turkey. As a boy Badr had herded the family's flocks of sheep all over the area, and he knew the land, the fauna and the flora like the back of his hand. He grew up with Salukis and Arabian horses and had kept them all his life. He was a passionate hunter.

It was a Friday, when he would normally hunt all day from dawn onwards, but as it was Ramadan he had started later – otherwise we would probably never have met him. He had been out the week before and had caught five hares with three hounds, but we were not so lucky this time. Though we found plenty of scrapes and droppings, we walked for more than an hour with nothing more to show for it than a tortoise that one of the hounds brought to us alive. Badr said it was very rare for a Saluki to retrieve at all. Then Liese suddenly screamed, 'Hare!' and the chase was on, with all five hounds running, the older ones showing the debutants the way. The hare gave them a good run but could not lose them, and eventually they brought her down, a big doe weighing some 3–3.5 kg. The Kurds were absolutely absorbed in the chase, shouting encouragement to the hounds and whooping when they caught it. Even Badr, who was not young and had already had a heart attack, was beside himself with excitement.

As we walked back to our cars he described what constituted a good Saluki, using

Guru as his model: it should have straight front legs, turning neither in nor out; and the toes should be long, not round like a cat's. The chest should be deep, should be visible through the front legs, not pinched, and should lead into a well tucked-up waist. The neck should be fine and the head well shaped. The hind legs should be well muscled. The Arabs had a saying: 'A Saluki should be built like an Arabian mare or a woman, with a fine head on an elegant neck, a well-developed chest and a good pair of thighs!' The coat colour was unimportant but the ears should be cropped to save them from being torn in running or fighting. The feet should be dipped in henna to toughen the pads. The appearance was less important than the working ability of hounds that had to earn their keep and give their owners satisfaction. For him, a good Saluki was one that coursed and killed. He would not keep one that did not kill. If the hound killed a hare, he would eat it, as he always said *'Bismillah'* in the prescribed fashion before slipping it. The hare would be boiled four times in fresh water and either grilled or cooked with tomatoes and other vegetables.

He had some strange ideas about mating: if the male was too tall for the bitch, put a stick under the bitch's waist to raise her up; if the dog was old or simply reluctant, put him on the bitch and tie his legs around her; and, if the dog was shorter than the bitch, stand her in a pit to equalise the height. Perpetuating good breeding stock was all-important. He admitted that he had once exchanged an Arabian mare of his own breeding and a water pump for a special dog he was keen on having.

He could clearly go on and on with an inexhaustible supply of information, and invited us back to dinner at his house in Hama to continue the conversation. We exchanged contact details and I promised to take up his further invitation to return to spend 'at least a month' with him hunting in the desert. We failed to find his house that evening in the darkened, sprawling town, but I remained in touch with him and continued my Saluki education with him for many years afterwards.

Our next destination was Syria's second city, Aleppo, which I had first visited as an Arabic language student in 1957. Then, as on this occasion, the Mazloumian family welcomed us into the famous Baron Hotel, where they had hosted in the past so many illustrious travellers, including Lawrence of Arabia and Freya Stark. They had managed somehow to preserve the atmosphere of the early 20th century, despite all the revolutions and upheavals in the interval, and amazingly the building has survived the internecine fighting of the present time, when so much of this once ancient and mysterious city has been totally destroyed. We spent three beautiful days exploring the many sights of the city and the ancient sites dotted all around; Salukis kept popping up in Roman mosaics or Arab murals in different places, and I was delighted to see in the museum a small bronze figurine of a Saluki-like hunting hound from ancient Ugarit dated around 1300 BC.

A long journey then lay ahead of us, eastwards almost right across the breadth of Syria to Tell Brak, where we were to join a British archaeological dig for a few days. En route, we visited the ruined Byzantine city of Rasafe, which once vied with Palmyra for the splendour of its buildings. We also crossed the Euphrates by bridge to the bustling town of Raqqa, which has since become notorious as the centre of the so-called Islamic State, and continued to Hasake, in whose jurisdiction Tell Brak lay. From there the massive bulk of the mound could be seen rising up from the flat plain all around. This was clearly Saluki country, and when I stopped for a chat with a man by the roadside he said there were at least 40 hounds between there and the dig. I enquired again in a little village and a man said that the gypsies in Hasake bred them but that his brother, called Salman, also had some. We followed his directions to his brother's house but Salman said he no longer had any, although if we cared to return the next morning we could go coursing with some of his family's hounds.

One of the attractions for me at Tell Brak was to see where British archaeologists

Saluki skeleton from Tell Brak c.2500 BC.

had excavated in 1987 what Professors David and Joan Oates described to me on a visit to Baghdad at the time as the earliest well-substantiated skeleton of a Saluki-like dog, probably dating from over 4,000 years ago. The late Dr Juliet Clutton-Brock at the Natural History Museum in London later told me that it was certainly of 'Greyhound build'. In a booklet on the find published in 1989, she made a detailed comparison of the skeleton with that of *Luman*, a Saluki whose skeleton is preserved in the Rothschild Collection at the Natural History Museum in Tring, southern England, which had been imported from the Tahawi tribe of Lower Egypt by the Honourable Florence Amherst in 1895. She wrote that the comparison was so close as to be almost identical and there could be little doubt that the two hounds were of the same type, albeit separated by four millennia. So, after a warm welcome from the archaeologists at the site and the allocation of a tent, we had to go and see where the skeleton had been excavated. Once again as I stood there, despite the howling cold wind, I was filled with the sense of the extraordinary continuity of the breed over so many years.

After a very cold night in the tent, we drove over to Salman's the next morning and found him shearing sheep. He dropped everything immediately and we set off to collect the Salukis and some other hunters. First we picked up a smooth red grizzle bitch called *Khowla*, who was stuffed unceremoniously into a sack with only her head showing and popped into the back of my car. Then we went to another place where we picked up a smooth cream dog, who joined the bitch in the back. She was in season (hence the sack), and I wondered how she would be able to run free with a male around her. In fact, when we started walking up the fields of winter wheat she got on with the business of finding hare, though the dog seemed more interested in her. Neither they nor we could put up a hare, though we walked for a couple of hours over the muddy ground. In the end, we had to give up as another storm was threatening ominously and we had quite a way to go over muddy tracks. On the way, we passed through several hamlets where there were Salukis, including one feathered silver grizzle bitch, very pretty despite its rather tatty coat. Salman said that most of the Kurdish hamlets around there kept a Saluki or two. Thus, we returned empty-handed but with the inner satisfaction of having coursed with similar hounds over similar ground to those ancient Akkadians who had inhabited Tell Brak over 4,500 years ago.

It was bitterly cold under canvas that night and we resolved not to tarry longer there but to push on southwards down the Euphrates to Deir ez-Zor, from where we could visit Doura Europos, the vast Hellenistic city laid waste by the Roman Emperor Aurelian in 271 AD. I made enquiries of the various Arab tribes round about there and at the imposing 8th-century Umayyad desert castle of Qasr al-Hair al-Sharqi, which once boasted a large enclosed gazelle park for the Arab dignitaries to hunt in, as well as at Palmyra, but nowhere did I see or hear of any Salukis. Today, when I contemplate the pictures of the wanton destruction at Palmyra wreaked by the so-called Islamic State, I am so glad that we saw it then in some of its former splendour. Although this first brief sweep across Syria had not produced as many Salukis as I would have liked to see, I was left with the impression, not least from my new friend Badr in Hama, that further investigation at a more leisurely pace would be more rewarding.

We still had many hundreds of kilometres to go to reach Muscat again and we pressed on with the minimum of stops until we were once again skirting the edge of the Empty Quarter, where we renewed contact with some of the Al Murrah tribe camped there. It was by then the big holiday at the end of Ramadan and everyone

Muhammad Ali Haidan Al-Marri with Najma.

was entertaining guests in their tents with tea, coffee and dates. As we went round, I spied peeping out from one of them the appealing face of a feathered tawny red puppy with a white blaze: hence her name *Najma*. We liked the look of her and, in chatting with her owner, I was amazed to find that he was an ex-policeman who had worked for our daughter's godfather in Doha! I felt that we were fated to meet him and *Najma*. We were hurried on to see several other puppies, all of them bitches, but *Najma* had taken our fancy. So back we went to have a proper look at her and to see if her owner, Muhammad Ali Haidan al-Marri, would let us have her. He told us she was eight months old and recited her lineage. She was Irish-marked, heavily feathered and robustly built, though only about 58 cm tall. He related how he had sold one of her siblings to the Ruler of Abu Dhabi for a huge sum and how difficult it would be for him to let *Najma* go. This was all part of the normal bargaining process and I played along, emphasising the Arab tradition of not selling Salukis to respected guests of the tribe and my willingness to compensate him for his loss with a gift in return. I offered him my binoculars, which he immediately put to his eyes the wrong way round so that everything appeared smaller! I corrected his error and he was delighted to hand *Najma* over to us in exchange, with just a length of wire in lieu of a collar and lead. She seemed to take to us immediately, followed us easily to our car, and jumped in without any fuss. This, we discovered, was typical of her: she was the steadiest and most obedient of all the Salukis I have ever known. She drove with us the rest of the way home without fretting and made the huge transition from a bedouin tent to an ambassadorial residence as if to the manor born.

Najma in Oman.

He has a blaze and his legs are white;

Chapter Seven

Extending the Saluki Footprint

Najma was a little unsure that first night but eventually she settled down with *Tayra* after the latter saw that she could not bully her in the way that she had *Ziwa*. I took them down to the beach early the next morning. *Najma* had probably never seen the sea before and at first kept very close to me. However, when she saw *Tayra* having fun racing through the shallows, she clearly wanted to join in. Not quite knowing how she would be off the leash, I let her go and she was soon playing with *Tayra* in the water as if she had done it all her life. I was delighted that, whenever I called *Najma* to heel, she came immediately. Amazing!

Over the next week or two I began to see the very positive effect that *Najma* was having on *Tayra* who, despite her poor relationship with *Ziwa*, had lost some of her liveliness through being on her own. Now, with a young and active playmate that was not in the least afraid of her, *Tayra* became almost like a puppy again and even imitated *Najma*'s obedience to the recall. But suddenly it all changed, and *Tayra* started to become really disobedient, refusing to come back at the end of our walks on the beach. It was as if she was asserting her independence of *Najma* and was determined to do her own thing; or maybe she was simply jealous of *Najma* and was seeking attention? Anyway, we made a fuss of her and she settled down again.

This was just as well, as I was about to head off to London for a few weeks by a rather circuitous route. I had been corresponding for some while with Dr Ali

Miguil, a Moroccan veterinary doctor who had written his doctoral thesis on the Sloughi in Morocco, and I planned to see him and some of these indigenous hunting hounds during a return visit to Morocco after an interval of some 30 years. I was curious to compare these hounds with the Saluki, a breed that shares the same name in Arabic but is regarded internationally as separate. I flew to the capital, Rabat, where Gordon Pirie, then at the British Embassy there, had made some useful introductions for me. In particular, I met

Ghazal at Volubilis.

the head of the Moroccan branch of the Society for the Protection of Animals in North Africa (SPANA), who kindly said that he would arrange for one of SPANA's veterinary doctors near Marrakesh to show me some of the Sloughis in that area.

But first I wanted to explore the area around Fes and Sidi Harazem where, according to Dr Miguil, many Sloughis were to be found. On the way to Fes I turned off at the ruined Roman city of Volubilis, which flourished between 45 and 245 AD as a great provider of agricultural products and wild animals for Rome's arenas. My embassy friends had once seen some Sloughis with a souvenir seller there and, as soon as I stopped my car at the entrance to the site I spotted a pretty little Sloughi puppy by his stall. He was about three months old and called *Ghazal*. He was an unusual colour, with a black mantle over a fawn base, with very distinctive fawn ears. Tied up to a kennel nearby was another puppy, a bitch about eight months old, called *Brjaa'*, also with a black mantle over fawn but with a white patch on her chest, which is seen as a fault in the ring but not among hunters in the field. The owner said that he bred Sloughis on his farm some distance away, mainly for hunting foxes and jackals, and showed me some skins for sale in his shop. He also sold his puppies to visitors for rather inflated prices.

I was less successful in my search in the area around Fes. Despite numerous enquiries in Sidi Harazem, where Dr Miguil had reported a Sloughi show had been held in 1985, and in other small towns, I drew a complete blank. Eventually a chance enquiry of a man by the roadside with a sheep led me to a small hamlet where I was greeted by a very fierce Sloughi called *Jinah*, a name favoured widely in Syria. He was six years old and so aggressive that, try as I might to photograph him in profile, he remained always head-on in an attacking position.

I continued my route to Marrakesh, a city that I had known well when I lived in Morocco in the early 1960s and which had lost none of its exotic charm in the interval. I had to sample again the delights of the old town centred on the *Jama'a al-Fna*, the Square of the Congregation of the Departed, so called from the days when public executions by decapitation took place there. Nowadays the square bustles well into the night with vendors of food, drinks and souvenirs, and entertainers with performing monkeys and snakes. I had hoped to visit Princess Francesca Rispoli, a leading Sloughi enthusiast who had established an important breeding centre just outside the city, stocked with the finest hounds she and others could find in Morocco. However, when I located it in the beautifully green Wadi Ourika and enquired after her, I was given the sad news that she had passed away about six months before and her remaining hounds had been either dispersed or put down.

I had arranged to meet Dr Abdelmoula Erridmane at the SPANA clinic in Chemaia, a small town about an hour's drive west of Marrakesh. When I arrived, he was examining a handsome cream two-year-old male Sloughi called *Dabbouh*. He told me that he often saw Sloughis at the clinic, as people knew that they could receive free medical attention there. They liked to keep their hounds in good condition as they had been encouraged by monetary prizes to participate in the regional shows arranged by the Moroccan Sloughi Club. Such a show in Chemaia two years before had attracted over 200 participants, which gives some idea of the large number of hounds in the region.

This kind of show seems to have been superseded in more recent years by wider hunting shows, where Sloughis and falcons are shown in their traditional roles in simulated hunts. I have attended two such shows, one in Meknes in 2010 and another in Sidi Mokhtar in 2012, in which large numbers of Sloughis took part.

Dr Erridmane had put the word out to Sloughi breeders at the local Thursday open market that he would be coming to see their hounds the next day, if they assembled at any one of three villages around Chemaia. We set off in his small but robust car for the first village of Mhadi, a good half-hour's drive away over rough dirt tracks. Here, however, the villagers seemed suspicious of our motives and refused to produce any hounds for our inspection. Hunting of game with dogs is banned under a French colonial law of 1844 that has never been rescinded since Morocco's independence, and Sloughis are supposed to be used only for hunting predators, such as foxes, jackals and wolves, but hares are also taken from time to time and the villagers may have been afraid that we were checking up on them.

There was nothing we could say to change their minds, so we moved on to Ouled Salem, where the situation could not have been more different. Here, Sloughis appeared from all directions and there were so many that it was difficult to keep track of them. They ranged from small puppies up to mature hunting hounds and came in all the standard colours, though most were brindle, called here *Khumri* rather than *Strati*, as Dr Miguil had recorded. One well-made black and tan dog had won the distinction of a first prize at a show in Rabat the year before, but I noted that the owner was not using it for hunting, preferring to keep it safe from injury for its show potential. This represented quite a change in the attitude of the villagers towards their hounds, generally kept purely for the purpose of hunting. While Dr Erridmane gave veterinary advice to the villagers, I took measurements and lots of photographs of what seemed to be a flourishing population of hounds.

We moved on to the next village, where everyone was at Friday prayers in the mosque when we arrived. The worshippers emerged soon after and many of the men joined us in a delicious meal of local produce: chicken stuffed with almonds and rice, followed by boiled mutton and a coarse rye bread, rounded off with yoghurt, walnuts and dates. The *Mulla* joined us from the mosque and blessed everyone by name, even me! Our host was the village headman, who came from a distinctive tribal group known as *Nuwasir* (singular *Nasiri*), and was regarded as *Sharif* (noble). Members of this group are known traditionally to be not only immune from rabies but also able to cure it by rubbing salt into the wound and licking it with their saliva. Dr Erridmane was naturally dismissive, but such beliefs are widely respected in the Moroccan countryside. Our host had only one Sloughi in his yard but gave us a guide to an even more remote village, al-Asalsala, where we would find many.

We continued across country and arrived at the house of the headman, who had clearly been waiting for us all day. As soon as we arrived I saw a sheep being slaughtered in the yard for yet another meal! It would be a long wait while it was cooked, so we set about exploring the village and its hounds. Our host had a small brindle puppy that was playing with a heavier puppy of roughly the same age, which appeared to be a crossbred Sloughi, called locally a *Barhush.* This led me to ask what measures they took to prevent accidental matings. He said they simply confined the bitch to the yard, but clearly accidents still happened. Dr Miguil recorded (Miguil, 1986) that sometimes a metal ring was inserted through the vulva to prevent mating but I did not see any evidence of this practice. Outside the house some 20 Sloughis had gathered, including some that had been shown successfully. This illustrated just how widely the show culture had penetrated, even into the more remote parts of the countryside. One of the hounds caught my attention in particular. He was a tall and heavily-built brindle called *Dabbouh* and was, according to his owner, 14 years old, making him a great rarity, since few hounds survive much beyond the end of their coursing career. He was of a type still used for hunting wild boar, which can do a lot of damage to agriculture if left uncontrolled.

Our second lunch of the day finally appeared about 5.00 pm and began with kebabs of liver with French fries before the main course of boiled mutton and rice. There were lots of eager hands ready to do justice to the generous repast. A glass or two of mint tea finished off the meal and we were on our way again back to Chemaia and Dr Erridmane's clinic, where a man had been waiting all day for treatment for his unusual black with white Sloughi. The colour suggested to me a touch of Galgo, a breed that was and is making increasing inroads into the Morocco Sloughi population from Spain. It was now evening and Dr Erridmane said he and his family had wanted to invite me to lunch, but he accepted that three lunches in one day was perhaps too much! So I returned to Marrakesh for the night.

14-year-old Dabbouh.

The next morning, I drove over the still snow-topped Atlas Mountains to Zagora, a small town on the edge of the Sahara, where Dr Ali Miguil was now in a veterinary practice. I was disappointed to learn from him that there were no Sloughis in that area but I was more than compensated by the chance to speak to him at length about his doctoral thesis on the Moroccan Sloughi, written in 1986, a summary translation of which I published (see Clark, 1995). He kindly gave me to copy much of his original research material, including many photographs. In general, he described a fairly bleak picture of the situation of the Sloughi as a result of crossbreeding and the ban on hunting edible game, which encouraged the breeding of larger and coarser hounds for hunting predators. He favoured the lifting of the ban to allow hunting with hounds at certain times of the year, and incentives to breeders to take part in shows.

He and his charming wife were generous hosts and showed me some interesting parts of the town, especially the colourful market, where nomadic Tuareg, looking magnificent in their distinctive indigo-blue turbans, rubbed shoulders with local Berbers and Arabs, and traders dealt in a bizarre mix of such things as herbal medicines, silver jewellery, false teeth and reading glasses. I could not resist taking a camel ride, passing a road sign pointing into the desert stating '51 days to Timbuktu'!

On my way back to Rabat, I stopped in Casablanca to call on Dr Mohammed El Baroudi, the then President of the Moroccan Sloughi Club. He took a more sanguine view of the situation of the breed. He said it was clear from the response to the annual show alone that there were good-quality hounds in sufficient numbers for the breed to be secure. His club had about a thousand members and organised an annual show, in which about 300 Sloughis took part. The local breeders were now alive to the possibility of financial reward from raising show-class hounds capable of winning prizes, so he felt that they had even more of an incentive to keep the breed pure and of good quality than the usual need to produce successful coursing hounds.

On the journey back to London, I mulled over the impressions I had gained from the local breeders and hunters during my week-long visit to Morocco. First, I was confirmed in my understanding that linguistically no distinction is made by Moroccans and, say, Iraqis in how they write or pronounce in their local dialects the name of their breed of coursing hound. The distinction in spelling between 'Saluki' and 'Sloughi' has been made by Westerners attempting to transliterate the Arabic. The Berbers have a different word – *Oska* – but the Arabic name predominates. Much has been made of the apparent physical differences between the two breeds. For example, it is said that the withers in the Sloughi are less prominent and the bottom line shows a longer sternum and a high tuck-up; yet I have seen many desert-bred Salukis with such characteristics and, by contrast, some Sloughis in Morocco with standard Saluki features. Indeed, Xavier Przezdziecki, a highly experienced French army officer and administrator in North Africa between 1929 and the mid-1940s, wrote in his comprehensive study of sighthounds *Le Destin des Lévriers* (1984) (translated into English in 2001 as *Our Levriers: The Past, Present and Future of All Sighthounds*):

> In Saharan regions of Morocco, the last refuge of pure Sloughis, there still existed some varieties with black coats, animals identical to those of the Near East, and whose owners bore the names of tribes or factions that have counterparts in the Syrio-Jordanian regions.

I did find some commonly represented differences between many of the Sloughis and some smooth Salukis, which I thought might be attributable to the need for breeding a more robust hound in North Africa primarily for hunting predators. For example, the Moroccan hounds often had a broader skull and sometimes a shorter tail, though such characteristics can also be found among some Salukis. Some differences were definitely more pronounced in Morocco, e.g. roseate ears (58% of the hounds examined by Dr Miguil), although such ears are officially frowned upon, following the imposition in 1937 by the French of lop-ears as standard; but even roseate ears also occur sometimes among Salukis. The brindle pattern is also much more common in North Africa, although it too occurs occasionally in Salukis. The clinching argument advanced for the division into two breeds is that the Sloughi is invariably smooth-haired, whereas the Saluki can be smooth or feathered. However, I discovered later that there was evidence that feathered hounds had existed previously in North Africa. Today in North Africa, feathering is associated with crossbreeding and hostility to feathering is now so deeply engrained as an indicator of crossbreeding that, even if feathered hounds appeared in litters or were reintroduced, they would be unlikely to gain acceptance among the breeders. It would seem probable, therefore, that the feathered Sloughi that was once part of North Africa's natural heritage is extinct. However, I learnt much later that, despite such circumstantial evidence of similarity between the breeds, analysis of samples of Sloughi DNA has indicated a genetic profile different from that of other sighthound breeds, though further research remains to be done before the relationship between all the various regional sighthounds has been unequivocally established.

Back in Oman again, I made a connection with Morocco of a different kind, which in a round-about way was to prove very helpful to me later on. I had given a lecture in Muscat to the Oman Historical Society about the Saluki's position in Arab culture and its sad decline in Oman almost to the point of extinction, the text of which I later published with illustrations in the bilingual glossy magazine of the local oil company. The article attracted a number of comments and questions from Omanis, among whom was a young shaikh from a prominent merchant family that I knew well. Shaikh Sa'ad had felt inspired to breed Salukis and sought my advice about where he could obtain a pair. I suggested that probably the easiest way was to approach the then Ruler of Abu Dhabi, whose large hunting kennels I had visited at al-Khazna, roughly halfway between Abu Dhabi city and al-Ain on the border with Oman. Some weeks later, Shaikh Sa'ad telephoned me to say excitedly that a pair of Salukis had arrived from Abu Dhabi and I must come and inspect them.

I went round as soon as I could, and standing on the lawn in front of his house was

Nisma.

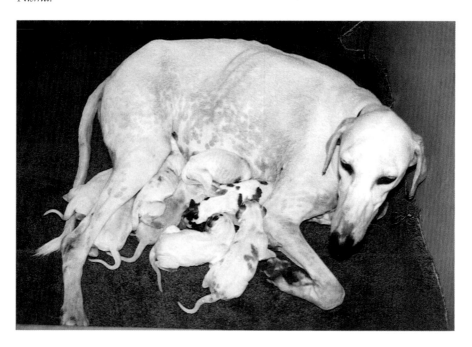

Shaikh Sa'ad with a pair of identical pure-white smooth Salukis. The only difference between them was that the male was slightly taller and more heavily built. They were about two years old and had been presented by King Hassan of Morocco to the Ruler of Abu Dhabi on one of his hunting trips there. Although the hounds looked healthy and well-fed, they were not in hunting condition and I was struck by the poor tuck-up of the bitch, which may have been due to lack of exercise. They had a lovely temperament – very gentle, unexcitable and sociable. They had the most beautiful dark topaz eyes. After I had examined them thoroughly, I congratulated Shaikh Sa'ad on his good fortune to have such a fine healthy pair, but he was downcast. He said that he could not breed them as they were siblings and asked if I could find a mate for the bitch. I recalled my unsuccessful attempts to mate *Tayra* with one of the Salukis held by the Royal Oman Police and suggested he might try there. He cheered up immediately, as he knew the police officer concerned, and would enquire. Some weeks later he called me again to tell me that he had taken the bitch, now called *Nisma*, to the police kennels, as she was in season, and within minutes of being introduced to the same feathered red grizzle that I had tried to use so unsuccessfully they had coupled without any difficulty. In return, Shaikh Sa'ad gave *Nisma's* brother to the police.

Over the next two months Shaikh Sa'ad followed to the letter the instructions I gave him on raising a litter, copied from Ken and Diana Allan's book *The Complete Saluki* (1991). He had had a spacious kennel made for the delivery, with infrared heating as it was January when, even in Muscat, the nights could be cold. One morning he called me to say he had been up all night attending the delivery of *Nisma's* four male and four female puppies. I went round to see them and found them suckling well. They were predominantly white, but several had black or grey markings and a couple had a touch of red about the ears. By the age of about two months, it was clear that two of them were different from the rest. While the others looked smooth-haired like their dam, the firstborn male and one of the females were developing a thicker coat. They were also showing different colours: the male a kind of apricot and the female a grey-fawn particoloured. They clearly reflected more the influence of the sire. His origin was not documented, but on one occasion the police told me they thought he was descended from Tunisian imports two generations back, though that seemed to me unlikely as Tunisian hounds are usually smooth; on another occasion, they told me they believed he was descended from British imports, which seemed more likely.

As the puppies were growing up, I received one day out of the blue a letter from a good Samaritan who had heard that my own hounds were in quarantine kennels not far from her home in England and had gone to visit them. She told me that she had taken some comforts to help them cope with the bitterly cold weather and promised to give me progress reports on them. At the same time, she said how much she wanted a desert-bred puppy. I asked Shaikh Sa'ad if she could have one from the litter and he generously agreed to let her have one of the remaining males, to whom I gave the name *Naseem* (the male version of his dam's name). Although I was heavily engaged in my own departure from Oman into retirement at the time, I somehow managed to make the arrangements for *Naseem's* export – without much cooperation from him! First, the journey home from Shaikh Sa'ad's had left my car in an indescribable mess, as his nervousness had had a disastrous effect on his bowels. Next, he injured his leg and had a limp. Then, 24 hours before his flight to London, he ate some rubbish in the garden, probably dropped by a scavenger crow, and fell very ill. I thought he was poisoned and called the vet. He gave him a couple of shots to stop the vomiting and said he would be fine the next day. Fortunately he was right, and *Naseem* was fine on the journey to London and into quarantine kennels, where the staff thought at first that he had a skin disease as they had never seen such a short-haired Saluki! His new owner was delighted with him and while he was in quarantine continued to keep a close eye on my own hounds' welfare too, until I returned home later that year and could see to them myself. One of *Naseem's* female siblings, called *Maha*, also went to an English family, who were living in Oman for a time but eventually took her back to England and successfully bred from her.

But I am getting ahead of myself. Towards the end of 1993, I was beginning to make plans for the remaining period of my time in Muscat before my retirement from the Diplomatic Service in June 1994. I found I had to use up before then several weeks of my annual leave entitlement and decided to spend some of it on a return visit to Syria. Since my fortuitous encounter two years before with Badr al-Barazi in Hama, I had maintained a correspondence with him, in which he repeatedly invited me to spend 'at least a month' hunting with him. So in February 1994 I flew to Damascus to begin an extraordinary week in his company.

Badr was descended from a long line of Kurdish Khans, or feudal chieftains, who originated in the area south-west of Diyarbakir in eastern Turkey but who migrated to

Hama, halfway between Damascus and Aleppo, in Ottoman times, so that the family now spoke Arabic rather than Kurdish as their first language. His ancestors built fine stone houses in a quarter of the town named after the Barazi family and acquired huge tracts of good farmland round about. Most of this property was redistributed under the agrarian reform of the early 1960s but enough remained to provide the family with status. As a young man, Badr had been made responsible for the family's huge flocks of sheep and roamed the great plains of Syria seeking grazing for them. He thus became acquainted with the ways of the bedouin and acquired their gift for reading nature. He had bred and hunted with Salukis for about 40 years. Previously he would ride Arabian mares of his own breeding to hunt, but the shortage of hares near enough to his farm involved travelling too far by horse and he had to resort to a pickup with a specially designed removable dog box on the back.

From Damascus I took a very comfortable Pullman bus for the journey in the still wintry sunshine to Hama, where Badr's son Fakhr met me with the news that the winter season had already produced some great coursing, with the record set at 21 hares in one day with four Salukis. We went first to his father's house, where I was welcomed by Badr and his family with a huge meal of Hama specialties of such variety that I soon gave up trying to identify the unfamiliar tastes and flavours as selected items were piled onto my plate with the injunction 'Eat!'. However, I remember in particular the delicious *kufta*, a kind of meatball as big as an egg but made with hare meat. Scarcely able to move, I was nonetheless eased into a pickup to go on a tour of Hama and to see the family farm outside the town.

Hama straddles the River Orontes and is one of Syria's oldest towns. The site has been inhabited certainly since Neolithic times and has been occupied by successive civilisations from the second millennium BC. Its visible monuments show little of its early Aramaean, Assyrian, Hellenistic and Byzantine history, though it is fertile ground for archaeologists. Badr recounted that a Byzantine sarcophagus had been turned up by a plough on his grandfather's farm. Until the uprising against the Syrian Ba'ath regime brought terrible destruction to Hama, the town still had some fine Islamic monuments, such as the 8th-century Great Mosque from the Umayyad period, the 12th-century Nur al-Din Mosque and the 14th-century Abu al-Fida Mosque. There was also a small museum installed in the beautiful 18th-century Ottoman Azem Palace on the banks of the Orontes. Above all, Hama was famous for its giant waterwheels or *norias*, which for centuries – with much creaking and

Hama's Roman water wheels painted by John Doyle, PPRWS.

groaning – raised water from the river into aqueducts for distribution around the town. When I was last there in 2009, only a few remained as tourist attractions. However, all these monuments have suffered in the civil war of the past few years.

Driving to Badr's farm, we were halted by a strange sight: two young men (Badr's nephews, as it turned out) were riding across the track on beautiful Arabian mares of Lebanese-Egyptian stock accompanied by a pack of harlequin Great Danes. With their studded collars and slavering jaws, they looked very fierce but they were really quite friendly when we stopped to have a look at the mares. Another of Badr's nephews had trained as a dentist in Romania and had brought back a pair of Great Danes, which he had since bred to produce this pack. We continued down the track towards a high-walled compound. I could hear the familiar howl of Salukis but there was also a deep-throated barking. Then I could see, on top of a building in the compound, two woolly bear-like dogs barking in a frenzy of defiance. They were Kurdish guard dogs; 'Only puppies', Badr said dismissively, 'and not yet full grown'. But they were big enough to cause me to be constantly on my guard as they circled around me looking for an opportunity to go for my legs.

They shared the compound with Badr's pack of three mature and two eight-month-old Salukis and a gorgeous coal-black Arabian mare with a white blaze bred on the Jazira plain in eastern Syria. The hounds wore padded coats against the bitter cold of winter, but they were undressed to show me their paces around the courtyard. The mare was also loosed and it became quite tricky to avoid the racing hounds, the flying hoofs and the attempted attacks of the guard dogs while I was trying to take photographs. Things only quietened down when Badr produced their food for the day – and every day – nothing but dry pitta bread! I was amazed that these hunting hounds could be in such wonderful condition on such poor food. The guard dogs wolfed down their share, while the Salukis chewed theirs more daintily. It made me think of the daily meat ration I fed my Salukis and I wondered who was right. I asked Badr if he ever gave them anything else. He said that meat made them fat and useless for hunting and bones made them fight among themselves. Bread, especially if dry, kept them lean and keen and they did not squabble over it. I argued that they would be even stronger if he gave them some minerals and vitamins, and he ordered the farmhand to give them crushed bones once a week. The poor diet might explain why, among dozens that week, I did not see a single hound much older than five or six years. We selected the three mature hounds for the next day's hunt: *Guru*, a smooth black and tan male that had been with us two years before; *Rogo*, a smooth red two-year-old male of outstanding physique; and *Mark*, a young smooth black and tan. All had their ears crudely cropped, as did all but one of the hounds I saw in the area.

The next day was bright and clear, with a piercingly cold wind. We were away soon after 7.00 am, with three of us in the pickup and five hounds in the back, the additional two belonging to hunters who followed separately. Our destination was an area about an hour's drive east of Hama, where the undulating ground was entirely covered as far as the eye could see with a sparse growth of sprouting winter wheat. The going looked hard. It had been a very dry winter and the shallow furrows in the stony earth with larger rocks scattered about gave the hares plenty of cover and us plenty to stumble over. We set off walking in line with *Guru*, a tall smooth grey grizzle called *Battah* and two others on the wings held on simple rope slips, while the powerful *Rogo* roamed free before us, constantly scanning the ground for any sign of movement. It was he

Cropped ears.

who put up the first hare after half an hour. All five hounds tore after it, urged on by our yells. The hare led the hounds away in a wide arc with the young men of the party running to keep them in sight, while we watched through binoculars. Soon one of them was signalling that the hare had gone to ground. It had drawn the hounds to a dry wadi full of holes in the rocks and had disappeared. We walked on, and again it was *Rogo* who started after another hare, which was quickly run down. Sadly, it proved to be a pregnant doe but there was no sentimentality about these hunters, who were more concerned about whether there was enough meat on it to make into the *kufta* balls they enjoyed so much.

Before we could move on, we had to settle which hound had made the kill. No one could really say, as it all happened so far off and only Badr with his binoculars and the young runners were anywhere in a position to see. This did not prevent everyone from arguing in favour of this or that hound, but eventually the consensus was that *Guru* and *Battah* were the fastest in the pack. Four more hares were coursed, of which two were caught and two went to ground. All the hounds were involved and, as each course was over at least 1.5 km, they had covered a prodigious distance by one o'clock, when we stopped for lunch – and to think that all that running was done on dry pitta bread!

Lunch for us was more a kind of feast al fresco. We squatted on the ground in the

Walking up.

lee of a wall for some protection from the cold north wind, while dish after dish was produced from the back of one of the cars: several kinds of meat dishes, accompanied by hummus, tabbouleh, baba ghanoush, pickles, yoghurt and various salads, all eaten with a twist of pitta bread in the fingers of the right hand. Fruit, bitter coffee and sweet black tea finished it off. The hounds looked on hopefully but there was little left over for them. We were not quite finished, however, as someone put on a tape of Arabic music in one of the cars and several members of the group performed the *dabke* circular dance, to ribald comments and much laughter all round. We should have called it a day, but some hours of daylight remained and naively I thought their polite question whether we should go on was seriously meant. So I agreed, and we went on for another hour without so much as a sight of a hare. It was only then that Badr revealed that they and the hounds wanted to go home. The hounds went back to their pitta bread, but for Badr and me the day was not yet over.

As a local leader, Badr held an open house each evening. From about 7.30 to 9.30 pm, friends used to drop in for coffee and gossip. Country people of his generation did not care much for television and made their own entertainment in the *majlis*. I was quickly initiated into the rules by the *majlis* jester: only one person was allowed to speak at a time and he could say what he liked. Someone would start off with an apparently innocent question to one of the older members, who seemed to act good-naturedly as the butt for the banter of the rest. The repartee would flow back and forth, with one speaker after another capping the wit of the previous one. Once a week, one of them was responsible for producing a simple supper and that night it was the jester's turn. Squatting on the *majlis* floor, we tucked into a delicious dish of pitta bread soaked in a kind of broth full of chick peas, eaten at great speed and almost in silence. The night before I left, they put on another exceptional meal in my honour, with speeches and poetry after grilled spicy *kibbeh* (balls of minced lamb pounded with cracked wheat and seasoning) served with lashings of sheep's yoghurt and hot bread – delicious! All good clean fun, of a kind we have virtually forgotten in the West.

But before then there was more coursing to be done. Badr had arranged with relatives in Aleppo that we would go up there for a day's coursing in an area towards the Turkish border where some hunters had reported many hares. First Badr took me on a tour of the Saluki fraternity in Hama. We went all over the town, turning often into quite simple houses with courtyards, which from the outside seemed silent and empty but on the inside were alive with Saluki puppies and mature hounds, horses, chickens and children. I saw some superb hounds of proven coursing ability. All were, by Western standards, very lean and muscular and with their crudely cropped ears they would win no prizes in the show ring; but that was not their purpose. They were there purely for coursing and to give pleasure in the chase to their very competitive owners, who were anxious to breed or own hounds that would be fast and effective enough to catch hares for the pot. Then we set off to drive to Aleppo, with *Guru* and *Rogo* in the back of the pickup.

Our first stop was at Khan Shaikhoon to see some well-known breeders there, but they were all away hunting. (This is the small town devastated by a poison gas attack in April 2017 and I wonder how many of the hospitable people I got to know there survived it.) So we continued towards Aleppo, stopping next at Barqoum, a small collection of beehive-shaped mud-brick houses, where we would leave our hounds for the night at the home of Abu Rifaat, who would be our guide the next day. It made me feel as if I had slipped back a couple of centuries as we sat on the floor of the single-roomed mud-brick house under twin beehive-shaped domes discussing the weather, the crops and the next day's coursing, while sipping sweet black tea from little glasses, served by his silent wife. Through the plastic sheeting that served as a window I could make out in the courtyard the vague forms of the hounds in their ungainly padded coats as they sorted themselves out in sheltered corners for the night. Then we went on to Aleppo, where we were to dine (feast?) with more members of the family before an early night.

The next morning was icy. Frost sprinkled the roof of the pickup, which refused to start until we pushed it. At least the exercise warmed us up. The hounds arrived from the farm, all six of them jostling and snarling in the back of the pickup as they sought room to lie in. In addition to Badr's two hounds, two farmers had brought *Jazzar*, a male feathered red grizzle; *Douman*, an almost black, slightly feathered male newly acquired from some gypsy breeders and on his first trial; *Qassab*, a beautifully shaped, slightly feathered cream-silver grizzle male not yet two years old; and *Tayra*, a dainty smooth black and tan bitch.

The hunting party numbered ten in three vehicles. We headed east-north-east from Aleppo towards the Turkish border, where the conditions looked perfect: clear blue sky, fields of winter wheat already several inches high and odd patches of rocky ground where the hares liked to lie up. But we walked for an hour without a sign of one. We walked for another hour, when a hare got up right in front of me and four of the hounds were slipped. Although *Guru* was first up to the hare, it was *Qassab* that, in a remarkable run, overtook *Guru* and turned the hare. *Guru* turned even faster, but again *Qassab* overtook as the hare led them back on their tracks before us. There followed a long straight run until both hounds seemed to seize the hare as one, with the other two hounds close behind. Badr's nephew Abboud, whom I had earlier convinced of *Qassab*'s qualities and who had purchased her from his farmer owner, was beside himself with delight that his hound had run so well against the seasoned *Guru*.

Our spirits rose after such a long and exciting course and we hoped we would find more hares; but it was not to be, until we were on the point of taking a break for lunch, when suddenly *Rogo* put one up. It certainly made up for the long hours we had walked and gave one of the longest and most exciting chases I have ever seen. It ran off in almost a straight line for several hundred metres until it reached a narrow road leading to a nearby village. Closely pursued by *Jazzar*, *Douman*, *Qassab* and *Rogo*, it zigzagged along the road before disappearing down the bank and under the road through a culvert. The hounds could barely squeeze through the pipe and, when they emerged on the other side plastered with mud, they had lost considerable ground on the hare. It promptly doubled back across the road and repeated the pass through the pipe with the hounds now well behind. It ran on up the road and disappeared among some outbuildings at the edge of the village but was flushed out again by the hounds into an orchard, where they finally pulled it down. Badr, meanwhile, had been driving the pickup in pursuit with Abboud shouting encouragement deliriously to his *Qassab* from the back, where he clung on perilously to the twisting and lurching vehicle. After so much excitement and a long day in the field, we broke for a wonderful picnic, which Abboud produced from his car. His wife had made all the delicious food herself and we were treated to a rare spread, including the popular *kibbeh bi-siniyeh* (pounded lamb with pine nuts and seasoning). Afterwards we tried two other places without any luck and the Hama crowd gave the Aleppans the thumbs down for their choice of ground.

I still had another day free before returning to Damascus, and Badr and his relatives took me early in the morning about an hour's drive east of Hama to an area called Mas'ada, where there had been good coursing before. We had *Guru*, *Rogo* and *Qassab* in the back of the pickup. We reached some ploughed land that looked promising and soon found fresh scrapes, but it took a long walk before the first hare got up and it led the hounds on a fine chase. It made for the road and zigzagged along it for a while before turning sharply to run behind a low stone wall, from which a fox suddenly emerged. The hounds were so intent on the hare they did not notice the fox, which trotted nonchalantly away. We could see the hounds streaming after the hare across a field, now joined by a farm worker who was running after them for all he was worth. They eventually caught it, but it was a very long run. Badr commented that the hounds were not running as fast as they could as they were tired from the long day before (and, I thought, a cold night shut up in a garage with nothing but bread and water!). That day we put up only one more hare, which gave the hounds another long run as they could not overtake it, and it eventually disappeared down a hole.

I was ready for my bed when we reached Badr's house, but it was not to be. A visitor had arrived – an elderly Kurdish shaikh from somewhere north of Aleppo wanted Badr's help in a difficult case in his village involving the murder of a madman and blood money. Badr listened attentively and immediately arranged for legal advice the next day. The old shaikh stayed for supper and for the night, all wrapped up in his thick felt cloak on a sofa – a reminder of the not too distant feudal past when the khan of a tribe was the natural recourse for help. Badr had responded to the appeal without hesitation and at his own expense.

As I boarded the bus for Damascus the next day, with Badr's entreaty to return every year ringing in my ears, I thought how lucky I had been to lift the veil for a

The hunt near Aleppo.

moment from a corner of this fascinating country rarely seen by Westerners and to enjoy the traditional sport of shaikhs and khans and their fine Salukis, just as it had been once upon a time, long ago. Today I am left wondering whether it will ever be possible to repeat such experiences in that poor benighted land, riven by civil war and the devastation wreaked upon it by the so-called Islamic State.

I spent only a few days in Muscat, sorting out a number of problems that had arisen in my absence and preparing for our farewell tour of Arabia before my retirement. Liese and I wanted to make a nostalgic journey round the Gulf, to take our leave of people and places we had long known and to visit some other places that might be difficult to reach later.

Our first objective was Doha, Qatar, over 1,200 km away across an almost endless wasteland. We drove first to the oasis town of al-Ain, just across the border in Abu Dhabi territory, where we had an early lunch at the embassy's bungalow there, discreetly out of sight as Ramadan had just begun. We drove on to the UAE–Saudi border, where our spirits were uplifted, as we were about to clear the last checkpoint on the Saudi side, by the sight of a fine-looking smooth red and white particoloured Saluki, with – unusually for a male – two small puppies running after him. When the border guards saw our interest, they immediately offered us the male but, tempting though he was, we could not take him on so soon in our long journey. Regretfully we waved the guards goodbye and continued towards the Qatar border.

But first we had to make a detour from the main road into the sands towards the little bedouin oasis where two years earlier I had acquired *Najma* from the tents of the Al Murrah tribe. The sun was already beginning to set as we approached the oasis and I feared we would arrive at just the wrong moment when the people would be breaking their Ramadan fast. In fact, we turned into the dusty square by the mosque with ten minutes to spare. As I pulled up, the headman, whom we had met before, appeared and welcomed us like old friends. He insisted we stayed for the *Iftar* – breakfast – which we agreed to do after we had had a quick look at the Salukis that we could already see running about. So, while I took my pictures of four or five of the typically smooth light sandy hounds of the Al Murrah and an unusual – for this area – feathered deer grizzle, our host waited impatiently for us to go in and eat. Liese had, of course, been whisked away to join the women in the harem; whereas I was taken to a room where the men gathered round a sumptuous spread of food laid out on the floor. First we ate dates and yoghurt, the traditional food for breaking the fast, and then we tucked into a variety of dishes, tearing off pieces of meat or dipping into bowls of rice only with the fingers of the right hand – quite tricky when it is piping hot!

When I had had enough I rose and washed my hands before squatting again, this time with the emir of the tribe for bitter coffee flavoured with cardamom, followed by sweet black tea. All the time the emir was reciting verses from the Quran, which made conversation rather difficult. Then a young man sat down beside me and began talking about his passion – hunting with Salukis and falcons. I showed him some of my collection of photographs of Salukis from different countries and was gratified that he picked out my *Tayra* as the best and an almost identical bitch from Morocco as the second-best – an interesting comparison. He picked out another smooth cream and white Al Murrah bitch I had photographed there two years before and said it was the premier hound of its day. He was surprised when I told him that in northern Syria the previous week we had been catching only five or so hares a day. He maintained that, when he went 'south' into the Empty Quarter, he would catch as many as 20. It was my turn to express surprise that there were so many in the desert, but he and another hunter assured me that this was so. But we could not tarry longer as we still had to cross two more borders and drive to Doha to be there in time for dinner.

Doha had changed out of all recognition since I had first visited it some 35 years before, when it was a sleepy little town. Now we drove though wide avenues past shopping malls in the modern Gulf style to stay with old friends at the British Embassy.

The next day I took up an invitation to meet one of the members of the ruling family, whose father had been a renowned hunter with falcons and Salukis. The son was himself a hunter and kept a pack of Salukis on a farm some distance from Doha, but he said that his father always liked to have a few hounds around him and would soon bring them for me to see. Sure enough, after a while the elderly shaikh appeared, followed by a smooth copper-red bitch, very muscular and broad in the chest seen from the front, and a tall, rather heavy-looking slightly feathered black and tan male. There was also another red bitch, which had never been on a lead before and had worked itself up into a lather trying to free itself. They showed me old photographs of the period when they used to go hunting in the desert every year for up to a month at a time.

The son then took me off to his nearby farm, where he kept a variety of wild animals and birds, including hundreds of gazelle and some oryx. He said he had also released some hares, which now lived happily within the protection of the farm's walls. But overall he thought there were few breeders of Salukis left. Those who kept them for hunting would take them to the Al Murrah bedouin for a month or two before the hunting season to get them into shape. Only the bedouin kept them all the year round, and in ever-decreasing numbers as they became more settled and left the nomadic way of life. How this depressing picture has changed in the interval! As I shall describe later, Saluki racing has become a major sporting interest of young Qataris, some of whom now maintain large kennels on a scale probably never seen before in the Gulf.

The next day we drove to Bahrain, across the spectacular curving King Fahd Causeway that links the island with the Saudi mainland, to stay with the ambassador, who had been best man at our wedding. He had made some interesting arrangements for us. First, the next morning we went to see the archaeological excavations at Saar, where a British team had been working for several years on this site that dates back to about 2000 BC, when Bahrain was known as Dilmun and was a major entrepot for trade, especially in copper from Oman for the city-states of Mesopotamia. We were guided round by archaeologists we knew from Iraq, including a young couple

I had married there in a consular ceremony. The site was impressive, with solidly constructed limestone-built houses and a columned temple.

On the way back, I stopped at a large house to ask for directions, and through the open gateway I was astonished to see some Salukis relaxing in the sandy pens of their kennels. They belonged to a member of the ruling family and we were allowed in to see them. There were two pairs, one of almost identical smooth red and white particoloureds like those of the Al Murrah and the other of a smooth white bitch in whelp, also of the Al Murrah type, and her tall feathered black and tan mate of a Persian-looking type that was once more commonly found on Bahrain. We saw some more of this latter type that afternoon when we paid a return visit to Shaikha Danah Al Khalifa's farm. We were greeted on arrival by Danah and an amazing sight – Saluki heads protruding through the fretted brickwork and over the top of the wall round her house in an ever-changing combination. Her pack then numbered 19 following the recent birth of two litters, one maintaining the old Bahraini bloodlines and the other the offspring of a pair of Saudi origin. So she had her hands full, but she kindly introduced them all to us and brought us up to date on events since we had last been there two years before.

We also called on some British friends who had rescued a brother and sister pair of feathered Bahraini-type Salukis. They exercised them on the beach with their Arabian mares, which kept them in good trim. In between, the ambassador had invited to meals old friends from my time in Bahrain as a debutant diplomat in 1957, and by the time we left my head was spinning with memories and impressions.

Our next destination was the British Ambassador's residence in Riyadh, which we would use as our base while we made contact with a number of people to whom I had introductions. At least that was the plan, but it was still Ramadan, when the hours of business are different and people move around a lot visiting family and friends. So we had time to visit the well-restored small town of Addiriyah, now a UNESCO-protected world heritage site, which was the original home of the Saudi royal family and served as their capital under the first Saudi dynasty from 1744 to 1818. I also succeeded in arranging to visit the kennels of one shaikh in Kharj, a small town about 100 km south of Riyadh. It was not easy to find his farm in the maze of plantations there, but at last we arrived and were shown over the extensive kennels by a farmhand. In a series of pens there were six or seven adults, a few well-grown puppies and a litter of about half a dozen puppies. Communication with the Indian farmhand was difficult, but he kept pointing to a big feathered copper-red male that he said was American and the sire of both sets of puppies, whose dams were Saudi. The combination looked good, but the proof would be if they stood up to coursing in the harsh conditions of the Empty Quarter, where the owner had told me he hunted in the winter. There was also an odd-looking small smooth bitch with an almost identical younger male with a brindle pattern on a light-grey background. Sadly, I could not discover from the farmhand anything about their origin.

A British friend had given me the name of another breeder in the nearby town of Ragheeb and we tracked him easily as I happened to chance on his son when I was asking the way. Hamoud Abu Naif turned out to be a dignified old man who welcomed us into his *majlis* with refreshments, despite Ramadan. He told us the sad story that he no longer had any Salukis as the last four had all been stolen and there were no more to be had in the vicinity. In any case, he was concentrating on his falcons, and had two brought in to show us. He made a striking picture with his own hooked nose by the side of the falcon's curved beak. He told me – and this was confirmed to me later – that under a new law hunting was allowed in Saudi Arabia only with falcons but no longer with Salukis or shotguns. He agreed that, if fully observed, the law would be bound to lead to a sharp decline in the population of coursing Salukis. This would be a loss to Salukis worldwide, for the bedouin pool of hounds represented an important source of the original breed. However, I suspected that the wily bedouin in the vast expanses of the desert would find a way of maintaining the breed. Certainly the law did not appear to have had any immediate impact at our next stop, and the introduction of Saluki racing in recent years has also boosted the breed's popularity.

It had been our intention to visit from Riyadh the Al Murrah tribe at the oasis of Yabrin on the western edge of the Empty Quarter, where other travellers had spoken of the fine hounds to be seen there, but we had suffered a puncture and I was wary of attempting a drive of 100 km each way across desert tracks without a backup vehicle. So we abandoned this adventure and turned east towards the Gulf and back to *Najma's* home oasis at Anbak. Once again, the headman welcomed us and insisted that we spend the night there as it was already late afternoon. But first he wanted to know whether I would accept as a gift the year-old red and white particoloured dog that had greeted us with great affection as we got out of the car. I felt honoured but, as tactfully as possible, had to decline because, much as I would have loved to have him,

Al Murrah Saluki.

it would merely have added to our existing problems of sending back to six months' quarantine in England our other two (female) Salukis.

We had hoped to meet *Najma's* breeder but he was away in the desert with his camels. His absence was indicative of how the human and Saluki population of the oasis was constantly fluctuating. In four visits there, we had hardly ever seen the same people or Salukis. The bedouin are heavily dependent on their camels and come into the oasis only occasionally. The rest of the time they are following the grazing with their herds, and their Salukis of course go with them. This time we saw the most unusual sight of a black and tan puppy, which must have been brought in from elsewhere, as such a colour is rare in the desert environment. It may have been brought by hunters from the north.

That night, as we sat in the headman's tent round the glowing brazier, I asked whether the story of the hunting ban was true. He confirmed that it was indeed in force. I asked how it was that I had seen at least half a dozen Salukis there that evening and there must have been many more out in the desert. He replied with a smile that they were merely pets! I imagined that it would be difficult to prove the contrary; and we retired to sleep in the newly furnished *majlis*, confident in the knowledge that the bedouin would find a way to balance their traditions with modern requirements.

We drove home to Muscat via the United Arab Emirates, where we said farewell to many of the friends we had made in the 1960s in Dubai, Sharjah, Ajman, Umm al-

Quwain and Ras al-Khaimah. We also took the opportunity to pay a visit to the kennels of one of the Dubai shaikhs, who was a keen hunter with falcons and Salukis in the Empty Quarter. He had some nice smooth Saluki puppies and several adult hounds, two of which had been imported from a well-known British kennel; but they had apparently found it hard to adjust to local conditions. He also had some Greyhounds for racing. The kennels were in a sort of wildlife park, with about ten cheetahs, though not trained for hunting, as well as all kinds of local fauna such as gazelle, foxes, wolves and birds of prey.

I went on to Sharjah, where I had an introduction to an American former diplomat who, while serving in Jeddah, Saudi Arabia, had acquired a pair of Salukis: a feathered tricolour male of English ancestry, though born in Jeddah, and a smooth red bitch with a white chest. At the age of eight, she had produced two puppies, a smooth female version of the sire and a feathered female of a most unusual colour – brindle stripes on a sandy background. Neither of the parents showed any sign of brindle, but it is possible that it was masked. The owner later took them back to the USA, where the brindle must have attracted some attention.

Soon afterwards, we had to face up to the departure of our two hounds for their six months in quarantine in England. We had decided to send them ahead of our own departure as we would be very busy in the remaining period extricating ourselves from Muscat after more than four years there. A local carpenter had made wooden crates for them with their own water supply for the long journey and, knowing the Houdini-like talent that Salukis have for escaping, I hoped that they would not chew their way out. They looked so forlorn at the airport and whined, making it all the sadder for us. However, they went off and, to our great relief, arrived safely the next day in London, where they were collected and taken to the quarantine kennels. We would not see them again for several months.

If I had known at the time about the experience of my colleague, Sir Alan Munro, with flying his Saluki *Mancha*, I would have had even greater concerns. Alan was posted as ambassador to Algeria in 1984 and arranged for *Mancha* to follow in the cargo hold of the thrice-weekly Air Algérie flight from London Heathrow airport; but on the appointed day, he failed to arrive. Alan then heard what had happened. *Mancha*, duly caged and sedated, awoke as he was about to be loaded onto the aircraft and somehow forced apart the wire frame of the cage. He then galloped off onto the airfield in the gathering dusk, and all landings had to be suspended until he was retrieved. That was embarrassing enough, but – incredibly – he did it again at the next attempt to fly him, closing Heathrow down once more! At the third attempt, *Mancha* was finally loaded, secured in an iron chest, but the pilot then decided that the aircraft was overladen. Something had to be left behind and it was a choice between *Mancha* and a large consignment of whisky, ordered by the government for the celebration of Algeria's forthcoming National Day. It was no contest, and *Mancha* was again left behind.

The Munros then decided he should fly out with their twin sons for the school holidays. At first the pilot was disinclined to take the troublesome animal on board, but finally agreed and off they went. However, when the boys arrived in Algiers there was no sign of *Mancha's* iron chest and no record of it! Only much later were the Munros called back to the airport to collect the iron chest, which had been bumping its way round the carousel for hours. As if that was not trouble enough, the sequel was that, having agreed to carry the dog, the airline remembered that foodstuffs packed in dry ice and animals are not allowed to be carried in the same hold. Consequently, a large consignment of fresh and frozen foods, destined for the British Embassy's staff, was offloaded and left to stand in the open on a hot night. It was then unfit for human consumption and the ambassador and his Saluki were far from popular! *Mancha* was oblivious of all this and thoroughly enjoyed terrorising the feral cats around his new home. He eventually died of old age, back in London again.

Brindle puppy in Sharjah, UAE.

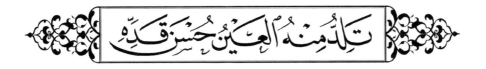

his excellent conformation is pleasing to the eye.

Chapter Eight

A New Beginning

I retired from the Diplomatic Service in the middle of June 1994 and on arrival at our new home in London we were immediately immersed in settling in and reordering our lives. We had chosen the house partly because it had a large garden and was within a few minutes of the huge unspoilt area of Wimbledon Common, where the hounds would be able to run free. I often used to joke that it was like having my own country estate, because I would go there early in the morning before people were about and let the hounds run to their hearts' content through woods and over fields, often in pursuit of the varied wildlife there – though in truth they had no need to go beyond the garden fence for that, as we were plagued by urban foxes and squirrels.

They had borne quarantine very well in each other's company, but were of course overjoyed on their release at the beginning of October to be free again. However, the long period of inactivity meant that they needed to be brought back to coursing condition. So every day, twice a day, I exercised them on the Common, and I even trained them to follow me on my bike. Occasionally I also tried running them on the nearby grassland of Richmond Park. However, here there was the unpredictable hazard of deer and, after a dangerous encounter with a majestic stag one day, I decided that the risk was too high. There would be other opportunities for them to exercise their hunting instincts, as we had applied to become members of the Coursing Section of the Saluki or Gazelle Hound Club (SGHC). Before I could enter them for coursing events, however, I needed to seek the agreement of the Kennel Club to their registration in the United Kingdom. They were both already registered with the Bahrain Kennel Club and, after scrutiny of their documentation, the Kennel Club agreed to register them.

The Saluki is a comparatively rare breed in the UK. A black and tan Saluki called *Zillah* is known to have been bred in the Zoological Gardens in Regent's Park in 1835 and a Saluki called *Tierma* is recorded at the Kennel Club as having won at a dog show in 1875. However, the breed started to become established only in 1895, when a pair imported from Egypt became the foundation of Florence Amherst's kennel. She became a prolific breeder with this pair and later imports, but the breed only began to become more widely known after the First World War, when returning officers from the British Army who had served in the Middle East brought back the Salukis they had acquired for hunting there. By 1923 there were sufficient numbers of Saluki owners to form the SGHC, and organised coursing was started in 1925 to preserve the breed's hunting skills in a very different environment from its natural habitat rather than let it go the way of some other working breeds and become exclusively for show. Rules were drawn up, similar to those of the National Coursing Club for coursing Greyhounds, which laid emphasis on testing the fitness, endurance, ability and stamina of the hounds in knockout competitions in which two competing hounds are awarded points by the supervising judge, usually mounted, under conditions that give the hare every opportunity to exercise on its home ground its considerable wiles to avoid being caught. In my later experience I observed that the kill rate of hares was very low, as the English or Scottish countryside generally provided plenty of cover for the hares to make their escape. Very often those that were caught were shown to be old and occasionally diseased; unless the latter, they all ended up in the pot.

To give members of the Coursing Section the chance to get to know us and our hounds before approving our application for membership, we were invited to join the Coursing Section at a meeting in the middle of October on a farm in Oxfordshire, which we accepted with alacrity as a wonderful opportunity to familiarise ourselves and our hounds with the very different coursing scene there from what we had been used to in the Middle East. The beginning was not auspicious. We set off from London in fog, and when we reached the designated farm it was so dense that we could hardly make out who was who. There was clearly no prospect of any action for a while, so we used the time to get to know the people and the hounds we would be associating with for years to come. They were all seasoned practitioners of the sport, and cast an appreciative eye over our newcomers. By chance, Nina and Philippe Adam were visiting from France. I had helped them to acquire a lovely little feathered cream bitch from Shaikha Danah Al Khalifa in Bahrain, so it was particularly pleasant to see them there and to hear how well she had adapted to life in France.

'Walking up', charcoal drawing by Terence J Gilbert, 1983.

We took an early picnic lunch as the sun was beginning to break through the fog and enjoyed a beautiful though inconclusive afternoon's coursing. The time before dusk was too short to complete the two eight-dog stakes but it helped us and our hounds to see how things were done in this carefully regulated sport, run so differently from the free-for-all of the Middle East.

A sterner test came shortly afterwards. The SGHC Coursing Section used to hold an annual competition against the Deerhound Coursing Club in Scotland. Although our hounds were still not qualified to run in formal competitions, we were invited to go along on the off-chance that they might be able to run in a trial. At the beginning of November we drove up to Aviemore, where the competition would be run on the nearby moors. It proved quite a shock to the system to be confronted with frost on the ground and snow on the surrounding mountains on our first morning. I kept wondering how our Middle Eastern hounds would cope with such unfamiliar conditions, particularly *Tayra* with her short hair.

The meeting was spread over three days and, as a number of Salukis had dropped out for one reason or another, the prospects of our hounds having a run at some point were quite good. The first two days were given over to separate stakes for the Deerhounds and the Salukis. On the first day we simply joined in the line walking over the deep heather to drive the hares forward for the slipper to release after them the two competing hounds. The object of the chase was the Scottish or blue hare, which is smaller than the brown hare and changes the colour of its coat to white in winter. This makes it easier to pick them out against the dark heather, when it is not covered with snow. Even so, the hare compensates for its visibility by exploiting the often treacherous ground, where the heather obscures the many holes and gulleys, into which the unwary could easily fall. The hounds seemed to manage rather better than us, though sadly one Deerhound broke a leg.

The next day, *Najma* was allowed to run as a bye in an eight dog stake for the Moray Purse. She was drawn against *Shamsa bint Sha'awa*, a feathered red bitch bred in Saudi Arabia by Mike Ratcliffe that looked very like *Najma* in size, shape and colour. They ran a very evenly matched course over a hill and out of sight but, to everyone's astonishment – considering this was her first formal coursing event – *Najma* ran straight back to the slipper as if waiting to go again! She and *Tayra* ran against each other in an informal trial and seemed to adapt remarkably quickly to these unfamiliar surroundings.

The last day was devoted to the Blanco Challenge – winning Deerhound against winning Saluki, another hound of Saudi descent owned and bred by Paul Sagar – which the Deerhound won in atrocious weather. We had had to leave before then to meet, at his Loch Fyne home, one of my heroes – Sir Fitzroy Maclean, whose adventures in Central Asia as a British diplomat immediately before the Second World War, described in his great book *Eastern Approaches* (1949), had inspired my own interest in that fascinating part of the world. He regaled us with stories from his adventurous career, especially when he was head of the military mission to Tito's Partisans in Yugoslavia. But we had to leave for our next destination – Paul Sagar's home in Oldham, where we had promised to see his latest litter of puppies. They were very tempting, but I had already decided we would attempt to breed from our own hounds.

Paul Sagar was a dedicated coursing man who, until his untimely demise, did much to raise the level of coursing Salukis in Britain, where there had been a trend for many years away from coursing in favour of breeding purely for showing. He maintained a network of farmers in the north of England who were happy to allow him and his friends to run their hounds over their fields. He invited us to join them one weekend in February on a farm near Marston Moor in Yorkshire, and it was such fun. It was not only that there were plenty of hares for the hounds to chase but, rather, the whole atmosphere of a day spent walking in the glorious countryside in congenial company, followed by a jolly meal in a friendly English pub. This came closer to what I had previously enjoyed in the Middle East. The fact that Mike Ratcliffe was in the company, with all his stories of coursing during his many years in Saudi Arabia, made the parallel even closer.

While I was there, I was pressed to return the following week to spend a day at the Waterloo Cup, the so-called 'Blue Riband of the Leash', run on Lord Leverhulme's estate near Altcar. Although restricted to coursing Greyhounds, it was the premium event of the coursing calendar, without equal anywhere in the world. It all began quite modestly in 1836 as an eight-dog stake, with the winner taking a monetary prize and a trophy. It was not until 1857 that it reached its established form of 64 Greyhounds competing for the Waterloo Cup, with the 32 first-round losers competing for the Waterloo Purse and the 16 second-round losers for the Waterloo Plate. It became such a sporting spectacle that thousands would turn up to see it, drawn partly by the opportunity to bet on the runners. It lost some popularity as other sports developed but when I arrived at Altcar that cold, damp February day the crowd of spectators standing on a raised bund on one side of the plain was enormous. Another, similar bund stretched along the opposite side to delineate the coursing ground, along which the driven hares would run.

Paul Sagar seemed to know everyone as, apart from anything else, he often worked as a professional Greyhound slipper. He took me into the reserved enclosure, where the atmosphere was more like that at Ascot races, with a line of Range Rovers from which food and champagne flowed. Sadly, the weather was unkind. The ground was so waterlogged that the courses were mostly straight runs, at the end of which the Greyhounds were snapping up the hares easily. The stewards moved the field to a drier area, but by early afternoon the rain had really set in, carried almost horizontally by the fierce wind off the sea, and no further coursing was possible that day.

Despite the conditions, I was glad that I had seen this historic Greyhound event, but I came away even more convinced of the superiority of Salukis. Yes, the Greyhound impressed with its explosive burst out of slips and its speed on the straight, but it looked almost clumsy by comparison with the agile Saluki when it came to working the wily hare and it tired much too quickly. I had occasion to reflect on an unexpected reaction to Greyhound coursing a few weeks later, when I took up an invitation from my Syrian friend Badr to join him for a week with the hounds in Hama.

When I was picked up by Fakhr, one of Badr's sons, from the bus station in Hama, he greeted me with the inauspicious news that the Syrian authorities had recently imposed a five-year hunting ban! When he saw my look of consternation, Fakhr grinned and with a wink assured me that everything would be all right. Later, after a huge family lunch, as Badr took me up to his farm he reassured me that the hunting ban was not being enforced and he believed it was directed towards stopping the indiscriminate slaughter of migrant birds with guns rather than the occasional coursing of hare by Salukis. At any rate, on our first excursion we overtook a car with the barrels of sporting guns protruding from all four windows – carried, according to Badr, by off-duty policemen! So we thought we would be in good company!

At Badr's farm I had expected to see some of the hounds I had seen the year before, especially his star performers, *Guru* and *Rogo*. However, neither they nor any of the other hounds were there. In their place were a very muscular smooth cream dog, also called *Guru*, his sibling, a smooth red bitch called *Khamleh*, a smooth cream bitch, one month pregnant by *Guru*, called *Shoha*, and a 14-month-old smooth black and tan dog with the odd name of *Martine*, after the old Martini–Henry rifle, which was much loved by the bedouin. What had happened to the other hounds and from where had these new hounds come? It was clear from Badr's answers that only the best hounds were good enough. Old *Guru* – that superb athlete that Badr had held up to me as his ideal hound – had passed his peak and had been given away. *Qassab*, who I thought had shown so much promise as a novice, had also been passed on as he lacked stamina, and another hound had died. No sentiment is attached to these hounds, and if they do not meet the overriding standard of efficiency in the chase they are not kept. Another hunter told me later that he had shot one of his most promising young hounds because it would wander too far away and had started to eat the hares it caught (probably, I thought, because it was not fed enough). It is a tough code, but one that does produce high-quality hounds.

Some of the new hounds at the farm had interesting backgrounds. The new *Guru* was one of the most powerfully built Salukis I have ever seen. The thigh muscles were so thick that from the rear he looked bandy. I took his measurements: height 68.5 cm, length 68.5 cm and the circumference of his chest a staggering 74.3 cm. Badr had heard of *Guru* from a friend in northern Syria, who regarded him as being without parallel. Badr had to have him and, as it happened, the owner owed Badr some money, so he went to collect his debt and, he hoped, the hound. However, the owner, who lived in a village on the border with Turkey near Ain al-Arab (Kobane), at first hid himself away. When he was eventually shamed into showing himself, he tried to keep the hound hidden, saying it was no good. Badr was not to be diverted, not even when the owner offered him his daughter instead of the hound! Finally, a deal was struck for about $150 and a new *galabiyeh* (garment like a nightshirt) – then a large sum for a Saluki in Syria. Prices have since gone through the roof because of the market for racing Salukis in the Gulf. Badr later gave the owner some more money and another *galabiyeh* to acquire *Guru's* sister, *Khamleh*. As for *Martine*,

Guru.

he came from another famous breeder in a village just north of Hama, which I was to visit later.

The coursing that followed the next day was wonderful but exhausting. We rose with the *muezzin's* call for the dawn prayer at 4.30 am. After a quick cup of Turkish coffee, we were ready to go, but in the Arab world time is elastic and some of the other hunters turned up more than half an hour late. Even so, we were on the road as the red rays of the sun began to light up the sky to the east, the direction in which we were heading from Hama. We were going to an area where Badr and his companions had not been for a long time in the Wadi al-Azib, which leads eventually to Palmyra, the magnificent desert city partly destroyed by the Roman Emperor Aurelian in the 3rd century and ruined further by the Islamic State occupiers in 2016–7. We arrived at around 8.00 am and set off walking immediately with Badr's four hounds, including *Shoha*, the pregnant bitch. The conditions were ideal: a gently undulating landscape for as far as the eye could see, with patches of growing wheat in the sand and gravel ground and the heat of the sun tempered by a cold wind. Crested larks, the songbirds of the desert, rose from the profusion of wild flowers, among which I recognised red anemones, tulips and blue muscaris from which our cultivated varieties originally came.

After half an hour the first hare got up and streaked away with three hounds, less *Khamleh*, in pursuit. It was a superb spectacle, as the hare was never more than about 460 m away. It was a long course of close to three minutes, with *Guru* repeatedly striking at the hare and eventually catching it. *Shoha*, though pregnant, was also in close contention. In dips here and there where rainwater had gathered, some patches of wheat were higher than others and from one of these a fox suddenly and unwisely emerged. The three loose hounds converged on it and, once again, *Guru* took the lead and seized it by the neck. *Martine* had never seen a fox before and it was interesting to see how he held back to watch how *Guru* dealt with it. We were to put up two more foxes that morning and both were despatched in short order by *Guru*, who suffered a terrible gash across his muzzle in the process. However, this did not prevent him from catching two more of the three hares we caught later. The remaining one was caught by *Khamleh* with a terrific burst of speed from a standing start over about 150 m: her speed was partly what so impressed Badr about her but, as he pointed out, it was also her stamina, as she still looked as fresh at the end of the day as she was at the beginning.

By then the sun was high and we were all in need of sustenance. Badr had prepared a sumptuous meal of *kibbeh* with a range of salads as we lounged on a hillock by the side of an artificial storage dam, used by shepherds for watering their flocks. Of course, the hounds received nothing; they had their usual meal of hard pitta bread when they got back to the farm. Here I enjoyed a small triumph, because my pleas the previous year that Badr should supplement their meagre diet of bread had to some extent been answered: he now allowed them some table scraps, principally chicken bones. One of the other hunters remarked that he could hardly give his hounds more than he ate himself, and for him meat was a rarity and bread his staple food. At least chewing the hard bread produces the whitest teeth in these hounds.

After returning the hounds to the farm, the day was far from over. After barely time to shower and change, I was taken to the hunters' *majlis* in Hama. Squeezed into a small room with benches round the walls was a fluctuating gathering of upwards of 20 people who had, or had once had, a keen interest in coursing with Salukis. The discussion was all about famous hounds and memorable courses, with their owners describing particular events in great detail. Every hound mentioned seemed to be described as unique in all Syria but, as always among hunters or fishermen, a little exaggeration was good-humouredly tolerated. The discourse was interrupted only by prayers, in which they all joined without ceremony behind the *imam* of the day, and for piping hot servings of *zuhour* (a kind of camomile tea).

Badr then whisked me away to his own *majlis* for his nightly gathering with any of his friends who cared to drop in. This time we were joined by a retired professor of Arabic literature famous for his prodigious memory of poetry and classical stories. I tested him on one of the pre-Islamic collection of poems called the *Muallaqat*, in which a pair of Salukis is described coursing an oryx (see Chapter Five). He thought for a moment and then began declaiming the very lines. Later he regaled us with a story about one of the caliphs of the Umayyad period in the 8th century with remarkable fluency – a performance well up to his reputation. I was then faced with another huge meal before collapsing into bed around 11.30 in the knowledge that it would be another short night, as we would be off again before dawn the next morning.

The *muezzin*'s call to prayer shattered my sleep but the prospect of another day's coursing soon had me on the move. It was Friday, the local weekend, and our group was joined by other keen hunters on their day off. We numbered about a dozen, with five hounds: *Khamleh*, who had finished so fresh the day before; *Battah*, a tall (68.5 cm), very lean dog I had seen the previous year; *Jinah*, a two-year-old feathered red grizzle; and *Raddad*, a 14-month-old smooth cream dog and his fawn grizzle sister

Abdul Jabbar with Showha, Martine, Khamleh and Guru.

Raddeh that I had seen as puppies the year before. Badr was resting his other hounds for another day. Our objective was an area even closer to Palmyra, where none of the other hunters had been before. We were following the directions given to us by one of the hunters in the *majlis* the night before, who swore that the area was very green and full of hares. Along the way we had to keep checking our route with shepherds, whose ferocious dogs flew at us from the black goat's-hair tents they were guarding.

Eventually we arrived at the hunting grounds and as we walked up we found plenty of hare scrapes and droppings, but no hares. After a while, the reason became clear: ahead of us, groups of bedouin women were gathering an edible plant, something like chicory, which fetches a good price in the market, and looking for highly valuable – and more elusive – truffles. Their activities had scared off the hares, so we turned to prospect an undisturbed area. Our change of direction was soon to be rewarded when we put up our first hare, which took the hounds in a wide arc before going to ground in some rocks. The hounds succeeded in flushing it out and it led them on a long chase before going to ground again. The feeling of frustration was soon dispelled when one of the hunters spotted a hare in its form. There was no question of driving it out and giving it 75 metres' law, as we would do in the UK: all the hounds were loose anyway, and they quickly ran the hare down. Another hare had taken three of the hounds way out of sight, when yet another broke cover right in front of me. The only available hound, *Battah*, was slipped and he put in a superb solo run, striking three or four times at the hare in the first few hundred metres before it eventually disappeared among some rocks, from which *Battah* pulled it out by the leg.

Meanwhile, *Khamleh*, held in reserve in the car, was brought out by Badr, who had spotted another hare in its form. There followed another excellent twisting solo course before the hare escaped down a hole. By then it was 1.00 pm and we were all feeling tired and hungry after our early start, the long journey and several hours in the field. So we wended our way back down the Wadi al-Azib towards the lake, where we had lunched the previous day. On the way, we drove by an expanse of green wheat that looked too good to pass up. It took another hour's gruelling walk under the high sun before we put up a hare. It gave four of the hounds (one had gone lame) a very good run before they pulled it down.

My friends reckoned that four out of the eight hares coursed was a respectable score and we all looked forward to the barbecue that was to follow. In remarkably quick time, the grill was glowing and the kebabs and *kibbeh* were turning on the spits. In customary Arab fashion, the vast quantities of food were attacked with great concentration and almost in silence. Only after we rose replete did the banter resume over glasses of hot sweet tea. It was late afternoon before we set off to return to Hama. We were also delayed by two punctures on one vehicle and a diversion to meet some gypsies we had seen walking back to their tented camp with four Salukis. My friends knew the gypsies and had bought Salukis from them before, as they are recognised as breeders of good hounds. They had a smooth black and tan dog with them that looked like a good courser, but the others were still too young to assess. I now wonder whether the gypsies, who used to be found in encampments on the outskirts of small towns across northern Syria, have managed to escape the attentions of the Islamic State fanatics.

The next day was gentler. We went on a tour of Khan Shaikhoon and Sawran, two villages north of Hama noted for their strong Salukis; Badr's *Martine* came from Khan Shaikhoon. We first called at a house where we found his identical litter brother and two delightful, playful puppies. I mentioned that I rarely saw more than two puppies from any single litter and wondered why there were so few. I was told that it was quite normal for a bitch to have between eight and ten puppies but it was usual to cull most of them at birth to reduce the strain of feeding them and the problem of later placing them.

At another house, where *Battah* had been bred, we found a superbly built two-and-a-half-year-old smooth grizzle dog called *Zingo*. He was already a proven courser and looked in top condition. He was with his identical litter sister, also a fine-looking animal, and two puppies of the same breeding and colour. In Sawran, we found another litter brother of *Martine* and two other less-distinguished hounds. Finally, we came back to a farm near Badr's own to visit a lawyer friend known for his rivalry with Badr to have the best hounds. He had four, of which a tall, strongly built smooth grey grizzle dog and a much smaller but very compact-looking smooth red and white particoloured dog were particularly remarkable. I had seen the latter and his two other hounds as puppies the year before and noted that they all seemed to have come on well. However, the lawyer was at a loss to explain his total lack of coursing success with his hounds. Over the past season they had not caught a single hare; either they did not find any or the hares went to ground. When he heard of our exploits over the previous two days, he looked even gloomier. He called Badr a magician when it came to finding good hare country.

Abu al-Ward with Zingo in Khan Shaikhoon.

In many ways, the Arabs are unpredictable and react in an utterly different way from what you would expect. I had taken with me as a gift for Badr a superb leather slip lead, crafted by Mike Ratcliffe. In the West, anyone would have been delighted to own it. However, Badr, while praising the workmanship and showing it proudly to his friends, merely relegated it to the wall of his house where he had hung various horse trappings. He never once attempted to use it, but kept to his usual simple rope poacher's slip lead. He gave me in return one of his pretty beaded collars, which I had presumed had been made by the ladies of his house until he mentioned that they were made to order by prisoners in the local gaol! I had also taken with me as a gift a couple of videos on Greyhound coursing in Britain, thinking that they might find our orderly procedures amusing. I seriously underestimated the reaction. About twenty people from the hunters' *majlis* crammed into a small room to watch the videos and went wild with excitement at every course. They admired the power of the Greyhounds and urged them on with whoops and yells. Each kill was registered with an explosion of noise loud enough to take the roof off! It took some explaining that the object was not so much to catch the hare as to score points.

I still had another day's coursing ahead. This time we had a gentler start, as the location was near to Hama. We arrived in the field soon after 8.00 am. It had rained in the night and the air was cool and fresh. However, the ground remained hard and stony, so much so that I feared for the hounds' feet. We had a long walk before *Guru* put up the first hare. We were in the centre of a bowl and the hare ran very conveniently in a circle around the rim, so that we had an excellent view as all four of Badr's hounds gave chase. It took them a full three minutes to bring it down. We then caught two more over shorter distances, *Shoha* going lame in the process before being honourably relegated to the pickup.

By then we had been going for several hours and the hounds were no longer fresh. The next hare gave them a punishing run over a long distance before escaping down a foxhole. One of the lads tried to dig it out with his hands but it had gone too deep and, in disgust, he blocked the entrance with stones. Just as we were thinking of calling it a day, a hare got up from under my feet and the three tired hounds gave chase. Over the first few hundred metres they followed closely the hare's every twist and turn. Then it became clear that they were falling further and further behind as the hare ran on strongly almost in a straight line. First *Martine* and then *Guru* slowed to a canter, and finally even *Khamleh* gave up. When we collected them, they were all hobbling. Considering all the circumstances, they had performed outstandingly. They received no treatment for their injuries from Badr, who merely said that a good rest would cure them. They only seemed to have recourse to a vet for something really serious, and treated simpler ailments themselves, including stitching wounds. However, they had given up traditional medicines in favour of modern preparations, for example for worming.

What a contrast all that was to the proceedings at the next Saluki event I attended, a few months later! This was the SGHC Open Show in a field near Burford in Oxfordshire, in which, for the first time ever, I would enter the ring with my hounds. It was an occasion not without a Middle Eastern connection because, by coincidence, I had been approached by Shaikh Jasim, son of the then Minister of Foreign Affairs of Qatar, for help in finding him a Saluki to take back to Qatar at the end of his studies that summer. As so often with open-air events in England, the weather was unfriendly, and we spent a lot of time trying to keep ourselves and the hounds warm in a cold wind under a leaden sky. Shaikh Jasim turned up and I took him round to meet some of the breeders with puppies and to see some of the hounds in the ring. The only hound that drew his attention and he was keen to buy turned out to be a young hound out of Mike Ratcliffe's Saudi import that was not for sale. So he went away disappointed.

I did not have much success in the ring either – *Najma* was placed sixth out of six entries! I overheard a member of the Saluki Establishment remark that she had an old-fashioned look, which I took as a compliment, though it was probably not meant as such. *Tayra* fared somewhat better, coming first out of three in a special entry for smooth Salukis, which were then still a rarity in the ring. They both won prizes in another special entry for imports from countries of origin. So we went home with some fine trophies, and mixed views on the merits of showing. It seemed to me that it was asking a lot of even the most experienced show judge to assess a hound purely on its appearance. The judge had to evaluate objectively to what degree the hound measured up to the written description of it in the breed standard on the basis of a quick physical examination and a short trot around and up and down the ring. This allowed no scope for testing its characteristics as a hunting hound. I resolved that I would put greater faith in the coursing field for evaluating my hounds and those of others. By then we had been accepted as members of the SGHC Coursing Section and I knew there would be plenty of occasions that winter for evaluating the breed in the field. I did not expect my hounds to figure among the trophy winners, as *Tayra* was already eight and a half and *Najma* four, but I would see how they matched up to their peers.

Before the coursing season began in late September, it was Liese's birthday and our children surprised her – and me – with the gift of a Jack Russell puppy! *Coco*, as they called her, was two months old and very lively. The Salukis did not like this intruder one little bit. *Najma* in particular could not take her eyes off her and if we had not kept them apart would surely have killed her. *Coco* showed the feisty characteristics of her breed and we thought that, given the chance, she would be able to look after herself in due course. However, this was not to be. Four days later she became seriously ill with vomiting and diarrhoea, and the vet could not save her. He diagnosed parvovirus and suspected that she had not been vaccinated and was already infected when she was sold. The pet shop where our children had bought her later admitted liability.

A week afterwards came a test of a more agreeable kind – the opening of the coursing season in beautiful weather on a large sporting estate in Gloucestershire. Both our hounds were entered in the first 16-dog stake for the Askalam Cup. *Tayra* was drawn first against a big dog five years her junior, though you would not have believed it when she flew out of slips and completely outclassed him. *Najma* was in the last couple of the first round against a young bitch half her age, but after a slow start she overtook her opponent and kept the lead all the way. So they both progressed to the quarter-finals. Here *Tayra* was drawn against the two-year-old *Asayaad Minua*, son of Mike Ratcliffe's Saudi import. She still acquitted herself very creditably, being first up to the hare and remaining in contention all the way. *Najma* again ran against a bitch half her age from Paul Sagar's coursing line and her experience carried her through. The hare got up near a dry-stone wall. *Najma* jumped onto the wall, saw where the hare was heading and made off in pursuit, with her opponent trailing far behind. On her way back, she put up another hare and coursed that till she lost it. She came back very tired.

I wanted to rest her before the semi-final, but was told she had to go back into slips or withdraw. I put her into slips against another young bitch and hoped we would not find a hare before she got her breath back. Fortunately, we walked for about 20 minutes before a hare was driven out of a cabbage patch. *Najma* was onto it immediately and pursued it till it disappeared over a wall, leaving her opponent far behind. But the judge ruled 'no contest' and they had to go back into slips again; poor *Najma* would have to run yet again. However, this was not to be, as we could not find another hare before dusk and the meeting came to an end. I was feeling very pleased with the way my hounds had performed on their first competitive outing. It was only when we reached home that I discovered that *Najma* had developed a swollen paw. She had kept on running without complaining. What a plucky little thing she was!

A couple of weeks later, we were back on a farm in Oxfordshire in very different weather. It was grey and wet and the going was very muddy. *Tayra* was not drawn, but *Najma* was drawn last in the second eight-dog stake for the Asphodel Cup against Paul Sagar's young bitch *Josephs Lily*, who was soon to become a coursing champion. However, on this occasion, *Najma* was faster out of slips and pulled quickly away. The course went into an adjacent field, where the mounted judge could follow, and he gave her the verdict. In the next round, she was up against Mike Ratcliffe's *Asayaad Minua* when the weather turned for the worse, with heavy rain making the going even stickier. We managed to put up a hare and *Najma* ran it well until she lost it in a hedge. *Minua* got onto it again and, hotly pursued by *Najma*, held off her challenge till the end in a wood. The meeting was then abandoned, but *Najma* had again done very well in conditions that were still strange for her.

Our next outing was less successful. We went to one of the vast estates in Norfolk, where the flat land is ideal for coursing. The weather was like spring, the going excellent and the hares fortunately plentiful as we needed a lot if we were to complete the card. The event was the 32-dog stake for the Sharif Trophy and both my hounds were entered. *Tayra* was drawn first against the same big young dog she had beaten easily the previous time in a short course. Here, on a huge field of stubble, things were different. She was slightly handicapped by her recent recovery from a cut foot but she was still first up to the hare. A long chase ensued in which she began to tire and the younger hound

The author at the 1995 SGHC Open Show with Tayra, and Sonja with Najma.

took over. They ran beautifully together and at the end of the meeting they were awarded a rosette for the Best Course of the Day – not bad for a nearly nine-year-old! Only on her return to me did I find that she was dripping blood from another cut to her dew claw and her foot looked swollen. *Najma* was also drawn against a young dog she had beaten easily before, but this time she seemed listless and did not run well at all. We managed to complete the event with a thrilling final, and all went home well content with a glorious day's sport. However, *Tayra's* foot concerned me and an x-ray showed that she had a fracture, which would keep her away from coursing for a while.

Najma seemed to recover her old energy and by the next meeting at the end of November on a farm near Burford in Oxfordshire she was in great form. She was drawn last in the third of three eight-dog stakes that day. So we had a lot of walking before she went into slips against a young bitch who did not seem to know what to do, and *Najma* completed a long course on her own. In the next round, she won easily against a veteran hound, but on the way back she put up first another hare, then a second and then a third, so she was pretty tired before I had her under control again. In the final, she was drawn against an enormous young dog that dwarfed her in slips. She was faster away but, with its huge stride, her opponent gradually took over and won. Still, *Najma* was the runner-up and claimed her first trophy – a silver spoon with a hare on it.

In the last meeting of 1995 before Christmas, *Najma* showed her determination and resilience. She was drawn last again in the third of three eight-dog stakes. It proved to be an unusual contest. Her opponent was a very young bitch and became confused when the hare doubled back to run through the line as we walked up. *Najma* had locked onto it immediately but balked when it went through a barred gate. It was declared 'no contest' and they went back into slips again. Again they were slipped on a hare that doubled back through the line, where the two contestants were joined by a loose hound that got in their way. However, the hare made for the barred gate and this time *Najma* managed to squeeze through, leaving the other two hounds gazing after her. But it was by then getting late and the meeting drew to an inconclusive end.

By the start of the New Year both hounds were fit again and we looked forward to the rest of the coursing calendar until March, but events took a sudden and unexpected turn. In January 1996, I was headhunted to set up and direct an exciting project in Bosnia, an area I knew well from serving for over six years in the British Embassy in Belgrade. The International Crisis Group, a well-funded nongovernmental organisation, proposed to establish a team in Sarajevo to monitor the implementation of the so-called Dayton Peace Accords between the warring parties there and to help bring about reconciliation between the various communities.

Before I set off, I managed to take the hounds to one last coursing meeting in Norfolk for the prestigious Cleve Cup. This was a 16-dog stake for nominated entries only and was followed by the Cleve Plate for first-round losers. My hounds were entered for the back-up eight-dog Norfolk Stake, which was run towards the end of the day, with mixed results. *Najma* made a very good start but had a nasty fall and could not make up the lost ground to her young opponent. *Tayra* was simply incredible! She was drawn against Paul Sagar's year-old bitch *Rose of Moray*, but the age difference simply did not show as, from start to finish in a beautiful duel, she was like *Rose*'s shadow and they even killed the hare together. *Rose* was the winner but they were both awarded rosettes for the Best Course of the Day. It was a good note on which to end before I took on my new responsibilities.

What fine jaws he has! What a fine muzzle!

Chapter Nine

Puppy tales

While I was in Bosnia I came back to London for consultations and found waiting for me two large US mail bags of enormous weight, containing my allotment of copies of *The Saluqi: Coursing Hound of the East* in recompense for the contributions to it of text and illustrations that I had made over the years since my time in Iraq, when Gail Goodman, the editor, had first mooted our collaboration on such a book. In the intervening years, she had had to overcome enormous odds, with the generous backing of Shaikha Danah Al Khalifa in Bahrain, to turn the disparate contributions of a number of authors into the major work of reference that it has since become on the desert-bred hound and its influence on the breed in the West.

After nearly a year of hard, unremitting work, I returned from Bosnia in October 1996 and reconnected with the coursing scene. My hounds had first to be brought back into condition after a lengthy period without the intensive activity to which they were accustomed. An event in November was of particular significance, as it signalled the end of an era and the start of a new one.

One frosty Saturday morning, we drove to an estate of huge proportions in Gloucestershire where, at ten years old, *Tayra* was to run in the Veteran Cup, which proved to be her last course. As always, she gave a spirited performance but lost a long course to a younger veteran. *Najma* was not running as she was in an interesting condition and I had decided to mate her with a young dog of Paul Sagar's breeding.

Paul kindly took her home with him to facilitate her introduction to *Cream Cracker* (*Kenine Tarazed* x *Kenine Tanoda*), a smooth cream two-year-old of part-Saudi descent owned by Mark Paulin. Two days later, on 23 November, Paul reported that the deed was successfully done and I could collect *Najma*.

Paul and I were especially pleased as we felt that we were also making a small contribution to the preservation of the Saluki in the West by the infusion of fresh genes from the Middle East. I had been made aware of the small number of foundation Salukis in the West through having meanwhile become a member of the Society for the Perpetuation of Desert Bred Salukis (SPDBS), of which I am, at the time of writing, a director), formed in the USA in 1987, whose mission it is to authenticate and register imported desert-bred Salukis. The SPDBS was recognised as a domestic registry by the American Kennel Club in 2002 and SPDBS-registered Salukis with a complete three-generation pedigree are admissible to the AKC stud book. Thus, for example, in 2016 the SPDBS received applications to register 25 Salukis, either direct imports or the offspring of imports, and the descendants of all the successful hounds will be able eventually to be fully integrated in the wider pedigree Saluki population. The Saluki is exceptionally fortunate in that it can resort to this still largely untapped gene pool in the Middle East and thus avoid the harmful consequences of close inbreeding experienced by other breeds. However, there has been and still is resistance in some quarters, where notions of closed stud books prevail, to such imports without a written pedigree, but the scientifically proven benefits to health from such outcrosses are slowly overcoming such prejudices.

Early in 1997, *Tayra* began to behave very strangely. One frosty morning we went for a long walk, during which she found a patch of heather and rolled around on it with obvious pleasure. She then set off at high speed, jinking and zigzagging as if in pursuit of a hare. That evening, we had guests to dine on some pheasants I had shot. *Tayra* slipped unobserved into the kitchen and delicately removed half a pheasant. It proved to be her Last Supper. The next day she could not move because of a large swelling on her breast. It was diagnosed as rampant breast cancer and we had to put her to sleep. That night Liese felt as if something had brushed along the side of the bed, just as *Tayra* would do in the morning to get us up. We imagined it was the final release of her proud spirit.

I had always had the feeling that she was only a half-tamed creature. Although she was very affectionate, she retained an independence of spirit that was at times impossible to control. She needed only to feel the sand between her toes and her head

'Tayra', watercolour by Gillian Heywood.

would go up in expectancy of the chase. Whenever I unclipped her lead, she would always spring forward as if coming out of slips and would sprint 50 metres. She could never have enough exercise and was always reluctant to come home if she had not chased and preferably caught something. Sometimes she would go off on her own or with my other hounds for hours when we were camping in the desert. She was truly *al-Hurr*, the free or noble one, and her departure left a huge hole in our lives. There were, however, the stirrings of new life in *Najma* to compensate for our loss.

Najma had borne her pregnancy lightly and was still energetically pursuing any squirrels that ventured forth from their winter hibernation on warmer days when, on 24 January, she did not want to go for a walk and started to show signs that her

Liese with her hands full.

time was near. She had some mild contractions, but it became clear that there was a problem. Around midnight she was so distressed that I had to rush her to the duty vet in our area, who quickly established that she needed a Caesarian section. One of her puppies was much larger than the others and was blocking the birth passage. Early the next morning, we went back to collect a still woozy mother and her seven healthy puppies – four boys and three girls; and so began an increasingly hectic phase of totally absorbing puppy-watching and caring for their dam.

I had built a large wooden pen that allowed plenty of room for the puppies and *Najma* to move around safely, while also giving her easy access to the garden. So, at least for the next few weeks, they were fairly well contained in one place. There were two grizzles, one feathered male and one smooth female, two smooth cream males with light brown patches on their heads, a very large feathered cream male and a smaller feathered cream female and a feathered red female. As they were seven, I decided to give them names based on the Arabic days of the week: *Waheed al-Ahad* (Sunday), *Thani al-Ithnain* (Monday), *Thalooth al-Thalaatha* (Tuesday), *Rabbaa al-Jarbou* (Wednesday), *Khamsa al-Khamis* (Thursday), *Sudous al-Saadis* (Friday) and *Sabti al-Sabt* (Saturday).

When they were about a month old, prospective owners from among my coursing friends came to inspect them, and four were quickly spoken for and left when they were two months old. I kept *Thalooth*, aka *Sally*, for myself, leaving only *Waheed* and *Sudous*. *Waheed* went eventually to a fell runner in Cumbria, who later reported that he had never before had a dog with such speed and endurance. *Sudous* went to a family in Italy, where he settled happily and later sired a litter. The house was restored to some kind of order again and I could begin to start training *Sally* to the outside world.

I had chosen *Sally* well, as things turned out. She struck me from the start as very calm and well balanced, like her dam. *Najma* was a ferocious hunter but was otherwise very relaxed and obedient. When *Sally* reached three months, I began walking her on Wimbledon Common without a lead and she kept close to *Najma*. This way she quickly learnt to respond to my calls and whistles, just as her dam did. She also learnt to hunt with her dam, and at six months she proudly caught her first rabbit in a joint effort with *Najma* on a trip to the country. Shaikha Danah Al Khalifa happened to visit us from Bahrain the next day and was duly impressed, as were Lev and Margret Tamp from Tehran when we met them a few days later.

Soon after, in June 1997 Liese and I went on an archaeological tour in south-western Turkey, travelling along part of the route taken by Alexander the Great in 334–333 BC. Among our companions were a former British ambassador to Afghanistan and his wife, Peers and Joan Carter. Somehow or other, a conversation with them turned to Salukis. As we talked, one of them produced from a book, where it served

Chipak as a puppy in snowy Afghanistan.

as a page marker, an old black and white photograph of what I took to be a Saluki. It was, in fact, a photograph of their own very special hound – *Chipak*, the Afghan name of a small falcon used for hunting quail. She had been given to them as a puppy from the royal kennels in 1968 by Princess Bilqis, daughter of the last King of Afghanistan, Zahir Shah. The Carters said that they had seen very few Tazis in Afghanistan, where they were considered as belonging to the Crown, rather like swans in Britain – indeed, they had to have a special licence to take *Chipak* out of the country.

Chipak went on many expeditions across Afghanistan with the Carters and proved to be an excellent hunter of hare and even marmots, towards which she used to creep until she was near enough to snatch them before they disappeared down their burrows. When the Carters returned to Britain in 1973, they encountered considerable difficulty in having her registered at the Kennel Club as an Afghan, and had to gather evidence of her lineage from members of the Afghan royal court, who had by then become dispersed in different countries after the revolution in their home country. But she was eventually registered as *Chipak Barqak* ('Chipak the Lightning').

Chipak engaged my particular interest because she was in so many respects closer to the northerly type of Saluki in appearance than to the average Afghan Hound, at least as we know it. Indeed, Mrs Daphne Gie's book *The Complete Afghan* seems to acknowledge that *Chipak* looked different, describing the head as stronger and the eyes a little more full than is usually bred in Britain and the coat conforming more to the Lochak type of Afghan, which is rarely seen in the West nowadays. Certainly, this photograph of her as a puppy shows a hound that is virtually indistinguishable from Salukis I had seen in northern Iraq, and illustrates how the Saluki shades into another variant that has evolved for hunting in the different conditions of the mountains of Afghanistan. Interestingly, Abdul Wali, the husband of Princess Bilqis, offered the Carters a smooth-haired Afghan Hound before they left but they had to decline it, as they felt one hound was quite enough to cope with in the very different circumstances of their retirement in Britain and registering it would have presented even greater problems.

But the future for hunting with dogs in Britain was by then becoming cloudy. That summer I joined with other coursing friends in a massive public rally in Hyde Park when about 100,000 people gathered to protest against the proposed ban on hunting with dogs. I also joined in an even bigger protest the following March, when a column of over 250,000 people wended its way through London to Parliament. Very unfairly, and against all informed advice, the protest and the well-argued case for retaining traditional hunting with dogs was ignored by the Labour government of the time and the ban was eventually enacted in law, though it did not take effect until 2005. So we had to make the most of the time left to us; and the disappointment was therefore all the greater when the SGHC ruled that my puppies would not be allowed to compete in coursing events until they were exactly a year old, which meant that they would not be eligible for the annual puppy stake 25 days before their first birthday. But at least I could show *Sally* in the Minor Puppy Class at the SGHC Championship Show in October, when she came third out of seven entries. Meanwhile, *Najma* was still competing and *Sally* always came along, learning the procedures in the process

In November 1997 I broke away from my coursing routine to go back to some of my student haunts in Lebanon and Syria on a tour arranged with a group of former fellow students. Among other places, we visited Baalbek, famous for its soaring columns and massive temples of the Roman era. Among the ruins I came across a number of locals who, by their dress, were country people and I asked them about Salukis in the area. It will be remembered that the dam of Brigadier General Lance's famous *Sarona Kelb*, imported to England in 1919, was called *Baalbek* after the place from which she came. One or two of the younger people did not even know what a Saluki was, and when I told them it was a hunting dog they said there were lots of them around. However, when I showed them photographs they admitted that their hunting dogs were retrievers. Some of the older men knew exactly what a Saluki was, but said they had not seen any locally for years. This was not so surprising, since the area had been the scene of intermittent strife for a long time and the whole of Lebanon had seen a phenomenal growth in construction, reducing the amount of open country to support a hare population.

While we were in Damascus, I managed to slip away for 48 hours and took a trip north to Hama. Sadly, my old friend Badr, with whom I had stayed in the past, had died since my last visit. Typically for him, he had driven up to his family's former home village of Ain al-Arab (Kobane) on the Turkish border to collect a black and white particoloured dog to add to his pack; but the excitement for this passionate hunter of having a new Saluki and the fatigue of the long journey had been too much, and he suffered a fatal heart attack. In all the confusion, the dog had escaped and was never seen again.

I had not been able to send word that I was coming, and arrived unannounced. However, I need have had no qualms about my welcome. In their traditional way, I was received by his sons like one of the family. They did not share their father's passion for Salukis and had given all his hounds away, but one of the sons, Fakhr, immediately took me around Hama to see some of them in their new homes. I was delighted to be reacquainted with some of them and their offspring. One of them was *Rogo*, a smooth black-masked red dog of great hunting ability. He had sired a litter of eight, of which only two had survived, with Badr's indefatigable smooth red bitch *Khamleh*. I was pressed to take one, but …

On the same farm I saw three offspring of Badr's great dog *Guru* and his elegant bitch *Shoha*, who had been pregnant the previous time I had been there. All three had the powerful build of their sire and were already coursing well. With them was the smallest Saluki I had ever seen, no more than 53 cm at the shoulder but well proportioned. She was nicknamed 'the Cat' for her small stature. We went to some stables where there were several racehorses and three Salukis padded up against the cold. Hama's first racecourse was under construction and, with an eye to the profits to be had from this very popular sport, many of the Saluki enthusiasts were going in for racehorses in quite a big way. All that would, however, have come to an end during the ongoing civil war. Among the hounds was a son of *Rogo*, who had recently caught four hares solo, so was clearly coming on very well.

By then it was getting dark, so we dropped in at the hunters' *majlis*, where I was greeted warmly by the old crowd, who regaled me with stories of their latest hunting exploits. At first it felt just like old times, but then they started to tell me that coursing had become much more difficult. Drought had caused poor harvests and they needed to spend more time trying to make a living from what was left. I showed them a copy of *The Saluki* magazine to see what they made of our British hounds. They were struck by the length of hair and assumed they came originally from Iran, where it was much colder, as their hounds did not look like that. I explained that these were mainly show hounds, but they did not see the point of breeding Salukis just for their beauty. The group's imam was concerned to see under the picture of one dog, written in Arabic, the name *al-Mutakabbir*, which is one of the 99 names of Allah. He said that it was offensive to Muslims to give a dog, even a Saluki, such a name. (I undertook to tell the owner, and did so; but she declined to change it, and the dog went Best of Breed at Crufts in 2000!) This reaction underlined how much care was needed in choosing an Arabic name. The Arabs tend to avoid proper names and to keep to purely descriptive ones.

Fakhr took me off to dinner with some of the family and arranged to take me in the morning to see some more breeders. We did not have a lot of success, as it was a Friday and most of them were out hunting. Indeed, I was pressed to join a merry band with about ten Salukis just setting off in a minibus. However, we were in luck at one stables. By a newly painted sign extolling the horses, the owner with a magnificent waxed moustache was parading up and down a dappled grey with a chestnut foal. He produced a photograph of the sire, which he said was an Arabian imported from England. Inside the stables we could hear a commotion as three Salukis were released from their padded coats and went racing around the yard. There was a beautiful smooth sandy bitch, the image of *Tayra*, with – unusually – intact ears and the gentle eyes and delicate air of a gazelle. He said he would breed her at her next season. I said I assumed he would use one of his two feathered dogs – a black and tan, called *Mirage* after the French aircraft, or a grizzle whose cropped ears like fluffy ear muffs reminded me so much of the famous portrait from around 1919 of Major C W Bayne-Jardine's import *Hama of Homs* who, with a name like that, must have come from this area. He replied that he preferred smooths and intended to use the son of *Rogo* that I had seen the day before. He believed feathereds were heavier not because of their hair but were fatter and did not run as fast. Certainly, in those parts most of the Salukis were smooth.

Time was running against me. I still had to join Fakhr's family for a huge lunch before catching the bus to Homs, where I was supposed to rendezvous with another bus carrying the rest of my group back from Palmyra to Beirut. However, their bus did not arrive and, after waiting for over an hour, I waved down a local one to

Tayra's double at a stables in Hama.

Damascus, from which I emerged two hours later smoked like a kipper from the fug of cigarette smoke of the other passengers. I jumped straight into a departing taxi for Beirut and arrived there minutes after my colleagues, who had just missed me at the rendezvous. We flew home exhausted at dawn the next day, and were so glad to be reunited with our hounds.

As *Sally* approached her first birthday, I was already giving her a run while out rough coursing with friends and I could see that she was shaping up well. As soon as she had had her birthday, I entered her in a Coursing Section event in Norfolk at the beginning of February, in which two of her siblings would also be running in an eight-dog stake. We hoped to see how their progress compared, but circumstances were against us. We had to wait until two other events were completed and by then it was getting late. *Sally's* sister *Rabbaa* (aka *Molly*), owned by Paul Sagar, won her heat easily. *Sally* and her brother *Thani*, owned by Kim and Lyn Ingram, were slipped on a hare that ran in a straight line for the woods, with the two hounds running neck and neck behind in a dead heat. And that was it, as it was too dark to go on. But at least the young hounds had had a run and returned quickly, so we were well pleased with their first official foray.

From the sublime to the ridiculous; the next day I had entered *Sally* in two classes at the SGHC Limited Show, where she came fourth out of four in one class and fifth out of five in the other! She was subsequently promoted to second in one class as a result of two disqualifications, and thus qualified for entry to Crufts the following month. But what really made my day was that a young man of Middle Eastern appearance came over and began questioning me about *Sally*, the only hound he had really liked at the show! He turned out to be a Saudi lawyer working in London, and he was very keen to acquire a Saluki. I suggested that he should first come to a coursing meeting to see the hounds in a more natural setting and, if he was still interested afterwards, I would introduce him to people with puppies. I invited him to join us at a coursing event two weeks later in Oxfordshire.

We were hit by a couple of ferocious squalls at the start, but then the sun came through and the hares came out. All the hounds had a good run and at the end I asked my Saudi friend what he thought. Despite being drenched and cold, he grinned and said that it was the best day of his life in England, and asked when he could see some puppies. I put him in touch with Roy Goodby, who was able to let him have a couple. I saw them later, installed in great luxury in a house near a park in London, but my friend's busy professional life did not leave him enough time for the hounds and, after they wrecked his sitting room one day, he decided he had to give them up.

Meanwhile, in March I had shown *Sally* at Crufts where, despite an ear infection and being in milk, she earned a Very Highly Commended, though placed fifth out of five. An American bystander asked whether I had ever thought of taking ringcraft lessons, so perhaps the fault was more mine! I put all such thoughts far behind me, as I went straight on from Birmingham to Yorkshire, where I spent the next day coursing with friends on the moors and we and all the hounds had a wonderful time.

I also kept the hounds fit by taking them lure coursing, and we even tried track racing. They took easily to both these sports, and were well prepared for the opening of the coursing season in September. I was curious to see how *Sally* and her siblings would fare on the bigger stage of competitive coursing. I need have had no fears on that score, as they all did brilliantly. Indeed, at the first meeting in Gloucestershire, *Sally* won the eight-dog Beaufort Stake and her first trophy. It was the start of a great season for her; but immediately afterwards I had to take some time away.

I had been able thus far to combine fairly well my business consultancy work with my sporting activities, but I could not pass up the invitation to go with Liese on a cruise for two weeks as a guest lecturer, especially as it was to parts of the Middle East where I had Saluki contacts.

At the beginning of October, we flew to Aqaba in Jordan, where we were to embark on our cruise ship a day or two later. I had managed to arrange to meet a bedouin of the Howeitat tribe living in the Wadi Rum, running down towards Aqaba from the ancient Nabatean site of Petra, which was made famous by Lawrence of Arabia in his *Seven Pillars of Wisdom*. It has magnificent scenery of towering sand dunes and multicoloured mountains. I wanted to see whether the Howeitat still had Salukis there, as they did to my knowledge in the 1950s, though more recent reports from travellers suggested that they had become quite rare. It was therefore without great hopes that Liese and I drove up from Aqaba to the agreed rendezvous with Dhifallah. Although raised as a bedouin, he had in recent years become a professional guide for camel trekking and climbing and knew the Wadi Rum intimately. He gave us a warm welcome and, over the inevitable coffee and tea, said that there was plenty of game in the area, including gazelle, and as a result the bedouin still kept Salukis for hunting. He usually had a couple himself but he had lost them and was looking for a replacement. He confessed that a lot of the hunting those days was actually lamping and that, even by day, the courses were generally fairly short. I thought this was probably because the local hare was the Arabian hare, which is much smaller than the brown hare that I knew from Syria and Iraq.

He drove us to meet Sa'id, an old bedouin who was a keen hunter and breeder of Salukis. He lived in a little breeze-block house, but we sat outside on rugs and

Fazza and her adopted puppies.

cushions under a tent in his yard with a pot of strong tea bubbling on the fire in a simple stone hearth. Sa'id first introduced us to *La'aban*, a medium (66 cm) muscular smooth black and tan dog of about four years. He had a nick in one ear 'for identification purposes'. He was used for gazelle and hare, but Sa'id said his bitch was better for hare. He called her name – *Fazza* – and a very small (under 58 cm), lightly feathered cream Saluki appeared from an unfinished outbuilding. Sa'id said she was very fast and turned quicker than *La'aban*. She appeared to be in whelp, but I was wrong. *La'aban* had sired a litter with a smooth red bitch that had had difficulties with feeding her eight puppies. Sa'id had taken three of them and put them on *Fazza*, whereupon she started producing milk within two days and took on the role of foster mother. I saw the puppies, then about a month old, and they looked fine.

I was impressed with Sa'id's control of the hounds. They ran freely around the yard, but at his word of command immediately jumped into the back of his pickup, evidently expecting to go hunting. I asked Sa'id if he had any preference for colour. He said that colour was unimportant but he had a slight preference for reds, as they seemed to bear the heat better than the blacks, which were at their best only in the early morning or the evening. He related that once, when *La'aban* was having a poor night at lamping, he had put ash on the tan pips over his eyes, which stood out in the moonlight, and after that he had no problems. I asked what they did when a hound became too old to hunt. He said that they just let them die naturally and he had had one that lived to the age of 16.

Further discussion in the tent was interrupted by the arrival of a burly bedouin with long locks curling from under his headcloth. He turned out to be a folk singer and composer who entertained tourists with bedouin music. He was also a hunter and had had many Salukis. He was full of stories, including one about a Saluki that had joined in a camel race over 10 km and came in first. Sa'id was clearly not very happy about the way the man was all the while handling one of his puppies, and repeatedly asked for it back. In the end Sa'id snatched the puppy from him and threw it in the dust as a sign of his displeasure. The puppy ran off unharmed and the visitor departed. Sa'id said the man was always travelling and his wife mistreated his Salukis in his absence. He would never, therefore, give him a puppy, but he was happy to give one to Dhifallah – and we drove away with the little thing sitting unconcernedly next to me. It was by then midday and very hot. Dhifallah said he wanted to show us many more hounds, but only if we promised to stay the night. We could not do that and had to forgo that pleasure, but at least I had a friend there who would turn out very useful on my next visit a few years later.

We boarded our ship in Aqaba and cruised on to Sharm El Sheikh, which lies on the southern tip of the Sinai Peninsula, where we went ashore. Our destination was the 5th-century monastery of St Catherine's, some three hours' drive away. We stopped halfway to admire the view by a small group of roadside peddlers of fossils and minerals. They told me they were of the M'zairy tribe, who kept Salukis in their village. We drove on, and on the horizon I saw the charming sight of a bedouin girl herding her goats with a smooth red Saluki trotting behind. At St Catherine's we were besieged by cameleers offering rides. They were from the Jabaliya tribe and also kept Salukis in their villages. Sadly, there was not time to go there.

While anchored next in Jeddah, Saudi Arabia, we went to see the camel market, where I found most of the cameleers were Sudanese. I was interested to hear that they too kept Salukis in their villages back home.

When we stopped in Hodeida, Yemen, we flew up to the capital, Sana'a, where I pursued the Arab tradition that says that the Arabic word Salūqī derives from the ancient Yemeni town of Salūq. There is a line in a poem by the 8th-century Umayyad poet 'Umar bin Suyaym al-Qutami that reads: '*They have with them hounds of Saluq, like horses, wheeling round in battle, dragging on their halters*' (Allen and Smith, 1975).

According to the 10th-century Yemeni geographer al-Hamdani, Saluq was identified with a place near modern Ta'iz, which was once noted as a centre for mining metal and making armour. Sadly, the location of this place is obscure. However, the area all around Ta'iz is very mountainous and seems hardly the terrain for coursing with Salukis. It is nevertheless curious that the Iranians call the Saluki *Tazi*, which is believed to be a corruption of *Ta'izi*, meaning someone or something from Ta'iz, i.e. an Arabian.

Our next stop was at Mukalla, serving the Wadi Hadhramaut in eastern Yemen, where I was intrigued to see in the museum in the former Sultan's palace an ancient, possibly Himyaritic, stone stele, depicting an ibex hunt with hounds. Professor Bob Serjeant's admirable little book *South Arabian Hunt* (1976) maintains that local village dogs rather than Salukis were used for hunting ibex. Outside the museum was a shop selling antiques that had a stuffed ibex in a glass case, so I asked the people milling about how they hunted ibex. Disappointingly, they all said that they shot them and knew nothing about hunting them with dogs. Bang went another tradition!

Our final port of call was Muscat, where we had lived only a few years before. I was

Stone stele in the museum at Mukalla.

delighted to meet ashore some of our old friends and their Salukis. These were mainly hounds descended from *Nisma* (see Chapter Seven). One of them, called *Maha*, a smooth grey and white particoloured, owned by Sue Heather, had been mated with a cream feathered dog bred in Dubai by Susi Leimbacher. Her smooth or lightly feathered grey grizzle puppies looked very good as they cavorted on the beach and made quite a contrast in type with their playmate, a rangy feathered black-masked red dog that I had helped the Heathers to obtain from the Tamps in Tehran. Some of these hounds eventually made their way to England.

It had been an interesting tour, but I was keen to get back home to resume the coursing season. It was quite a shock to go from the clear skies and warmth of the Gulf to cold and wet Wiltshire, where a week later I took the hounds for some rough coursing on the Downs by way of preparation for a big two-day event on the estate of a friend of mine on the Scottish borders in Berwickshire. The main event was the Moray Trophy, for which 20 hounds were entered, including *Najma* and three of her offspring. The estate was vast and we were able simply to walk forward in line for many kilometres, driving out the white-coated hares as we went, though the foul weather of rain turning to snow was against us. The Salukis responded magnificently in such trying conditions. *Najma* excelled herself, winning her first round and beating her own son – *Thani* – in a short course when she snapped up the hare in front of him. She was eventually knocked out the next day by her daughter, *Molly*. Meanwhile *Sally* sailed through her first two rounds on the first day and two more rounds the next. Her sister *Molly* had done equally well in the other half of the draw, so the two sisters faced each other in the final. Meanwhile, the backup stakes for the Moray Purse – for losers in the first round of the Moray Trophy – and the Dava Trophy (for losers in the second) were being run off, and *Thani* also reached the final of the Dava Trophy.

Then the weather closed in again and the rain came pelting down, so that, as we sat in our cars, I thought that we would never be able to run the three finals. But then came a break in the clouds and *Sally* and *Molly* went into slips. We soon put a good hare up and away they went, with *Sally* opening up a gap first of one length and then two as they raced up to the brow of a hill and over the top. The judge was right there and pulled the white flag for *Sally* – she had won the historic Moray Trophy, with a kill

Sally and her trophies.

too, so I took the hare as my trophy. Next we ran the final of the Moray Purse, which was won in great style by Vance Page's *Kenvee Jacob*, who somehow managed to catch two hares in the process. Finally, *Thani* ran against his aunt *Salamara Girl*, owned by Ian Charlton, and won the Dava Trophy too. So all three siblings did very well at the start of what proved to be a very successful season.

Two weeks later in Wiltshire, *Sally* beat her brother *Thani* in an eight-dog stake to win the Michael Lyne Trophy. Then, in the first meeting of 1999, she was on tremendous form again, winning a hard-contested 16-dog stake and the Yorkshire Wolds Trophy. The next month, *Sally* was nominated for entry in the prestigious Cleve Cup for 16 Salukis, run in Norfolk. She demolished all the opposition in the preliminary rounds and reached the final against a seasoned adversary in *Kenvee Jacob*. This time they pursued a hare that went through a hedge and ran along it, with *Kenvee Jacob* on the far side and *Sally* running parallel on the near side. They eventually emerged into a field where her opponent pulled the hare down and won the course and the event, leaving *Sally* to take the runner-up's silver Knightellington Goblet.

But then disaster struck. A week later, *Sally* won easily her first round in the Asphodel Stake in Wiltshire, but on the way back she put up first one hare, then a second, and finally a third, all of which she coursed. It was only when she returned to me that I saw that she was limping, and on examination I found that she had cut one of her pads badly. So that was that, and I had to withdraw her and on the way home take her to the vet, where she needed six stitches under full anaesthetic. I was so disappointed, because it meant that she would not be able to compete the following week for the Lady Gardner Memorial Trophy for puppies – which was won by her brother *Thani* – nor in the final meeting of the season, the 32-dog Sharif Trophy. My only consolation was to hear later that *Sally* had been declared joint winner of the Victor Henderson Memorial Trophy for the Saluki winning the most courses in the season, and her brother was runner-up. *Sally* was also awarded the Bayt Shahin Trophy for the best progeny of an import.

On that relative high note, I took off for Tehran, where I would join a two-week tour by the Royal Society for Asian Affairs as the group's rapporteur. This took us to many fascinating places all around Iran and ended up where we had started, in Tehran. Here I took time out to visit Lev and Margret Tamp at their home. They had also invited some Iranians active with Tazis, so I learnt a lot about various efforts to study, preserve and promote the Tazi in Iran. During the time of the last Shah, members of the German community had established a Tazi Club and a registry, issuing pedigrees. That all came to an end with the fall of the Shah in 1979, though Margret Tamp had continued to hold the stud book. There was much talk of reviving the club, but nothing came of it. I tried to encourage one of the Iranians there, an academic in the environmental field, to organise a hare survey as a basis for establishing the Tazi population, but though he agreed enthusiastically and I even arranged some funding for him, it too came to nothing in the end. But at least I was able to see and lay hands on the Tamps' beautiful Tazis and admire their photographs of hunting with them on horseback. The hounds were generally bigger-boned and more heavily feathered than Salukis in the Arab world, but the basic characteristics were undoubtedly the same as those of Salukis. Indeed, it could hardly be otherwise, as Iran shares a long border with Iraq, across which there was frequent interchange of hounds, among other things, and I had seen similar hounds among the Iraqi Kurds.

Sadly, during that summer some unpleasantness, which had been simmering for a while, was beginning to show itself among the coursing members of the SGHC. It

The Tamps' Tazis in Tehran.

looked as if some of the Old Guard, who seemed to regard coursing as a mere adjunct of the show scene, resented the fact that the coursing events were being dominated by members from outside the show community, who actually prepared their hounds for working rather than showing. The Old Guard wanted to maintain the status quo ante and did their best to find reasons for unseating various members of the Coursing Committee, including me, so that they could resume charge. It all came to a head at the Annual General Meeting of the Coursing Section in June, when all the various objections were soundly defeated by the acclaim of the majority; but the rift between the two camps was deep and boded ill for the future. However, the Committee had done its job of securing a full programme of events for the winter season ahead, including no fewer than three two-day meetings.

An even sadder event occurred the following month, when my German father-in-law passed away at the ripe old age of 94. Liese and I flew over to Germany for his funeral and to sort out his affairs. Among other things, he had left Liese his car and we decided to make the most of it by driving over to Ost-Friesland, some 320 km away, to stay with Edgar Berghaus, a great expert on Turkish Tazis, with whom I had been corresponding for some time. It was a glorious day for the drive beyond the Elbe River to Glueckstadt where, in the middle of nowhere, Edgar and his partner Marlene lived in a converted barn along with their 28 Salukis. Most of the hounds were of Turkish descent, but a few were of mixed Turkish-American (Jen Araby) bloodlines. Edgar ran a removals business based in Cologne, where by chance one day he had seen his first Tazi being walked in the street by a Turk. He made contact, and as a result paid several visits to Turkey to learn more about the breed and to bring back some good specimens from which to breed.

The hounds were quartered in part of the barn where the cow stalls had been, with fenced pens outside and access to a large field beyond. They looked in excellent condition, and some of them had won just about everything on the racetrack and at lure coursing, live coursing being banned in Germany. One of them had recorded the fastest-ever time of any Saluki on the track. Edgar admitted that he had to fatten them up if he wanted to put them in the show ring, as they were too lean and muscular for the judges. Their regime was very healthy: one meal a day of raw meat and intestines with rice or cereals. With the help of his beautifully documented albums of photographs, he took me through his fascinating experiences with the hounds in Turkey and in Germany, so that the time flew by and it was suddenly midnight. I still had time the next morning to take lots of pictures of the hounds, one of which, a feathered cream dog of excellent proportions, would have made a good match for *Sally*.

This gave me something to think about as we drove back home. My imagination had also been fired to the extent that I felt I had to visit Turkey to see these hounds in their native habitat. I had already had a foretaste in 1988, when driving across Turkey back to Baghdad from home leave. As we had stopped to take pictures of the historic Ishak Pasha's Palace at Doğubayazıt near Mount Ararat, a heavily pregnant smooth grizzle Saluki had walked right in front of my camera and my cry of 'It's a Saluki!' remains recorded on the soundtrack of the cinefilm I was shooting at the time. Later, as we descended from the mountains towards the border with Iraq, we passed a Kurd with a horse and cart on which sat a crop-eared smooth Saluki puppy, while trotting along behind came a smooth black Saluki, evidently in season as she wore a kind of leather apron over her hindquarters.

The new coursing season began in late September, but we got off to a bad start with *Sally* at the first meeting through injury. She and her two siblings all made it through the first round, but in the next I could see that she was not running well and when she came back to me I saw a nasty gash in her leg with a loose flap of skin hanging. I had to bind it up with a bandage and take her off home. She was all right again in time for the SGHC Open Show in mid-October, where, after coming last at her previous appearance in the ring, she came a creditable second out of 14 in the Post Graduate Bitch class, thus qualifying her for Crufts again but also demonstrating what a subjective business showing is.

However, she was in trouble again a week later while we were rough coursing up in Yorkshire. Both she and *Najma* had some lovely runs but at the end, when they had caught a hare, *Sally* lay down and screamed. One paw was packed hard with mud and small stones, and it looked as if she had developed cramp. After I had massaged her leg she could walk again, but the paw was badly swollen. I thought the paw had healed over the following ten days, but the day before we were due to go to the next meeting I was woken early by a terrible howling. I found *Sally* trying to walk on three legs as she could not put the injured foot to the ground. So we went back to the vet, who diagnosed an infection and prescribed antibiotics. There was no way she would be fit to defend her title in the Michael Lyne Trophy 16-dog stake. This was particularly disappointing, as I had worked hard through friends to secure permission for the meeting on a new estate in Norfolk. The Sharif Trophy was run the next day on another estate in Norfolk, where the honour of *Najma*'s progeny was upheld by *Molly*, who was runner-up in the final of this 28-dog stake.

Sally's foot injury was bad enough, but a week later she started vomiting and could not keep any food down. The vet wanted to conduct an internal investigation with a barium meal and an X-ray and tried, but, he said, *Sally* had been 'uncooperative' and he merely prescribed some tablets, which seemed to do the job. So I made the decision at the end of the week to travel up to Scotland to enable *Sally* to defend her title to the Moray Trophy.

We were to run over the same vast estate in Berwickshire as the previous year. On the first day, the weather started very cold but bright and there was ice on puddles here and there. The heather varied from short to about 45 cm high and was very springy. Fortunately, there were plenty of hares, easily visible in their white winter coats, as 23 hounds were entered for the Moray Trophy and we were also running the two backup stakes, the Moray Purse and the Dava Trophy. By the end of the first morning, *Najma* and her three offspring had all done very well. *Sally* had got through three rounds and into the final of the Moray Trophy, where she would run against her brother, *Thani*. Their sister *Molly* was in the final of the Dava Trophy. *Najma* had got through a couple of rounds before her age caught up with her. At a celebratory dinner that night with the estate gamekeepers, the judge awarded the Best Course of the Day to *Sally* and Martine Cazeau's *Alsayaad Nabzan* in a thrilling semi-final.

The next morning was very frosty but bright, and *Sally* and *Thani* were first in slips. A hare got up almost immediately and away they went, with *Sally* in the lead in a straight line for a wire fence, where the hare simply disappeared. The hounds cast around unavailingly and the judge ruled 'no course'. Then the hare suddenly reappeared out of a drainage pipe and *Thani* caught it, but too late. We continued with the final of the Moray Purse for hounds beaten in the first round of the Moray Trophy, which was well won by Michael McCormick-Smith's *Glenoak Huchithra* from Rosie Lewis's *Knightellington Zafa*. Then we ran the final of the Dava Trophy for hounds beaten in the second round of the Moray Trophy, which was won quite easily by *Molly* from Ian Charlton's puppy *Indira Asal C'har*. Then *Sally* and *Thani* went back into slips for their final. *Thani* got away slightly ahead, but *Sally* caught up and went by and they raced almost neck and neck until *Thani* went forward and grabbed the hare, which was just enough for the judge to award him the course and the trophy. We still had plenty of daylight left, so we ran another stake for 20 dogs and had lots of good coursing, with *Molly* emerging as the winner. So, all in all, *Najma's* offspring had covered themselves in glory.

Before and after Christmas, we got a lot of rough coursing in with small groups of friends in different parts of the country. It was what I really enjoyed most – to spend the day in some glorious countryside with congenial people who ran their hounds seriously but good-humouredly. The atmosphere was so different at the next big official meeting in Norfolk in February 2000, to run the 16-dog Cleve Cup, where there was a lot of dissatisfaction about the way dogs that were not up to standard were being nominated for this most prestigious event; one was a nine-year-old veteran and two had not run competitively for the previous two years. Even the landowner

Thani leads from Sally out of slips in the final of the Moray Trophy.

commented on the disparity between the dogs. This was compounded by one or two decisions by the judge which did not look right. Sometimes the judges, who are usually mounted, are obstructed by hedges and prevented from following the course as closely as they would like, and the spectators might have a clearer view. I had had high hopes for *Sally* as she had been runner-up the year before and was on top form, but, having won her first two rounds easily, in the semi-final the course was awarded to her opponent, who not only 'lurched' (did not follow the line of the hare but anticipated which way it would run and was lucky) but was overhauled and soundly beaten by *Sally*, but sadly out of sight of the judge.

In the middle of February, we ran two meetings back to back and they could not have been more different. In the first, we simply could not find enough hares, though we tried everything; whereas on the same farm the next day they were popping up fairly regularly and we were able to run two stakes. *Sally* reached the final of the 16-dog Beverley Cup and everything pointed to a thrilling end to the day. A hare had been spotted sitting in the middle of a field and the slipper took the two finalists down to one end while the gallery stayed higher up on a track with a full view down below. It looked the perfect setting – red-coated slipper, emerald-green field of sprouting wheat and a cream and a grizzle in slips illuminated by the rays of the setting sun. But as the slipper moved forward, the hare simply disappeared. We all trooped down and walked up the field, but we could not find another hare before the light failed, so the stake was divided between them.

Two weeks later we were all back in Oxfordshire for the last meeting of the season, which proved – unintentionally – to be momentous in the history of British coursing. First, we ran the Lady Gardner Memorial Trophy for puppies, but there were only three entries and the final was won easily, and appropriately enough, by Lady Gardner's grandson, James Lewis, with his powerful dog *Dakhilak Shalm*. We then ran the 16-dog Kerrison Trophy stake, which, after some excellent courses, resulted in a final once again between *Sally* and her brother *Thani*. *Sally* was, as always, very fast away and led up to a hedge. She went through first and Kim Ingram was already congratulating me on a win as we went to collect the hounds, when the judge returned and pulled the flag for *Thani*. He had put in a lot of work out of sight beyond the hedge, where only the judge was in a position to see. It was a disappointment, but at least it was kept as a family affair. Sadly, in the background an incident had occurred that was to have serious consequences.

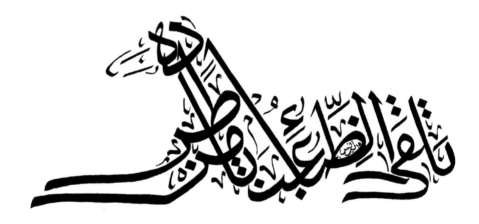

Gazelles are really in trouble when he is hunting! – Abu Nuwas

Gazelles are really in trouble when he is hunting!

Chapter Ten

Schism

In March 2000, I was elected to the Committee of the SGHC Coursing Section, which was to give me a bird's-eye view of the unfortunate events that began to unfold thereafter. But immediately after my election, I was far removed from any such considerations when I went on an educative visit to Tunisia with Liese, Adrian Phillips, a close friend and long-time Saluki enthusiast, and his student daughter. I wanted to see if we could discover some of the ancient historical background to coursing in North Africa, which was in part described in a Tunisian version of a medieval Arabic text that I was about to translate into English (published in 2003 as *Al-Mansur's Book On Hunting*), as well as see some of the contemporary hounds.

We started in the elegant Bardo Museum in Tunis, which holds, among other things, one of the world's best collections of Roman mosaics from all over Tunisia, particularly in the distinctive North African style that emerged during the 3rd century AD as decoration for the private houses of rich landowners and farmers. This style reflected scenes from everyday life, notably from the hunting field. Horses and hunting dogs were highly prized and, just as we would celebrate some favourite horse or hound with a painting, so they celebrated them in mosaics, often recording the animal's name, as in a mosaic from Oudhna in which the Saluki *Ederatus* ('Ivy Leaf') courses a hare, while his companion *Mustela* ('Weasel') courses a jackal. *Ederatus* is a brindle, indicating the existence of this pattern among these coursing hounds during

Mosaic from Oudhna in the Bardo Museum, Tunis.

the Roman period. Indeed, we saw brindles in several of the mosaics, suggesting that it was as common a pattern then as it is among Sloughis there today. Other mosaics illustrated the various ways of hunting with hounds, sometimes in tandem with falcons or driving game into nets.

But we were anxious to see the real thing and moved on to the south, passing on the way through a small town with the evocative name of Sloughia, though none of the inhabitants whom I asked could explain its origin. Our objective was Douz, on the edge of the Sahara, where I had read an annual camel festival (known formally as the Festival of the Sahara) was held in an arena and coursing boxed hares, rather like park coursing in Ireland, was put on as a kind of sideshow. On our arrival, I asked a man offering camel rides to tourists where I might find some hounds and he took me to a nearby house. He went inside and emerged with a robust cream dog. While I was taking photographs, the woman of the house could not restrain her curiosity and came out to have a look. She overcame her embarrassment before a foreign stranger and told me that her dog was about a year old and hunted gazelle and hare. He was not as refined as some of the hounds I had seen previously in Morocco, with his

Robust Sloughi in Douz

broad skull, thick neck, roseate ears and ill-defined tuck, but he was certainly powerfully built and looked as if he would acquit himself well at coursing.

Through the courtesy of the local tourist office, we went on to see Salem Gharsala, a well-known breeder who, according to the local guidebook, exported his hounds to the USA, Germany, France, Libya and Saudi Arabia. He was away at the time, but we were warmly welcomed by his vivacious wife and their children, who paraded his two breeding bitches before us in the room where we drank mint tea. One was *Rakkala*, a very small cream bitch, looking very Whippet-like, with her roseate ears, tiny feet and thin tail. She was seven years old but looked older, with her drooping stomach from many pregnancies. Like all the other hounds we managed to measure, she was taller than long, though measuring only 61 cm by 58.5 cm. The other, her four-year-old daughter *Mania*, was almost identical but slightly bigger at 63.5 cm by 61. She wore a curious belt contraption around her tuck, which was joined on one side by a strap to her collar 'for securing her', we were told. She bore a circular brand mark for identification on her rump. The hounds were easy to handle but did not look in hunting condition.

While waiting for Salem to return, we went to have a look at the collection of desert animals in the Douz Zoo. Much to our surprise, one pen was labelled in Arabic '*Salūqī*', and inside were four hounds. The only dog was extremely ugly! He had both ears cropped to the base, which emphasised his broad skull and thick neck on a squat frame with little tuck, and he had three parallel branded lines on his front legs. This form of branding is common in Algeria where, according to a French veterinarian, François Giudicelli, in 1975 over 40% of the hounds that he saw were branded in this way. The reasons given to me later that day – that it made them run faster and prevented cramp – were the same as given to Giudicelli. In fact, my overall impression was that the Douz hounds had a lot in common with those studied by Giudicelli in Algeria, which was not surprising in view of the proximity of the border. Indeed, Salem told me later that this was where some of his hounds came from. The three bitches in the pen were more attractive: one was red, one was cream and the third was her almost identical three-month-old puppy, sired by the dog. The only time they were allowed to run free was when they took part in the festival.

In the afternoon, we picked up Salem, a cheerful and passionate hunter, and drove to a nearby house, where we were introduced to a fine brindle dog measuring 66 cm by 63.5, called *Fayed*. He was the offspring of Salem's old bitch, though it was hard to see any resemblance, and a brindle dog bred, said Salem, by a German couple in the north of Tunisia. Salem showed us photographs of others from the litter winning at shows in Germany and France. They all seemed more substantial than their dam and had floppy ears instead of her roseate ones. Salem then took us to a relative's house where, inside the *majlis* curled up on a cushion, was a very gentle cream dog with cropped ears and 'go-faster' stripes branded on his front legs.

Sloughi with cropped ears and branded legs in Douz.

As we were sipping mint tea, Salem asked me to drive to another house and bring back the hounds from there. These were another cream dog and a tiny tan bitch with black masking hairs. She was again of the Whippet type, the like of which I had not seen elsewhere; but obviously hounds of this size must be suitable for hunting in the local conditions or they would not be bred. According to Salem, all these hounds were used for hunting hare, gazelle and fox, but not jackal as it was too dangerous. This was different from Morocco and Algeria, where jackal hunting is what has enabled the breed to survive the restrictions of the French colonial game-hunting laws.

We said goodbye to Salem and, as it was still early, I decided to take Adrian Phillips to see the cream dog I had seen previously, but the house was shut up. However, a passer-by on a motorbike volunteered to show us other hounds nearby. First, we saw a hulking red three-year-old dog with a broad, heavy head, thick neck, terrier-like ears and ill-defined tuck. While chatting with its owner, we were approached by two lads who took us to see another tiny cream bitch, measuring only 51 cm by 48.5, with the same Whippet-like appearance, that seemed to be living under a pile of rusty iron bars and pieces of cloth. The lads wanted to take us further into the oasis to see more, but it was getting late and we had seen enough of the local type of hound not to be

Crop-eared Sloughi in Douz.

impressed; but we did not have the opportunity to see them perform, which is what their breeders would say counts most. Apart from the brindle, which was partly an exotic in Douz, none of the hounds matched the appearance of the breed favoured in the show ring. On the other hand, they bore a striking resemblance to an historic drawing by Jean-Pierre Mégnin, the well-known French cynologist, in 1890 of a hound of Libyan origin, which might suggest that the type is endemic to the area.

On my return home, it was not long before the divisions in the Coursing Section began to open up wider. Although I had been present at the last coursing meeting of the season in February, I was unaware of what was later claimed to be an altercation between a member and the slipper over the manner in which his hound had been slipped, allegedly, unsighted on the hare. However, at the first meeting of the newly elected Coursing Committee in June, I was chosen to be its chairman and was immediately confronted with an instruction from the SGHC Committee to penalise by suspension from the Coursing Section the member who, it was claimed, had abused the slipper. The Committee decided that it had no alternative but to suspend temporarily the member concerned while the matter was investigated. Our meeting was followed immediately by the Annual General Meeting of the Coursing Section, and there was an ugly scene as the suspended member sought to be present in order to defend himself from allegations from other members, all of which were based on statements made weeks after the event and some by people not directly involved. The situation at the AGM was all the more regrettable in that it should have been the happy occasion for the formal presentation to the member concerned of the Victor Henderson Memorial Trophy for winning the most courses in the season, with a Saluki of my breeding.

The Coursing Committee subsequently carried out a full investigation into the alleged incident, for which, it was claimed by the SGHC Committee, there had been a precedent in 1995, though this was found to be false. Both the slipper and the alleged abuser denied the alleged altercation, which, according to the rules, should have been addressed at the time by the stewards of the meeting, if anyone had felt sufficiently aggrieved to raise the matter at all; but no one did. The Coursing Committee therefore considered that, in the absence of supporting testimony from the two principals in the alleged incident, the complaint against the member concerned should be dropped. The Coursing Committee recommended that the SGHC Committee accept this judgment. However, the SGHC Committee chose instead at a meeting in August to suspend without explanation the whole Coursing

Section until the next SGHC AGM, thereby depriving members of competitive coursing for the intervening season. This arbitrary decision was greeted with dismay by the majority of the active coursing members who, after informal deliberation, reached a consensus that it was unacceptable.

Hence we broke up for the summer in some disorder, and August proved to be a month for some heart-searching decisions on more than one level. First, on a personal level, a trip up to the Lake District to see Ian and Sue Charlton's litter of six one-month-old puppies that their bitch *Salamara Girl* had had with Kim and Lynn Ingram's *Thani*, bred by me, posed the question whether we should have one. I was slightly concerned because of the degree of inbreeding; *Salamara Girl*, already a product of a brother–sister breeding, was *Thani*'s aunt. However, the pups looked healthy and one little cream bitch seemed particularly feisty; and she was, after all, *Najma*'s granddaughter. We left it that we would think it over, not least because we had thought of breeding *Sally*, although our first attempt with one of Mike Ratcliffe's Saudi-descent dogs had been unsuccessful.

Then, on a wider level, a group of the core coursing people from the Coursing Section held an informal meeting to consider how to react to the suspension of coursing. There was a general reluctance to make a clean break with the SGHC and a preference, rather, to go for a loose arrangement of coursing meetings in the coming season to maintain the fitness of the hounds and to see what the SGHC proposed at the next AGM in March 2001. We thought we could acquire access to sufficient land to make it possible to hold a series of competitive meetings through the coming winter season under Coursing Section rules but not in its name. This was particularly important, as four of our hounds – Paul and Joanne Sagar's *Molly*, Kim and Lynn Ingram's *Thani*, my *Sally* and Ian Charlton's *Salamara Girl* – had (in that order) already been selected, before the suspension of the Coursing Section, to represent the SGHC in an invitation event called the Millennium Champion Saluki Stake, to be run in mid-December within the framework of Greyhound 2000, described as 'the most exciting Greyhound event for over a hundred years'. Although the Coursing Section was by then suspended, the National Coursing Club confirmed that the invitation to our hounds to participate in this great event still stood. So we needed to keep our hounds in top condition if we were to put on a good show for coursing Salukis.

In a happier frame of mind with this solution, I looked forward in September to a return visit to Syria with Liese and a group of friends who did not know the country.

While the group went off to the Roman sites at Bosra, I went on a mission to rediscover Lady Jane Digby, a remarkable woman of the 19th century with an acquired taste for Salukis. As described by Mary S Lovell in her excellent biography *A Scandalous Life* (1995), Lady Jane was born into an aristocratic family in 1807 and married well but early. She abandoned her husband and children for an Austrian prince; was married a second time to a German baron, with whom she had two more children; and had liaisons with the King of Bavaria, a Greek count (with whom she had another child) and an Albanian brigand before finding happiness in Syria with a bedouin shaikh 20 years her junior, with whom she lived until her death in 1881. She met the shaikh, Medjuel el Mezrab (as she wrote it, but more correctly Mijwil al-Misrab) when he acted as her escort on a journey across the desert from Damascus to Palmyra. He stood out in his magnificent robes with a hooded falcon on his wrist, which Mary Lovell describes as being used for catching birds and game as fresh food on the journey, 'as would his salukis – the elegant hunting dogs of the desert – which always travelled with him'.

Mary Lovell had generously thrown open to me her research papers, where I searched in vain for further references to Lady Digby's Salukis. I felt there had to be some, because Mary Lovell had written about Lady Digby's house in Damascus:

> All her pets lived happily alongside Medjuel's elegant salukis and the watchdogs. The salukis must have been extremely well trained, for sometimes Jane had tame gazelles living in her garden, brought to her as abandoned kids by the bedouins, and the gazelles seemed to dwell happily with the salukis which had been bred to hunt them.

But all I could find was a small pencil sketch that she had made of a desert encampment, in the foreground of which is a pair of Salukis. I also drew a blank at the Digby family seat in Dorset, where the current Lord Digby kindly opened up the family archives and collection of her magnificent watercolours of her travels. I resolved to see what I could find out in Syria.

An old friend of mine with an encyclopaedic knowledge of Damascus, Fatie Darwish, took me first to see Lady Digby's former house in the old quarter and then her burial place. The house had sadly fallen into disrepair, though here and there were signs of its former grandeur. Where she had once lived with her extended family, retainers, horses, Salukis and livestock, there were some 30 families packed in. One family showed us traces of the expensive, probably hand-made, wallpaper, a handsome ceiling rose inset with mirrors and an octagonal rotunda on the roof, where she must have sat in the evening to enjoy the cool breeze. The face of an old man living there lit up when I mentioned hunting with Salukis, and he recounted stories of his youth in the 1950s when he had escorted the American Consul into the desert to hunt gazelle. There was little else to lighten the gloom of a scene of dust and decay.

Her grave was also sad. Her remains lie buried under a fine, well-maintained tombstone in an otherwise neglected cemetery, with an inscription, apparently carved by her husband, which read in Arabic: 'Madame Digby al-Misrab'.

I rejoined our group to go to Palmyra, where I had arranged for a guide to take me to visit the Misrab tribe, who were said to be quartered some 65 km from there. However, on our arrival the guide told me that they had moved on and were too far away for me to visit them in the time available. The guide was intimately acquainted with her story and referred to her always as 'Umm Laban' ('the mother of yoghurt'), by which she was known for her creamy complexion. He related that the shaikhs of the tribe were scattered between Homs and Saudi Arabia, and he did not believe they had Salukis any more. I had to leave the trail there for the greater appeal of a couple of days with my coursing friends in Hama.

On my arrival in Hama, my old friend Fakhr al-Barazi greeted me with the unexpected question: had I ever attended an Arab funeral? It turned out that an old member of the coursing community, whom I had know from previous visits, had died and was about to be buried. So, without even dropping off my luggage, I was hurried off to the cemetery just in time to see the corpse in its simple winding sheet being laid in the ground. There were hundreds of mourners present and I was able to meet at one go most of the hunting fraternity, who extended invitations to see their Salukis, offers that I accepted with alacrity. The next 24 hours passed in a whirlwind of activity.

We went first to Sawran, a village north of Hama, where I saw many hounds I had never seen before, though I had been there only two years earlier. It was an extraordinary sight, as we rounded a corner, to see about a dozen hounds pegged out on long chains on a hillside, like pasturing horses. They were nearly all powerfully built smooth black and tans with cropped ears, looking rather like Dobermanns. Nearby were two smooth particoloureds with large patches of a kind of olive brown on a cream background. Running loose was a feathered tricoloured dog rather reminiscent of Brigadier General Lance's famous hound *Seleughi*, the sire of *Sarona Kelb*.

Salukis in Sawran.

From there we sped on to Khan Shaikhoon, where in the fading light I was greeted with a scene that I thought had disappeared forever from those parts – a gypsy encampment of some half a dozen tents, before each of which I could just make out the reclining shape of a Saluki. Fakhr said that he had been negotiating there for a puppy but, so far, the owner would not consider parting with it. He took me to see it. It was now dark, so a car was driven up to illuminate the tent with its headlights and there, lying in the dust, was the puppy. She was unattached and rose to meet us with a wagging tail. She was a feathered black and silver of about seven months, a lovely gentle creature that allowed us to handle her with no sign of fear. The gypsy was asking a large sum by Syrian standards and would not bargain, because he did not really want to part with her. We had to leave her, with regret, for a long evening of feasting and storytelling back in Hama.

The next day we went on a tour of the Hama Saluki breeders, when I saw one or two hounds I recognised from before, but most were new to me. One breeder presented me with two beautiful collars embroidered with coloured beads. He had a young puppy with him and I noticed that its dew-claws had been removed, something I had never seen before in the Middle East. He said this was traditional in his family and was done at the same time as the ears were cropped, at the age of about a month.

The author with Najma, Sally and Filfil al-Hamra.

I asked what had happened to the older hounds he had had before. He said that he never slaughtered them when they became too old to course, but either gave them away or simply let them go to be taken in by anyone who wanted them, or to fend for themselves. A few would be kept for breeding. But as a general rule the hounds had to be able to earn their keep. He started them coursing at about ten months, and certainly no later than 11 months since he believed a hound would not be a good hunter if started late. He fed them only one meal a day, consisting of bread soaked in fat, with eggs, bones or leftovers. They certainly looked fit and keen, though I did not have the time to see them run, as I had to rejoin our group for the journey home.

The autumn proved busy, as we began to put in place arrangements for our coursing meetings leading up to Greyhound 2000. A few of us undertook the task of reconnoitring a number of farms and estates where informal soundings suggested that we would be welcome. Our first meeting was in the middle of October, which was particularly significant for me, because Ian Charlton would deliver to me the puppy I had meanwhile agreed to take from him. We ran two eight-dog stakes that day and my puppy, now named *Filfil al-Hamra*, and one of her sisters walked the whole day with us. We followed up with a two-day meeting in Norfolk, when we ran two eight-dog stakes on the first day and a 20-dog stake on the second. All the hounds had plenty of runs, and both we and our hosts were delighted with the congenial atmosphere to which everyone had contributed.

A couple of weeks later, in November we put on another two-day meeting on the Scottish moors where, with a large turnout in excellent conditions, we were able to run a 22-dog stake with two backup stakes on the first day and another 20-dog stake on the second. All the four runners in Greyhound 2000 performed very well and were shaping up nicely for that major public event. I was, however, a little worried about *Najma*. She had also run well for her age but she seemed to be turning her right front foot increasingly outwards. A local vet in Scotland opined that she must have had a trauma there at some stage, resulting in the detachment of the inside tendon. There was some callusing on the joint and she was compensating by turning her foot out. He thought surgery would be too traumatic at her age and recommended no more coursing.

Meanwhile, the SGHC Committee had decided that the best way forward was to call a joint meeting with the suspended Coursing Section Committee on 10 December 2000, subject to certain preconditions. However, the suspended Coursing Section Committee felt unable to meet these preconditions, so the SGHC cancelled the meeting. A quorum of the Coursing Section then responded by requesting, under the SGHC rules, the convening of a Special General Meeting to discuss a proposal to dissolve the Coursing Section and to leave the way open for the establishment of a new independent coursing club; and the SGHC duly set arrangements in train to hold the requested SGM the following February.

All my attention was then concentrated on getting ready for Greyhound 2000, in which 128 Greyhounds would compete for the Millennium Trophy and special invitational stakes would be run for other sighthounds. It started on 10 December in Newmarket, with a pedigree Greyhound show, followed by a parade of all the runners. An exhibition of famous coursing Greyhounds, paintings and memorabilia depicting 'The Greyhound through the Ages' was also mounted. There was also Greyhound racing one evening at Swaffham Greyhound Stadium. The coursing started on 11 December near Newmarket and continued there and near Swaffham over the next three days, with the final rounds run on 14 December at Six Mile Bottom near Newmarket, together with the semi-finals and finals of the Whippet, Deerhound and Saluki stakes. The weather was perfect, with the sun shining from a clear blue sky for the last 24 Greyhounds. Some of them were beginning to show the strain of the long competition and they were glad of the break provided by running the semi-final of the Whippets. Then we moved to another field, where the remaining Greyhounds ran, followed by the Deerhounds and the Whippets. It was getting later and later and I thought we would never run, but eventually Paul Sagar and I were called to bring forward the two sisters, *Molly* and *Sally*, in the first semi-final.

Molly had been running very well in our private meetings but it was *Sally* that flew out of slips first to build up and hold a lead of two lengths as she turned the hare. *Molly* tried to get in but *Sally* clung on to the lead until they lost the hare in some rough grass. Her brother *Thani* then had an easier win over *Salamara Girl*. This meant the final was to be between *Sally* and *Thani*, but the sun was already sinking as they went into slips. Annoyingly, the beaters drove two hares past the slipper, so he had to wait until they had gone and a single hare came through. Once again, *Sally* streaked away from slips and raced into a clear lead up the field, turning the hare in front of the stand packed with spectators. She put in a couple more turns before catching the hare and was declared the winner. However, as Kim Ingram and I ran forward to pick up our hounds, another hare came by and the pair of them took off again and gave a brilliant demonstration of Saluki coursing in front of the stand. The hare then made for a hedge and into another field, where *Thani* eventually pulled it down and retrieved it.

By the time we had collected them, the trophies were being handed to the owners of the winners: *Daylami*, owned by the Osborne House Syndicate and trained by Michael O'Donovan, won the Greyhound Millennium Cup 2000; *Chyton Repetition*, owned by Mrs Dewhurst, won the Millennium Champion Whippet Stake; *Coronach Pennys Chieftain*, owned by Mrs Sharp, won the Millennium Champion Deerhound Stake; and my *Thalooth al-Thalaatha* won the Millennium Champion Saluki Stake. All the winners received engraved crystal rose bowls and we all trooped off highly delighted, not only with the results but also with this huge demonstration of the popularity of coursing at a time when it was under threat. We got some very good media coverage, as we did again just a few days later when about 5,000 of us marched down Whitehall to protest at the Second Reading of the bill to ban hunting with dogs.

It was while I was still basking in the glow of *Sally's* success that the director of a wildlife film company contacted me again to firm up the arrangements for me to act as technical adviser for a film on the desert-bred Saluki to be shot in the Middle East under the working title 'Running with the Wind'. The director, Wayne Lines from South Africa, his cameraman, administrative assistant and I were due to arrive in Marrakesh, Morocco, in late January for nearly a week's filming. However, just

The author with Sally and the Millennium Cup.

to complicate things for me, on the morning of my flight *Najma* and *Sally* became locked in a ferocious fight with a large urban dog fox. *Najma* did for it in the end, but sustained a nasty bite under her eye, while *Sally* had a bite to her leg; and both hounds were covered with fleas. Fortunately, I had *Filfil* on the lead or she would have been literally blooded. So, before I could set off I had first to get them to the vet for some shots of antibiotics. In my haste to get away, I found at the airport that I had picked up Liese's passport by mistake; so more panic! Anyhow, I made it and we spent the next day in Marrakesh going through the various scenarios; basically they wanted lots of action and local colour.

With the assistance of some of the contacts I had made on my previous visit to Morocco, I arranged for the team to go first to a picturesque, typically Moroccan mud-brick village, Si Ali Mousa, not far from the small town of Chemaia. Although there were only a few suitable hounds there, the villagers showed us some magnificent Barb horses and we agreed we would come back the next day to film them in their traditional robes and armed with old matchlock rifles, as if riding out to hounds. On a cold but bright morning, we returned to Si Ali Mousa, where the headman had arranged for four splendidly caparisoned Barbs and about seven or eight hounds, freshly decorated with henna, to cavort on a nearby plain as if engaged in a hunt. The hounds were difficult to motivate until someone produced a tame rabbit and waved it about in front of the camera, whereupon the riders and the hounds charged alarmingly towards us, turning away only at the last moment in a cloud of dust. The cameraman was delighted with the footage.

After lunch in the village, we made arrangements with the Nuwasir to organise a hunt near their village the next day. I had originally discussed a proper jackal hunt, but the villagers said that this was too difficult to arrange spontaneously. Instead, a fox had already been trapped for us and was being held in Chemaia. The idea was that we would bring it back to the Nuwasir, release it and film their hounds in pursuit. However, the cameraman insisted on ethical grounds that the hunt should be filmed in two, separate halves: first, he would film the fox racing across the landscape after its release and then, once it had escaped, he would film the hounds running in simulated pursuit. Explaining such niceties to the villagers was my task, and they clearly thought we were mad!

Before dawn the next morning, we collected the hunter with the fox in a reeking sack en route to the Nuwasir village. We went off to a wide wadi, green with winter wheat, to set up the camera, while the villagers and their hounds gathered on a hilltop just out of our sight. We assumed that the fox would run away from us down the wadi to where there was cover, but the creature surprised us by turning round and running back through where we were lined up into the view of the villagers. There was then no stopping them from releasing their straining hounds and we suddenly had a real fox hunt, though too far off for the camera. The fox realised the danger and turned away to the cover below, which it reached safely before the distant hounds could close in. The hounds had done incredibly well to cross some vicious-looking rocks to reach the wadi without injury to their feet, and on their return were ready for us to film them separately, walking up with their owners and being slipped on an imaginary fox, as if they were really coursing. So, in the end, honour was satisfied.

However, some other villagers wanted to be in the film and promised to take us on a real hunt. Early the next morning, we met up with eight of them, with eight hounds, and drove out to some fields of sprouting winter wheat. They went round to the far side and walked up in line towards the camera, with one hound running loose ahead of them. As they approached, it put up a fox and pulled it down after a short chase. We then moved on to a walled plantation, where we were told to wait outside while the hunters went in to beat out any game. They used a short-legged terrier-like mongrel for getting under the bushes. Before long a fox broke cover and jumped over the wall, but jumped straight back again. It did this twice before deciding to make a break for it. However, a couple of hounds had been stationed outside the walls and they were quickly onto it. The local farmer was delighted, as foxes do a lot of damage to livestock and are regarded as pests. The cameraman was equally pleased with some good natural footage, though we also did some repeats in slow motion of the hounds jumping over the walls.

*Mounted hunter
at Si Ali Mousa.*

As we ate our picnics with the hunters, I was thinking about the harmonious relationship between them and their hounds. They came when called, knew their hunting business and were handled affectionately by their owners. I noted one hunter was even cuddling a handsome cream, black-masked dog with one hand, while sipping mint tea from a glass with the other. It was a colourful scene to end on and the film director was very happy with the film in the can. However, it was only the beginning and we planned other forays into the Middle East.

Back home again, there was time for some wonderful coursing in Norfolk before the fateful Special General Meeting of the SGHC on 11 February 2001 under the aegis of the Kennel Club to discuss our proposal to set up a coursing club free from oversight by the SGHC Committee. I was deputed to make the case before a large gathering and was seconded by Chris Lewis of the Knightellington Kennel. The Secretary of the SGHC responded and rejected our proposal as unconstitutional. A few people spoke from the floor, more in sorrow than in anger. The proposal was put to a secret ballot and was duly defeated by a margin of three to one, with the majority of club members not involved in coursing voting against and the sizeable minority of active coursing members voting for. As a formality, the SGHC Annual General Meeting in March confirmed the reformation of the Coursing Section with the rump of the old membership, who had brought about the schism, and the way was then clear for the rest of us to get on with forming an independent coursing club.

What a fine hound you are, without equal!

Chapter Eleven

A Brave New Start

It was not the best timing to embark on a new coursing venture. Foot-and-mouth disease stalked the land, and with all the restrictions on movement in rural areas it was difficult to exercise our hounds and to find venues for future meetings. In a way I was lucky not to be living in the country, as there were no restrictions on exercising my hounds off-lead in the London parks surrounding our home; and I also took them to some lure coursing events that summer. So, with time on my hands before the winter season, I formulated some plans to extend my exploration of Salukidom by organising a visit to Central Asia.

Ever since qualifying as a Russian interpreter in the Royal Air Force many years before, I had nurtured the ambition to travel along the Silk Road. I had been particularly inspired by Fitzroy Maclean's exploits in his autobiographical book *Eastern Approaches* (1949), but the Cold War denied any chance, particularly for a British diplomat, and my career had in any case taken me in a different direction in the Middle East. However, since the collapse of the Soviet Union in 1991 and my retirement a few years later, all kinds of possibilities had opened up. As so graphically described and illustrated by Heinrich Moser in his *Durch Central-Asien* (Through Central Asia) (Moser, 1888), Uzbekistan was a country where historically the local rulers had hunted with hounds that resembled Salukis but were called Tazys, and neighbouring Kyrgyzstan also had some intriguing hounds with a rather hairy Saluki shape that were called Taigans. So I devised an itinerary for Liese, a small group of friends and me accordingly, and in September 2001 we took off.

We began on the northern side of the great Kara Kum Desert in the remarkably preserved walled oasis town of Khiva in western Uzbekistan, which today is largely deserted and locked in a time warp. The start appeared auspicious, as I soon spotted a *Berkut* (Golden Eagle) sitting on a stand. The *Berkut* is traditionally used for hunting right across Central Asia and is often used in tandem with Tazy hounds. My hopes were soon dashed, however, as the boy in charge of the bird said that it was merely a tourist attraction and wanted payment for photographing it!

Khiva has known periods of greatness from about the 5th century but it owes most of its monumental buildings to the 17th–19th centuries, when it was the seat of a series of khans, who derived their wealth from the transiting caravans and the slave trade. It was the latter that brought the Khanate into conflict with Russia and later the Soviet Union, of which it was forced to become part in 1924. The Soviets brought the railway to the nearby town of Urgench and developed it at the expense of Khiva, which led to the gradual abandonment of the old town. Much later the Soviets restored it as a kind of living museum.

From there we crossed the Oxus River, or Amu Darya as it is now called, on a rather alarming, ramshackle pontoon bridge and drove parallel with the river on the southern side of the Kyzyl Kum, the Red Sands, which stretch all the way north to the receding waters of the Aral Sea, en route to Bukhara. It was 11 September, a day I shall never forget for an event that changed the world. After a wonderful afternoon spent walking round old Bukhara and being spontaneously invited to join in a hilarious wedding party, we retired to our hotel and switched on the television at the moment the devastating terrorist attack on the World Trade Centre in New York was being shown. We thought at first that it was some kind of horror film, as the commentary was in Uzbek, but then it became clear that this was for real, and we were all stunned into silence as the implications began to sink in. But life goes on …

The next day we were due to go on to Samarqand, but I had noticed on the map an area not far from Bukhara that was designated as a gazelle nature reserve. I reasoned that if gazelle, or *Djairan* as they are called locally, were indigenous, hunting hounds might also be found there. We stopped at the entrance to the reserve and I went in to speak to the director in charge, but bounding to greet me came a hound that was similar in colour and build to my *Tayra*, though taller and with slightly turned-back

The Salukis in My Life

Here, There and Everywhere, From the Arab World to China

Foreword by
Sir Alan Munro KCMG

SIR TERENCE CLARK KBE CMG CVO joined the British Diplomatic Service in 1955 at the age of 21. He had just completed his National Service in the Royal Air Force where he had served as a Russian interpreter during the start of the Cold War during the reigns of Winston Churchill, USSR leader Stalin and US President Truman.

Fluent in English and Russian, he decided to learn Arabic, beginning at the School of Oriental and African Studies in London before transferring to Lebanon. His expert language skills made him an invaluable asset to Britain and for much of his diplomatic career he was involved with the Middle East both in the region and at the Foreign Office, serving in Bahrain, Jordan, Syria, Morocco, the United Arab Emirates, Oman and

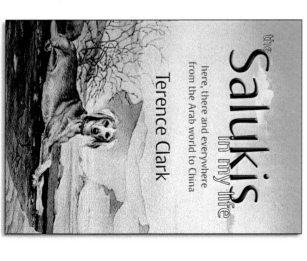

the
Salukis
in my life

here, there and everywhere
from the Arab world to China

Terence Clark

He remains closely connected with his friends and past colleagues in the Middle East and is at present Vice-President of the Anglo Omani Society and Chairman of the Friends of the Basrah Museum.

Sir Terence is the author of several books and many articles on the history and politics of the region and *The Salukis in My Life* is the first book to show how this beautiful breed have inspired and enhanced his career. Part-memoir, part-travelogue, the book explores in lively and unprecedented detail Sir Terence's fascinating life story interlaced with the history of the breed all over the world.

His commitment to the study, enjoyment and preservation of these 'Companions of Kings' encouraged him to take on positions across the world and introduced him to extraordinary people and places. Indigenous to the Arabian peninsula, the desert-bred Saluki has for centuries been revered, and remains as highly valued today for its elegance and intelligence.

Sir Terence's passion for Salukis is infectious – whether for hunting, showing, coursing, breeding or simply companionship, the reader of this beautifully illustrated memoir cannot help but share the love.

Price: £22.95
Publication: 6th March 2018

BIC: BM:WSX:WTL:WNG:
memoirs: field sports: travel writing: animals

Signature Books Representation (UK) Ltd
Tel: 0845 862 1730
sales@signaturebooksuk.com

Press Enquiries: Taslima Begum
Tel: +44 (0) 208 399 7736
taslima@medinapublishing.com

Hortaya near Bukhara.

ears. On closer inspection, it looked more like what the Russians call a Hortaya, a coursing hound rather like a small Greyhound that they believe may have descended from an ancient Scythian breed. Another hound lurked in the background and in a nearby pen was a whole pack of them. They were all smooth-haired with roseate ears and showed a range of colours: black and white, red, cream, white, sandy with faint brindle stripes and blue and white. They had come originally from Russia but I suspected that they had been crossed at some stage with local Tazys, as their haunches were not rounded like a Hortaya's and the straight topline and prominent ilia were more like those of a Tazy. The director claimed they were used only for finding fallen game in the reserve, but I asked myself – did they fall or were they pushed? These were undoubtedly sighthounds, not scenthounds! In another pen were some orphaned gazelle.

In Tashkent, the capital, I had arranged to meet a young Russian from the Uzbek Dog Club, hoping he might be able to show us some Tazys. However, he drew a rather depressing picture of the local hunting scene. In his club he could count on his fingers the number of Tazys, Taigans and Borzois, because of the sharp decline in hunting after the departure back to Russia of many of the ethnic Russian population since independence from the Soviet Union. There were many more in Kazakhstan and he thought we might see some as we drove through part of it en route to Bishkek, the capital of Kyrgyzstan. We had no luck there and Kyrgyzstan, which is 85% mountainous, did not look very promising either – but there I was wrong.

The beginning was not encouraging. I had the address of a Russian Tazy breeder in Bishkek and with some difficulty found his house; but he had moved back to Russia with his hounds. We drove on across scenery more like that of the Wild West. The snow-capped Tien Shan Mountains could have been the Sierra Nevada and everywhere people were on horseback, some rounding up great herds of horses or sheep. Our objective was a yurt camp high up in the mountains close by the former Silk Road caravanserai of Tash Rabat. As we approached the beautifully restored stone-built building, a dark shape glided towards us; it was a black bitch with chestnut highlights in her thick fur and brindle on her legs. She was a Taigan, the first I had ever seen, and her owner said she was about three years old. She had a broader skull than a Saluki and a shorter tail with a distinctive tight curl, said to be characteristic of the breed and apparently formed by the fusion of the last two vertebrae. She was very friendly, and followed behind us as we went for a walk up a valley hoping to get a view into China.

On the way back, we came across a yurt belonging to a woman to whom we had given a lift to Tash Rabat. Her warm and friendly greeting was echoed by a year-old red and white Irish-marked Taigan. She had a somewhat waddling walk due to her very broad chest, which I attributed to the need for large lungs in the thin atmosphere of the high mountains. I was told that Taigans also have a higher number of red blood corpuscles, for the same reason. The woman produced for us a tiny black three-week-old Taigan puppy from the mud-brick house in which they lived in winter, when the temperature descends to minus 35° C. The woman's husband, who was packing up their yurt to move, joined us and said he hunted on horseback with his hounds for hare, fox, marmot and mountain goat.

Further down the valley, a man came running from a yurt to invite us in. He told us that there were more Taigans nearby, and we

Taigan at Tash Rabat.

made a slight diversion to where some men were building a mud-brick house. As we approached, three Taigans came rushing out to greet us – a mainly black, heavily pregnant four-year-old bitch, a similar year-old dog and a year-old black and tan bitch. They all looked in excellent condition and one man said Taigans lived to 18 years, but I found that hard to believe in the harsh conditions of the mountains. A little further on, I spotted another Taigan outside a small house on the other side of a fast-flowing stream. Some young lads appeared from the house, jumped lightly onto horses and rode furiously across the stream to meet us, with a five-month-old black Taigan gambolling around them and an old, heavily feathered brindle Taigan lurking in the background. They were fascinated by my pictures of Salukis and Tazys and pressed us to go back home with them, but we needed to return to our yurt for what proved to be a bitterly cold night – and this was September!

The next morning, the icy wind had dropped as we took the road towards the vast Lake Issyk-Kul. On either side of the road we passed bucolic scenes of herds of horses, sheep and cattle – and even a few yaks. At one point, we overtook a young lad walking by the roadside with a beautiful black and tan hound that looked more like the old Bell-Murray type of Afghan than a Taigan. He spoke no Russian, so I could not quiz him about its origin. Further on, I spotted a familiar black shape silhouetted against a white farm wall. We drove over for a closer look and found a very handsome black and white Taigan bitch. The woman of the house invited us to see her puppies in a kennel at the back. Her little daughter went inside and brought out five two-week-old puppies

of different colours: one black, one black-masked red, one black-fringed fawn and two fawn with black masking hairs. All the while their dam was circling anxiously around her puppies,

Kyrgyz with Taigans near Tash Rabat.

Taigan puppies near Naryn.

and I made the mistake of stepping too near them to take a photograph. The next thing I knew, she had bitten me in the back of my leg, not seriously but tearing my trousers and drawing blood. So we beat a hasty retreat. My companions were fearful of rabies, but I reasoned that the owner would not live with a rabid dog and a farmer who came up to us confirmed that the dog was vaccinated against rabies. So I dressed the small wound and we continued on to spend the night by the lake.

On the way back to Bishkek for our flight home the next day, we stopped at the small historical museum in Cholpan-Ata, where I found some wonderful old photographs of hunting scenes, showing splendid mounted hunters with eagles and Tazys and an intrepid hunter with a flintlock rifle standing over a magnificent snow leopard with a Taigan at his back. How much has changed in the interval; there are now only half a dozen eagle hunters left in Kyrgyzstan and the snow leopard has almost disappeared.

On my return home, various friends in Russia sent me pictures of their show Taigans, which looked considerably different from those I had seen in Kyrgyzstan. The Russian hounds were taller and less robust, with a much longer and denser coat. I could not imagine them hunting in the snow with all that weight of hair. They looked too refined for their purpose. Some told me that the Taigan was under threat in Kyrgyzstan from crossbreeding and changes in the lifestyle of the people. Certainly I saw a few dogs that looked as if they might have been crossed; but on the other hand I had the impression that, as a result of the collapse of the previous Russia-oriented economy, people were returning to the land and their former lifestyle, which included breeding Taigans capable of fulfilling their purpose in a harsh environment.

I came back to London to some good news. First, my translation with Muawiya Derhalli into English of a medieval Arabic hunting treatise, *Al-Mansur's Book On*

Filfil al-Hamra, Lure Courser of Merit.

Hunting, was being printed. This was especially welcome, because it meant I could concentrate on completing my part of another book, to be called *Dogs in Antiquity*, which was in preparation with my co-authors Professor Douglas Brewer and Adrian Phillips. Second, the producer of the proposed film on desert-bred Salukis wanted to discuss the next locations for filming in Syria and Jordan in the spring. So that was something to look forward to, as at home there was still only lure coursing – at which *Filfil* was so successful that she rapidly earned the title of Lure Courser of Merit – and some occasional rough coursing as we headed into the New Year and, at last, the first meeting of the new Saluki Coursing Club (SCC).

We began in style in Oxfordshire, where our host welcomed the SCC to his farm with a stirrup cup. We were due to run two eight-dog stakes, but at first the hares were hard to find and the prospects did not look too good. Then we moved onto some set-aside land and the hares were popping up frequently, so that we were able to run both events, with all the hounds acquitting themselves well after a long layoff. There were no trophies this time but we were all more than satisfied with the organisation of the meeting and the convivial atmosphere. We were not so lucky a couple of weeks later, when we ran two eight-dog stakes in Wiltshire but could not complete them as the weather closed in and stopped the proceedings.

The following week, *Filfil* had a narrow escape. We were going to run three stakes down in Wiltshire, with a special event for puppies at the beginning. We had gone down the day before and, while exercising the hounds, we had put up a hare that *Filfil* coursed through a couple of fences. It was only as we were going back to the car that I noticed something hanging from her chest. On inspection, it was a flap of skin, torn on some barbed wire. I took her straight to a local vet, who did an excellent job of stitching her, without a full anaesthetic. The next morning she was full of beans and, after taking veterinary advice to grease the wound well with Vaseline, I decided to put her in the puppy stake, as it would be her only chance to run in this event. She reached the final, in which she was only just beaten by her much bigger brother *Skidaw of Saba*, and there were no consequences for her wound. We also completed a veteran stake and another eight-dog stake, and got home quite shattered.

We managed another good meeting in Oxford for two eight-dog stakes, before ending the season on the high note of a two-day meeting in the Scottish Borders, where we had an excellent turnout of 20 runners. The weather was kind and the hares plentiful, and we all enjoyed some great coursing. I was especially pleased because *Filfil* had made a full recovery from her operation and won the backup stake for first-round losers. We all went home delighted with the success of the SCC in its first season and confident of its future viability.

In the middle of March 2002, I set off once again for Damascus, where I was due to rendezvous with the film team. Everything was complicated from the start. My flight was stuck at Heathrow airport for five hours because of a suspect piece of luggage, so that I eventually arrived at dawn, quite exhausted. The film crew arrived afterwards and had to use all their cash as a deposit for the eventual export of their film gear. They were unaware there were no cash machines in Syria, so I had to bail them out with the help of a Syrian friend. Then the Ministry of Information insisted that we should be accompanied on location by a minder, who lived in Homs. As we would be filming in Hama, we would have to arrange to ferry him to and fro. Finally, we were able to leave Damascus and travel to Hama, where my old friend Fakhr collected us from our hotel for a discussion over dinner of the filming arrangements. He insisted on taking us afterwards to see the new Barazi family *majlis*, built by one of the family resident in the USA in a splendidly refurbished Ottoman building around a large courtyard, with a grand salon, furnished with a Barazi family tree and antique weapons on the walls, and a separate, beautifully panelled anteroom painted with arabesques in the Damascus style. A number of old friends were there, who were delighted and very proud to hear that their hounds would feature in our project.

The weather was really against us the next morning, as we set off very early to meet Fakhr and his uncle, Abdulhamid, who were in a lorry with three Salukis in the back: *Guru*, a four-year-old smooth cream dog, *Jukha*, a two-year-old red bitch and *Risha*, a ten-month-old feathered black and tan bitch on her first outing. We drove through steady rain towards Qasr ibn Wardan, about 65 km north-east of Hama, where I had first met my late friend Badr al-Barazi ten years earlier. Here, the farmers scratch the surface of the stony ground in the dips and hollows, where a little more moisture might be retained for their winter wheat. It is the type of terrain that suits the hare. On the otherwise barren and windswept plain fading into the desert, it has a source of food as well as some shelter from predators such as hawks and foxes – but sadly not from lampers from the town, who come by night and shoot indiscriminately.

We stopped for breakfast, eaten in the vehicles while rain poured down, and the crew doubted that they could do any filming. But eventually the rain eased a little and I went off with the two hunters and their Salukis to walk round in a half-circle in the hope of driving a hare in front of the crew. As we turned to come back towards the camera, a hare got up right in front of me and we slipped the hounds. The hare made for the track on which we had come and ran straight past the camera with two of the hounds close behind, providing some excellent footage. We tried another beat but the rain came down even heavier and we called it a day. Our minder, who had spent the whole morning sitting miserably hunched up in the car, was thoroughly alarmed when I told him that we proposed to spend the next couple of nights in a tent in the desert. He asked me to call his boss in Damascus to excuse him from accompanying us. So we got rid of him, even though we had already decided that camping was not on in that weather.

The next day was cold but at least it was dry, and we were up before dawn for the long drive towards Raqqa on the Euphrates, to an area where the authorities had bulldozed an earthen wall around a vast expanse of semi-desert in an attempt to keep the wandering shepherds and their sheep and goats out and to allow the natural vegetation to regenerate. This policy had been very successful but had infuriated the bedouin, who regarded the land as their traditional grazing ground. The regeneration had also encouraged wildlife, and my companions spoke rapturously of coursing 14 hares there one day, though managing to catch only two, as the denser ground cover made it easier for the hares to escape. So we set off with high hopes of some exciting action, with four hounds: a young feathered black and white particoloured dog, whose owner was very proud of his hunting prowess; *Qassab*, a young feathered black and tan dog with the fierce look of an eagle; and two very lean, mean-looking smooth grizzles.

After two hours' walking without so much as a sign of a hare, I began to wonder about my friends' stories, but then, way out on the flank, the black and white dog, which had been running loose, got onto a fox, coursed it and killed it on its own. Soon after, a hare got up and gave the black and white and the black and tan a long chase, with the former just snatching it in the end. However, the black and tan injured a leg on the viciously stony ground and had to be retired. In fact, we all withdrew to the cars, as we had forgotten entirely about breakfast and were in urgent need of sustenance. The respite was short-lived, as the hunters were keen to get on and we needed more footage. After another long slog in the teeth of a bitterly cold wind, we eventually put up another hare, which all the hounds coursed, including the black and tan, which had made a rapid recovery. By this time, we had had enough and just wanted to escape from the relentless wind. A deserted hovel provided some shelter, while kebabs were miraculously produced and grilled over a most welcome fire. We still had the long drive back to Hama ahead of us and decided the next day would be a rest day, especially for the hounds.

Wayne Lines was keen to see some more hounds, so we went on a tour of some of the surrounding villages. In no time at all we must have seen at least twenty hounds, including a beautiful litter of seven plump two-week-old feathered puppies. Six of them were almost black but would be black and tan like their sire, and just one was red like their dam. This breeder's hounds were all well-feathered and more like the *Sarona Kelb* type than most of the hounds in the area. Indeed, nearby another breeder had only smooths of a type that reminded me of Dobermanns – enormously powerful hounds that some of my friends disparaged as too heavy for serious coursing. That was my reaction too, though I remembered their equally powerful grandsire, who had been a formidable courser.

One of the breeders showed how the hunters decorated their hounds with henna, a green powder from the dried and pulverised leaves of a bush that, when mixed

Applying henna to the feet.

with water, imparts an orange dye to the skin and hair. The Arabs use henna for dyeing their hair or beard and for making patterns on the back of women's hands at wedding ceremonies. They also use it on their hounds' feet, not only for decoration but rather for toughening the pads and for treating injuries. Henna helps to heal more quickly by reinforcing the skin's keratin and deterring invasive bacteria and yeasts. The powder is first moistened with water into a paste and then applied thickly to the feet one at a time, when each foot is bound up with cloth and encased in plastic sheeting to keep the moisture in and left for 24 hours. I was surprised that the demonstration hound stood there completely relaxed and would apparently not attempt to tear the coverings off overnight. I knew from experience that my own hounds would rip off medical dressings within minutes! All the time we were watching the ceremony, more and more hounds kept appearing, with quite a number of puppies among them. I was sorely tempted by a very promising young tricolour bitch that even had intact ears, but the problems of importation and registration were too great to bear thinking about.

There was to be no more relaxation. The next morning we were up again before dawn for a final day's coursing in another area where cultivation meets the gravel desert. It was a fine day, and pleasantly warm. We had four hounds with us: *Qassab*, *Guru* and *Risha* from before, plus a young smooth black and tan dog, also called *Guru*. We were in luck this time. We quickly put up a hare that was pursued and eventually caught by all four hounds after a long chase. The hunters went straight on, and over the next couple of hours we coursed three more. By then the hounds were tiring and had provided some brilliant action for the camera as well as food for the pot. So we picnicked among the wild flowers that had burst forth after the rain, while the hunters danced with joy.

We returned to Damascus well content with the filming but, once again, we had to grapple with the restrictive Syrian bureaucracy before we could fly out to our next location in Jordan. The Ministry of Information summoned Wayne Lines and me that evening and demanded to see the film before its export would be authorised. The officials had thought that it was a simple matter of rewinding the film, like a video, and projecting it onto a screen. We had to explain that it was a negative that had first to be developed before it could be viewed. This caused great consternation and a lot of telephoning to higher authority until, eventually, the officials relaxed and gave us the clearance we needed for Customs. Whew!

On arrival in Amman, we met up with the film's new director, Dereck Joubert, and his wife, representing National Geographic, which had meanwhile come in to finance the production. I outlined to them the plan to drive down to Wadi Rum, the long sandy valley that weaves through the rugged mountains to Aqaba on the Red Sea. Here I had arranged for Dhifallah, a local bedouin, to provide everything that we needed for filming; and he did not fail us. He took us to a traditional goat's-hair tent in a magnificent setting at the foot of a steep bluff deep in Wadi Rum, where we were welcomed by his mother, who looked after the livestock in a pen close by, and a couple of his friends who would act as extras in the filming. The action would be provided mainly by *La'aban*, a six-year-old smooth black and tan dog, *Hizza*, a smooth cream bitch and *Warda*, a two-month-old smooth almost-white bitch, who proved to be the star attraction. *La'aban* was from the north, near the Iraqi border, and *Hizza*, who was one month pregnant, from an area towards Sinai; they both had rather broad heads and roseate ears like some hounds in North Africa. *Warda* was bred in Wadi Rum and had a lovely nature. She was sharp and strong and I would have gladly had her.

The issue that was bothering me was how we were going to present the hunting hounds of Arabia (which was to be the new title of the film) when, as we discovered, hunting mammals was banned in Jordan. However, Dhifallah had got it all worked out. He would show us how they used to train and hunt with their hounds by simulation. First, he brought up the Wadi Rum a colourful train of camels with the two mature hounds running in and out of them to show how the hounds learnt to trot in the shade provided by the camels (though if it became too hot for them on the sand they might be lucky enough to be carried in panniers on camelback). In this fashion, they once travelled the length and breadth of the Arab world, where sometimes they might be given away to local dignitaries or used for breeding with local hounds, so that, then as later, the breed would be constantly spread and renewed far and wide.

The next day we went out with another bedouin who had brought along *Warda*'s dam, her grizzle sister and her black and tan brother to see their method of hunting, which was quite different from that practised in Syria. Here it was all about tracking. The soft sand showed up clearly the tracks of all manner of creatures and, as we walked, the bedouin eagerly pointed out where the hedgehog had gone, where the lizard had slithered and, at last, where a hare had hopped. We followed the tracks until they were obliterated by the drifting sand being whipped up by an approaching sandstorm. We retreated to a more sheltered spot, where the bedouin released a tame hare for the puppies to chase as part of their training. We also found the back-filled entrance to a jerboa's hole. The bedouin showed us how they used to dig out jerboas for the Saluki puppies to practise on. They would cover the entrance hole with a headcloth and stamp or bang on the surrounding ground to frighten the jerboa,

Our bedouin hosts in Wadi Rum with Warda.

Camel train in Wadi Rum.

which would come shooting out of its hole and become caught up in the headcloth. If they caught one, they would tie a stick across its back to prevent it diving back down its hole and release it for the puppies to chase.

Back at our tent, one of the bedouin described their standard for the Saluki, using *Hizza* as a demonstration model: the muzzle should be long, the jaws strong, the ears floppy and close to the head, the chest broad and deep, the tuck-up high, the shoulder muscles long to carry the legs backwards when galloping, and the thigh well muscled; the tail should reach down to the hock; and there should be space for three fingers between the shoulder blades and four fingers between the hip bones. As he finished, it was prayer time and he needed to wash his hands, as he had been handling a dog, even though it was a Saluki, which is not regarded as *najis* (unclean) like common curs. There being little water there to waste, he simply dug down into the sand until he reached a moister level and proceeded to 'wash' his hands with the slightly damp sand. After a sumptuous dinner of a whole goat roasted over the fire, as we sat drinking tea around the campfire one of the bedouin said to me in all seriousness that the number of puppies in a litter depended upon the number of ties – one puppy for each tie! I wondered whether this was a reflection of the fact that litters tended to be small. I asked whether they ever cropped the puppies' ears, as is so common in northern Syria. They said they might crop the ears of guard dogs to be more alert, but the Saluki was not a guard dog, so there was no need to crop them.

The bedouin are essentially pragmatic and do not let dogma stand in the way of necessity. This was demonstrated again the next morning, when a sad sight greeted us at Dhifallah's house in the village: the pretty feathered sister of *Warda's* dam appeared with four small furry puppies pursuing her for a feed. She had been mated unintentionally by one of the big guard dogs that hung around there. The puppies were therefore termed '*Luqis*' (crossbreds) and would not be used for hunting, but would be distributed among the shepherds to protect their flocks. Their dam would be kept, as having had a crossbred litter would not affect her usefulness as a hunter.

By coincidence, we found that the track up the Wadi Rum from the village was filled with a cavalcade of vehicles, and Dhifallah discovered they were going to attend the release of a small herd of oryx into an area designated for wildlife. This was too good a photo opportunity to miss, so we raced around the line and got to the site before the release started. Our cameraman managed to shoot some good footage as these large beasts came bounding out of their travelling boxes and raced up a side wadi. I asked the director of the oryx project about hunting in Jordan and he confirmed that all hunting of mammals was banned, but at the same time he admitted that it was difficult to change old habits and to monitor the wilderness. Dhifallah agreed that there would always be some hunting with Salukis for the pot but this was not as big a threat to wildlife as that posed by hunters with guns. In any case, the bedouin liked to have a Saluki or two around, much as they kept a camel or two in the backyard as a symbolic link with their nomadic past.

The film team flew out of Aqaba with lots of colourful footage for the editing room and proceeded to Egypt and the Emirates for some further filming, in which I was not involved. I was called upon again, much later, to help with the film script before the completed version of *The Hunting Hounds of Arabia* was finally screened by National Geographic – not exactly as I would have liked it, but overall it helped to counterbalance some of the false impressions of the Saluki in its native habitat, and for that I was grateful.

I was able to make some further contributions to that same objective throughout that summer. In May, I was invited to speak at the Sighthound World Congress 2002 to celebrate the centenary of the Belgian Sighthound Club at the Sportpark Terjoden, Brussels. I was given a slot on the first day to make an illustrated presentation on the history and development of the Eastern Saluki, which seemed to be well received by the audience, among whom were some of the great names in the European sighthound fraternity.

The next month I was invited to give a similar address at the Saluki Club of America's National Specialty at the Kentucky Horse Park, Lexington. This was a great opportunity to meet many of the Saluki enthusiasts whom I knew so well by name. I was also asked to judge the colourful native costume event, when exhibitors dressed themselves in all sorts of quasi-bedouin gear and paraded with their hounds, some of which looked as if they could have stepped straight out of a bedouin tent. This was followed by an exhibition of desert-bred Salukis, where I saw a number of very familiar-looking hounds, before it was my turn to speak. All the tickets had been sold for the 150-seat theatre, and a very knowledgeable audience kept me going with questions long after the advertised time. The whole event was also filmed and put on sale by SCOA afterwards. So, all in all, I reckoned the desert-bred Saluki had had a very fair hearing in the USA.

I was also able to bang the drum a bit for the desert-bred Saluki at an event the following month while on a visit to Liese's former home in northern Germany. Astrid Soechtig had invited us to Siek, where there was a very well organised racing meeting on a circular track. A notice about my visit had been put up in the clubhouse and a lot of very keen enthusiasts, some with country-of-origin hounds, quizzed me at length about Salukis in the Middle East. Among them was a German couple we had known in Baghdad in 1998, who had brought back a Saluki from Sulaimaniya and had his son there. Small world! Seeing these hounds performing made me long to get back to running my own, but the start of the coursing season was still some months away – and first, Central Asia beckoned again.

My guest is guided through the perils of the night

Chapter Twelve

A Different Perspective

On my first trip to Central Asia the previous year, I had searched in vain in Uzbekistan and Kyrgyzstan for what the Russians call the *Srednoaziatskaya Taza* (the Central Asian Tazy). I had wanted to compare these hounds, of which I had seen only pictures, with Salukis, with which they seemed to have a close similarity. So I devised an itinerary that would take me and a small group of companions along another part of the Silk Road, starting in Kyrgyzstan, continuing through the Uighur Autonomous Region of China and finishing in Kazakhstan. Through the medium of the Internet, I had established contact with some sighthound enthusiasts in Kyrgyzstan and Kazakhstan, so that this time I did not have to leave it to chance to find the hounds.

At the end of August 2002, we landed in Bishkek, Kyrgyzstan at 4.00 am, yet even at this unfriendly hour we received a warm welcome from Almaz Kurmankulov and Nurlan Mamyrov of the Kyrgyz Taigan Society. Almaz kindly accompanied us over the next two days to show us some specimens of this rare breed, starting on a farm on the outskirts of Bishkek that belonged to Manas, a leading breeder of Taigans and horses. As soon as we arrived, a typical black and white Taigan bitch, evidently in whelp, came out to greet us from an enclosure where her five-month-old puppies and a German Shorthaired Pointer puppy that she was fostering were doing their best to climb out to join the commotion. They looked plump and healthy, as their dam was being well fed on the meat and dairy products from the farm. Two of these puppies were going to Spain as a gift to King Juan Carlos, and I wondered what they would make of the very different conditions there. Next to the puppies was a beautiful golden Akhal Teke champion endurance horse, and in the background I could see several more dark shapes of Taigans in the rays of the early morning sun. All were black and white and had the typical broad chest and head and a tight ring in the tail. I collected some hair samples from the females for Dr Peter Savolainen's ongoing study of the mitochondrial DNA of the region's sighthounds. Almaz was carrying his own record with the details of many of the two hundred or so Taigans that he had seen and registered with his society as Kyrgyz Taigans. Each hound had an individual sheet, recording its origins, parents, colour and essential measurements. Drawing on his record, Almaz easily identified most of the hounds I had photographed on my previous visit, including the bitch that had bitten me, which had won a third prize at the annual Taigan show held that November. As we went along, he meticulously added the details of the new hounds that we came across.

Our next stop was to have been the society's own breeding centre near Ak-Terek on Lake Issyk-Kul, but Almaz said that only one bitch was there, as the others had not yet come down from the mountains, where they spent the summer with the nomads. Rather like the practice of transhumance in Switzerland, the flocks and herds were taken up into the high pastures in summer and the Taigans went with them, fattening up on marmots and other game before the onset of winter, when they returned to their villages around the lake. We therefore decided to take the opportunity of observing a different aspect of the Kyrgyz hunting tradition – with eagles. I had hoped we might have the chance to meet Tenti Djamanakov, one of the great eagle hunters, but Almaz said he was too far from our route. So he took us to see another hunter, Zarnai Sagenbai, in the foothills of the Tian Shan Mountains.

We drove for several kilometres on a dirt road that eventually petered out, and we had to continue on foot to where, nestling in a hollow, the hunter's yurts were. As we approached, we were greeted with the screams of a golden eagle sitting on a perch in the late afternoon sunshine. Zarnai and his wife, who was dressed in her colourful Kyrgyz national costume, came out to welcome us. He agreed to put on a demonstration of his skill for us. Dressed in a dark-green velvet cloak with gold braiding round the edge and the typical tall white felt hat of the Kyrgyz, he mounted his sturdy horse with the hooded eagle on his right leather-gloved arm, supported

Zarnai Sagenbai, Berkutchi.

by a wooden two-pronged fork on his saddle. The bird was quiet now in its hood as Zarnai rode up to the top of a rise. He then unhooded it and cast it aloft. The eagle gained height and then plummeted at awesome speed down the valley to where a boy was whirling a lure at the end of a rope. It was only a training flight, but even so it was an impressive display of the eagle's majesty and power. Zarnai said with regret that he was one of only six eagle hunters left in the country, two of whom were his sons, and it was a problem to find others to maintain the tradition. There was no shortage of eagles – indeed, we saw several at close quarters as we continued our journey to Naryn for the night.

We planned to spend the next day meandering slowly up the old Silk Road towards the Torugart Pass into China, taking in half a dozen places on the way where Almaz expected to find Taigans. However, our luck was out, as Almaz established at the first stop that, for a variety of reasons, none was available. So we pressed on to our yurt camp by the old caravanserai at Tash Rabat, where I had seen my first Taigan the year before. On arrival there, Almaz heard about some Taigans with nomads about 30 km up the road towards the border. While the others relaxed, Almaz and I set off with the Russian camp supervisor in his ancient VW Beetle to try and locate them. We soon reached a checkpoint where armed border guards wanted to see our passports, but my companions did not have theirs with them. It looked as if we would be out of luck again, but an officer came over and after some parleying with Almaz in Kyrgyz he pointed towards a white building a few hundred metres away, where he said we would find some Taigans.

We pressed on with a sigh of relief. It was already about 5.00 pm and the light was beginning to fade as we approached the building. Immediately the now familiar shape of a very hairy, almost black Taigan appeared from round a corner. It was followed by a black and tan with a top knot that looked as if it was stiff with gel. Both were bitches and had puppies. Behind the building, I was surprised to see the puppies emerging from a hole in the ground. This was where they had been born and now lived. It took a little while to get used to the idea of Taigans living underground, but the more I thought about it the more I realised what good protection a snug hole would give against the cold nights in the mountains. Each bitch had two puppies and they looked in good condition. As I took some pictures, a young boy came up and offered to show us where there were some more in a nearby valley.

Almaz Kurmankulov, President of the Kyrgyz Taigan Society.

So off we went across country, bouncing over the rough ground and the occasional hard rock. At one point, we sank down in the mud in a gully and had to push the car out. It was getting darker and I was beginning to be worried about how we would find the way back at night. We went on and on, with the snow-capped Tian Shan slowly turning pink in the setting sun, until the boy said at last that we had arrived. We stopped at the edge of a steep bluff and could see below in the valley a single white yurt with smoke rising from its chimney. As we walked down, at least half a dozen Taigans streamed out to meet us. A couple of bitches were accompanied by their roly-poly puppies, grown fat on a diet of marmot caught by their dams and regurgitated to feed them. Another bitch had whelped just two days before, and growled menacingly from her hole in the ground when we came too near. The woman of the yurt paid no attention, simply grabbing hold of her collar and pulling her out so that we could see the three little puppies inside. We were then kept busy measuring, recording and taking hair samples, so that the time flew by. We had to forego the proffered hospitality and retrace our steps to the car, and we just managed to reach the checkpoint again as night fell. To this day, I have no clear idea of where we had been, but I suspect that it was in no-man's land.

We spent the night in yurts at the camp and continued the next morning on the road over the high Torugart Pass into China, but regretfully without Almaz, who had stayed behind to continue his survey of other Taigans in the area. How I wished I had such a dedicated contact as him in China! Although I was armed with a brief in Chinese on what they call *Xigou* ('slender dogs'), my enquiries produced only puzzled looks and shrugged shoulders. I was assured that there were no such dogs in the Uighur Region – indeed, they asked what was the point when there was nothing left to hunt. A walk through the fascinating old bazaar in Kashgar soon revealed stalls laden with the furs of all kinds of exotic animals, such as Arctic fox, lynx, wolf and even a tiger. The owners claimed these came from Siberia, but I dare say some had been hunted on the Chinese side of the Tian Shan. Over the next ten days or so, as we went through the oasis towns along the Silk Road and crossed the forbidding Taklamakan Desert to the verdant Tarim Basin and the legendary tombs at Dunhuang, we did not see a single dog of any description.

The last leg of our journey took us from Urumchi to Almaty, the former capital of Kazakhstan and still its largest city. Konstantin (or Kostya, as he is known) Plakhov, a biologist at the Institute of Zoology, picked me up from our hotel and took me

Roshan and her puppies at Askar Raibayev's, Almaty.

to meet Askar Raibayev, President of the Dog Breeding Federation of Kazakhstan and a big businessman. As we walked into his house, I was totally taken aback by the unexpected sight of *Roshan,* a beautiful black-fringed red bitch suckling her eight puppies in the centre of the room. Equally surprising was the sight of a ginger Siberian cat walking calmly among them. Askar told me about the efforts of his federation to preserve the native breeds of Kazakhstan, not only the Tazy but also the Tobet or Ovcharka, a huge shepherd dog. He himself hunted regularly on his estate with both Tazys for hare, fox and marmot and Tobets for wolves. He kindly offered to take Kostya and me to the Šunkar Breeding Centre, run by Viktor Bulekbayev in the foothills above Almaty. Šunkar (pronounced 'Shunkar') means 'falcon' in Kazakh and the centre has an impressive collection of Central Asian raptors, some perched in airy aviaries and others sitting out on blocks in the sunshine. Some of the birds had been brought there to recover from accidents before being released back into the wild. The centre also bred Tazys and Tobets, and there were some splendid specimens in their well-presented kennels. Several adult Tazys and some delightful cream puppies were also running free in the safe environment of the centre. The dogs were sold for quite high prices to contribute to the running costs of the centre, which seemed to be doing a good job of maintaining the breeds to a high standard.

Back in Almaty again, Liese and I went straight out to lunch with the European Commission delegate, to whom we had an introduction from a mutual friend in Damascus, where he had previously served. Among the other guests was Renato Sala, an Italian archaeologist who had worked for years in Kazakhstan and had made a special study of its ancient rock art. He gave me a beautiful photograph of a petroglyph from about 1100 BC at a famous site called Tamgaly in the Chu-Ili mountains north-west of Almaty, showing a prick-eared, curly-tailed dog attacking a Marco Polo sheep, which looked very like the images I had seen of similar-looking dogs in petroglyphs in Saudi Arabia. He also gave me a plaster reproduction of another one, showing a more Saluki-like long-limbed hound with a long, feathery tail. He made the very interesting point that it was unlikely that the Saluki came originally from the north-east steppes, since it was known to have already been in existence in the Middle East at a time when the steppes were still under the ice cap.

After lunch, Askar sent his car to take Kostya, Liese and me to see some more hounds in Almaty. The first stop looked at first most unpromising – a block of flats – but then a head popped out of a window that looked just like my *Sally*! Living on a balcony on the second floor were two adult, very Saluki-like cream Tazys, with their three three-month-old puppies. It was all a bit congested in the small flat, so we moved on to Kostya's bungalow, set in a yard surrounded by a high corrugated-iron fence. I was struck first by the sight of an enormous red and white Tobet, called *Zhendet*, looking rather like a St Bernard but with cropped ears and tail. Racing around madly and barking was a little terrier, while sitting quietly in a separate pen was a small cream

Tazy apparently of the Turkmen type with her four three-week-old puppies – two cream, one black and white and one red overlaid with black. From the bungalow emerged two quite aggressive male Tazys, one cream and the other a black and tan that looked totally Saluki. Kostya was clearly doing his bit to preserve and promote the Kazakh Tazy.

Tazy in Almaty.

As we flew home later, I could not help thinking about the Kazakhs' claim that their hounds constituted a discrete breed. Having now seen Tazys in the flesh, I could see that some of them showed some superficial differences, e.g. a tendency towards a slightly shorter tail with sparse feathering and a stockier appearance, but their general conformation and characteristics seemed to me to be like those of many Salukis in the Middle East. Clearly some more research was required. I had collected a lot of hair samples for Peter Savolainen's project in the hope that the mtDNA would shed some light on the origins of these hounds.

I got back home in time to take part in another huge demonstration against the proposed Hunting Bill, when over 400,000 protesters marched from Hyde Park to Parliament. It was said to be the biggest demonstration ever to be held in the United Kingdom, but it was soon shown to have been all in vain. In mid-November, the Queen announced in her speech at the opening of the new session of Parliament the government's intention to bring forward a bill to ban hunting with hounds. I joined in another massive protest organised by the Countryside Alliance in mid-December but, barring a miracle, the writing was now on the wall for coursing hare with our Salukis.

Against this background, the Saluki Coursing Club resolved to make the most of the time remaining to it and embarked on its best season ever. Everything went perfectly, with good weather, plentiful hares and large turnouts, so that we were able to run three eight-dog stakes at a time. It was a particularly proud moment for me at the end of the season, when *Filfil* was declared the overall winner of the Knightellington Jacket for the Saluki winning the most courses. Although on the small side, she had such a fighting spirit that she put everything she had into coursing – and she kept our freezer well stocked!

Filfil's success was, however, overshadowed by *Najma*'s increasing infirmity. Her spirit was irrepressible and, despite her painful leg, she was still engaging in battles with the fox and squirrel populations that plagued our garden right up until mid-summer, when a rough encounter with a squirrel reduced her to hobbling. My vet said there was nothing more he could do for her except amputate the leg, and with a heavy heart I had to agree with him that at her age it would be best to end her suffering. It was a terrible wrench to let her go after so many years as such a sweet-tempered member of our family. I was so glad that *Sally* had inherited her nature.

At the start of the new coursing season, *Najma* came back to haunt us in a most peculiar way. A small group from within the Saluki Coursing Club had accepted an invitation from the Portuguese Galgo club to run our hounds against the local Galgos in an experimental trial, which we thought might be repeated in future years to offset some of the effects of the expected hunting ban at home. Adrian Phillips, who had a house in Portugal, set up all the arrangements, and our group assembled at the harbour in Plymouth to take the overnight ferry to Santander in northern Spain. Imagine, then, our consternation when I submitted *Sally* and *Filfil* to the controller to have their microchips read and checked against their pet passports and *Sally's* number was found to be incorrect! I could take her out of the country but not bring her back! I called our vet who had implanted the microchips and it became clear what had happened. *Najma* and *Sally* had been chipped on the same day, and somehow the two sets of registration papers had been mixed up in the clinic, so that *Najma* had *Sally's* pet passport and vice versa. There was nothing to be done in the time available, so we had to abort our trip and, after seeing off the others, drive miserably back home.

Saluki v. two Galgos in Portugal.

However, all was not lost. The other members of the club were holding a big coursing event in Norfolk and we were able to take part there, while my vet sorted out the mess and compensated us for all our trouble.

The group in Portugal was keen that we should go out, but there was no ferry available. So, with the proceeds of our compensation, we parked the hounds with a friend, caught a flight to Portugal and hired a car to take us to a big hunting estate in the Alentejo region of central Portugal. The weather was perfect – sunny, but not too warm because of a keen wind. The sandy running ground was overlain with quite long dry grass, dotted here and there with cork oaks and rocky outcrops, providing plenty of cover for the hares. The home team consisted of five hunters and two gamekeepers on horseback and a slipper on foot, with an assistant behind him ready to bring up the next runners from the horsebox full of Galgos that kept within range on the many well-graded access tracks. There would normally have been three mounted judges, but they had decided not to judge the event as the running style of the two breeds was thought to be incompatible. A Galgo course is largely decided on the run-up, with points being scored only after 35 seconds, provided the course lasts more than 55 seconds – otherwise, it is a no course. Long-range performance and stamina are less important.

Without my two hounds, we could muster only six Salukis; and one was a veteran. We formed a line with the horsemen, put a Galgo in slips with Ian Charlton's *Shiraz* (*Filfil*'s big brother) and set off, not knowing what to expect. The Galgos were reputed to have awesome acceleration out of slips, like Greyhounds, but were less able to manoeuvre, especially on rough ground. However, when the first hare got up, it was *Shiraz* that blasted out of slips first, and never lost the lead to the Galgo over a long course. Salukis 1–Galgos 0. Next came Mike Alsop's *Safi* (*Filfil*'s sister) with a red brindle Galgo. The two hounds came out of slips together and ran side by side, with *Safi* gradually pulling ahead, but the hare disappeared in the long grass before the 55-second limit. By Portuguese reckoning it was a no course, but by ours it was another Saluki win. Robert Belgrave's young dog *Howie*, who had won the SCC puppy stake earlier in the year, was entered against a black and white Galgo. Again, the Saluki led all the way in a long course and pulled the hare down. Salukis 3–Galgos 0. The hare was smaller than the European brown, weighing only about 2 kg and closer in appearance to the Scottish blue, though not in colour. They were very fast over this terrain and gave our hounds a good run.

Next came Adrian Phillips' five-year-old *Qita*, who was never a sprinter and we thought she would not challenge the Galgo, but we were wrong. She certainly trailed several lengths behind as they disappeared around a hilltop, but on the way back she closed the gap and as they raced along a dirt track the lead changed several times and they pulled the hare down together. We reckoned honours were even. We then gave Ian Charlton's *Sandy* (*Filfil's* mother) a go, but the hare ran backwards through the line and the hounds were slipped unsighted. That left only Robert Belgrave's little Iraqi import *Windy* to run against a much bigger Galgo. She exploded out of slips and seemed to leave the Galgo standing as she raced into a big lead down towards a lake, where she appeared to drown the hare! Another win for the Salukis: 4½–½!

By then we had all had enough, and gratefully accepted the Galgo club's invitation to the estate's administrative centre for an enormous typically Portuguese meal. It had been quite a day, and had certainly laid the basis for an annual competition. More coursing was planned for the next day, but the weather changed overnight and the landscape was blotted out by heavy rain. Instead we pottered around seeing the sights of Lisbon, where I found an antique ceramic wine jug with a hound for a handle coursing a hare on the lid – which I thought helped to compensate for the absence of our hounds.

On returning home, I engaged in another busy coursing season. Sadly, the last meeting in Gloucestershire had to be cancelled as the ground was frozen so hard that it was feared that it would put at risk the judge's horse. However, some of us were staying overnight at the farm anyway and, once the sun had come up and thawed out the land a little, we were able to give our hounds a final run on a glorious day. I had to be careful with *Sally* as she was approaching the peak of her season and I intended to mate her with Martine Cazeau's half-Saudi dog *Asayaad Nabzan*; but, though he came to stay with us for a couple of days and was keen, she refused to have him. Sad, as that was her last chance.

That brought the SCC coursing season to a less than satisfactory end. We had had to cope not only with adverse weather and a shortage of hares but also the extra competition for entries in events. The SCC was becoming the victim of its own success, and too many owners were applying for places for their hounds at meetings. To cope with the demand, we had to put on more three eight-dog stakes and sometimes there were not enough hares, but it all helped to keep up interest in a working breed that was under existential threat in the UK.

A few weeks later, I was back in Morocco to see some more hounds under an existential threat of a different kind. Liese and I took a couple of friends who did not know Morocco to stay in one of the beautiful *riad*s in the old quarter of Marrakesh, owned by a French friend of ours. *Riad* means literally 'garden' but it has come to be used for the old houses built around a central garden that have been converted into small boutique hotels. They are very evocative of traditional Morocco, but provide a high standard of comfort and cuisine. It made an excellent base for exploring not only the delights of Marrakesh but also the surrounding area of the Atlas Mountains. It was also within easy distance of Chemaia, near where we had filmed two years before.

My Moroccan veterinary friend was expecting us to visit him and he took us back to the village of Si Ali Mousa, where we had shot some of the film. As we came into the dusty central square, familiar faces greeted us and we were welcomed back like old friends. I had brought copies of photographs I had taken the previous time and the villagers were thrilled to have them. But I did not recognise any of their hounds – they were all new young ones. I asked what had happened to the others and was told that they had died; yet, almost in the same breath, they told me that their hounds normally lived to ten or 11 years! I guessed that, as in other parts of the Arab world, where people live at bare subsistence level, they simply did not retain beyond hunting age those hounds that could no longer earn their keep, but either gave them away or turned them out to fend for themselves.

Although they were so poor, the villagers quickly served fresh pancakes and mint tea, and pressed us to take eggs as gifts. We moved on to one of the Nuwasir villages where we had also filmed, and had a similarly warm reception. Here too, I could not recognise any of the hounds from before – they were all new, but already very well trained. They did their owners' bidding or posed quietly for my camera in such a harmonious atmosphere, though I wondered where they would be in two or three years' time.

I contrasted this atmosphere with something rather different a couple of months later, when I was using my Russian language to guide some friends around Moscow and St Petersburg. I had made contact through the Internet with a Tazy breeder in the latter city and took the opportunity of visiting her briefly one afternoon. It was an unforgettable experience. She lived alone on the seventh floor of a hideous grey, graffiti-daubed block of flats in a desolate estate of similar blocks, with six mature Tazys that seemed to fill every available space. She was passionate about her hounds, which,

In the village square at Si Ali Mousa.

despite the unsuitable environment, had won many trophies and awards for coursing as well as showing. She would take them by train, one or two at a time, to events all over Russia. They looked fit and well, but this urban existence clearly required great sacrifices from their owner as well as a high degree of adaptation by the hounds.

That winter, with the hunting ban looming closer, we pulled out all the stops to have as full a coursing programme as possible. Almost every other weekend from October until 17 February 2005 – the day before the hunting ban took effect – we either held an official event or did some rough coursing. We were determined to enjoy every last moment while we could.

I was slightly handicapped for a while mid-season, when *Sally* had a nasty accident. We were walking through some parkland near my home when suddenly a fox ran across our path. I had just put *Filfil* on the lead and was about to clip *Sally* on too, but I was too late. She shot away after the fox and disappeared into a dense clump of bushes. Then I heard a scream of pain and the sound of a car skidding. *Sally* came running back, but I could see she had a wound in her shoulder and was in shock – only the adrenalin was keeping her going. Fortunately, my car was nearby and I soon got her

Natalia Leshchikova and her Tazys in St Petersburg.

home to inspect her properly. I guessed that she must have collided sideways-on with a car, since 'HONDA' was spelt out in black on her thigh. I feared she had done some internal damage to her shoulder and took her immediately to the vet, who diagnosed no broken bones but a deep wound that needed stitching and some bruising along her ribs. It was a lucky escape, and a month later she was coursing again. But it was the end of an era and we needed to reflect on how to cope with the ban.

by my brightly burning fire or by the barking of my dogs,

Chapter Thirteen

The Way Ahead

The hunting ban took effect at the end of the 2004–5 coursing season, so we had plenty of time before the following winter to work out a new strategy for preserving the characteristics of our breed. We held a meeting under the auspices of the Countryside Alliance with representatives of the other sighthound coursing clubs, where the atmosphere was very gloomy. The cause looked hopeless unless the government could be persuaded to repeal the law – and there were no prospects of a change of heart in the short term. The law did present some possibilities for using dogs to flush game to guns or to falcons, and we would have to consider with landowners whether we could work something out without falling foul of the restrictions.

In the meantime, I had a very full programme of overseas visits in view. I had been planning a return visit to Syria with Robert Belgrave, a member of the SCC who was keen on importing a Syrian Saluki to Italy to join his Iraqi import. But the news from the region was increasingly disheartening and we came close to aborting the trip. My long experience of the region encouraged me to think, however, that the situation always looked worse on the outside and I knew that, once in Syria, we would be in the safe hands of old friends – and so it proved to be.

Syria, like England, was experiencing a late, rather cold and wet winter, and the signs of spring were hard to find. The mountains between Syria and Lebanon were still draped with a thick covering of snow that fed the Barada River, flowing cold and grey through Damascus. The penetrating wind was cold, too, and I was glad I had brought warm clothes. We were met by Basil Jadaan, President of the Syrian Arab Horse Association, who also bred Salukis. He had kindly arranged a programme over the next few days to introduce us to some of the Saluki breeders, together with Micaela Lehtonen of the well-known Qashani Saluqis kennel in Finland and her Danish surgeon friend, Dr Kristina Strålman. After a lightning tour of the sights of Damascus and an introduction to some of the culinary delights, Basil took us off the next morning to see his own hounds, housed temporarily in kennels on a building site while new purpose-built kennels were being constructed elsewhere. We were welcomed by two very friendly smooth tricolour two-year-old siblings, called *Ghazal* and *Tayra*, originally from Hama, north of Damascus. They were typical of so many of the hounds we were to see later in and around Hama and Aleppo – small by British standards, light, athletic and with cropped ears. The bitch had only one ear cropped, as is often the case. Both hounds were remarkably relaxed with strangers as, with the assistance of Dr Strålman, I began collecting hair samples and mouth swabs for Dr Savolainen's sighthound study in Sweden. This calm reaction to the somewhat intrusive handling to which we subjected them was a notable feature of the hounds that we encountered and spoke volumes for their stable temperament.

However, the calm was soon interrupted by a bouncy five-month-old smooth black-masked red male puppy called *Khattaf*, that was destined to join Micaela in Finland. He, too, came from a well-known breeder in Hama, to where we were soon to head. The scene was completed by about half a dozen boisterous two-month-old Turkish Kangal puppies, frolicking in their kennels. These huge guard dogs have a reputation for ferocity and I had had occasion before to be wary of them, but as puppies they were easy to handle and to take DNA samples from. We were to see their huge sire later near Hama, and there was no question of taking a mouth swab from him! He was on a stud farm, where we stopped for a traditional bedouin meal with a local shaikh, who was prominent in the Syrian Arab Horse Association. After lunch, he laid on a parade of some of his finest horses as well as something different. He bred all kinds of pigeon, for which his daughter made pretty earrings of coloured beads that were threaded through the ear socket on one side.

After heavy overnight rain, the next day – a Friday and the local weekend – was fine and bright for a visit to the Hama racetrack, where many of the Arabians we had seen were trained and raced at that time (all that has stopped in the present civil war).

We had come to see some Salukis kept there, including *Tayra*, the smooth red dam of Micaela's new puppy, and two of her other puppies – a smooth red bitch and a white dog with almost orange ears. They were so cute that it was difficult to prise my companions away, but we needed to move on to the farm of one of my old friends, Ghanem al-Barazi. He showed us first a litter that had been born the day before and then two beautiful red puppies, a bitch and a dog with a fine white blaze. Kristina immediately fell for the dog and Ghanem, with typical Arab generosity, offered it to her as a present. What none of us knew at the time was that the puppy was sick and a few days later, despite heroic efforts by the new owner and a vet in Damascus, it died, probably of parvo. Kristina was heartbroken.

Ghanem's puppies in Hama.

It was then approaching midday and the hunters were returning from a morning's coursing in the area around Hama. As we arrived at one house, a small car pulled up and an incredible number of men and hounds tumbled out. Suddenly there were hounds bounding about everywhere, glad to stretch their legs again. It had been a meagre hunt, with only one hare between them, as a heavy squall had cut short the proceedings. Among the hounds were a smooth black and tan dog in a colourful coat and *Jinah*, a powerful smooth cream dog, who had sired the sick puppy. On we went to another house, where we saw three nice bitches with another handsome black and tan puppy wearing a beautiful beaded collar, made by gypsies. Ghanem then took us off to lunch in Hama within sight of the ancient Roman wooden waterwheels that once lifted water from the Orontes River into a network of aqueducts serving the town; but now they are merely a tourist attraction and turn with a mournful creaking and groaning. Suddenly, in burst another old friend, Abu al-Ward, who was a mine of information on Salukis. Without hesitation, he rattled off the three-generation pedigree of Micaela's new puppy, *Khattaf*, and set out plans for us to see other breeders on our way north to Aleppo the next day.

While the others rested, Ghanem took me to the Barazi clan's imposing *majlis*, which I had visited before but to which it was always a pleasure to return to meet the other people who had dropped in for a chat and to exchange news with them. It was by then about 9.30 on a cold and wet night, and we still had to go to another stud farm about 25 km from Hama. We followed a slippery, muddy cross-country route to the farm, where our host received us in a large black bedouin tent – with space heaters! Here we tucked into another great mound of mutton and rice, while the talk went on about horses and Salukis. I tried to explain how we coursed back home, but the idea of a competition to test the hounds rather than merely to catch the hare was very strange to them. With my head spinning with all the sights and talk of the day, I finally got to my bed about midnight.

It was raining hard the next morning when my old friends came to collect us for the short drive to Sawran, but by the time we arrived the sun was out again and we could enjoy the local hounds. At the first house, the yard had a mud-brick kennel with a car tyre in the middle as a doorway, through which tumbled several puppies, among them one particularly strong specimen. He was snapped up immediately afterwards by the agent of a Saudi prince from Riyadh, who, we discovered later, was following us around and buying up all the hounds we admired most – for huge sums, by local standards. The drain of Syrian Salukis for hunting and racing in the Arabian Peninsula was already under way.

In the next village of Khan Shaikhoon, one breeder had a wide selection of hounds, including a striking red grizzle youngster that did a prodigious jump over the yard wall to join the other Salukis running loose outside. There was also a nice smooth red puppy that ended up in the boot of Ghanem's car as a gift, no doubt to replace

Original kennel in Sawran.

the one he had given to Kristina. One of the breeders explained his breeding practice in familiar terms. He never inbred, as experience had shown that the offspring were never as efficient as the parents. He preferred to take his bitch to a good dog when she was about two years old. For him a good Saluki was an efficient hunter with a long muzzle, a wide and deep chest, strong thighs, straight long front legs, small tight feet and a whippy tail. He started hunting with the bitches at about 10–11 months, but held the dogs back until they were a year or even 18 months old. He normally cropped the ears at about one to two months, but he could not explain why – it was just customary. The hounds did not normally retrieve, which was hardly surprising as, usually, several hounds were released at once and would dispute the kill, unless prevented.

On we went to another breeder, with a handsome but lethargic cream dog. It is rare to see sick Salukis but this was obviously one. The hounds are not usually vaccinated or inoculated and, if one falls sick, it either recovers or dies. At the next house was something I have never seen before or since – a display of pairs of hares' ears spread out in a pattern over a window grille as trophies of the chase! There were some beautiful lightly feathered tricolour hounds there, but we were summoned inside for tea. Micaela and Kristina were taken into the harem, where they had a hilarious time trying to make themselves understood with sign language. We could have gone on to see other breeders but we still had a long drive to Aleppo, where we arrived in time for a late lunch by a tinkling fountain in a beautifully converted khan. Our host was one of the big horse breeders and we had to go and see some of his stables before we could finally relax and digest the impressions of a crowded day.

Farmstead near Zirbeh.

The next morning was beautiful and we drove to Zirbeh, a small town about 25 km from Aleppo, from where we took a dirt track that led to a small farmstead, and were greeted by a feathered cream Saluki that popped out of a beehive-shaped kennel. About another half-dozen Salukis emerged and ran around, one of them retrieving a tortoise to us. Carpets were produced and, as we sat drinking tea, the owner confirmed that he, too, never inbred but went out to a hound that was capable of catching up to five hares a day. I asked whether he culled the old hounds and he was rather upset, saying that he never culled the old or the young, since it was against the teaching of Islam. So I asked why there were never any old hounds around. He replied that he sometimes had hounds that lived to at least ten years and they simply lived on the farm until they died. His regime for healthy hounds was simple – milk and eggs up to the age of seven months, when they switched to a diet of pitta bread and olive oil. They looked fine on it and he promised we would see them run the next day.

On the way back, we dropped in at another farmstead that was positively alive with Salukis of all ages, milling around among the poultry as small children fed them scraps from the kitchen. Robert Belgrave was so taken with one smooth grizzle puppy, despite it having one cropped ear, that he refused to part with it until I told him the owner was asking $1,000 for it! However, he was so smitten that, later on, he arranged to acquire the puppy and she joined him in Italy and eventually in England.

The Scandinavians were going back to Damascus at this point, whereas Robert and I were going to continue around Syria. But first we were to enjoy some coursing in the area of Zirbeh with Qayyad, a bedouin guide, and Ahmad, the son of our horse-breeder host who was keen on acquiring some Salukis. Our transport was late to pick us up so, by the time we reached the farmstead, all but the farmer and one Saluki had already left. A young lad on a motorbike appeared and took the remaining Saluki on a lead to try to catch up with the others, while we followed behind, picking up three more Salukis as we went. I was amazed that the Saluki trotted beside the motorbike, but it was clearly accustomed to it. That is how many of the hunters work with their hounds these days, as I was soon to discover. We had to abandon our vehicle as it could not negotiate the rutted track and Robert and I mounted pillion behind two hunters and took off across country with the Salukis running alongside us.

Soon we reached a suitable area of rocky outcrops between fields of sprouting winter wheat and olive trees and began walking up, with three hounds on slip leads and one running loose, searching for signs of hares. Signs there were aplenty, but in the space of about two hours we did not put up a single hare. However, Qayyad maintained that he could take us to a gypsy encampment where there were at least 50 Salukis, and we could go hunting there in the afternoon. Robert dropped out to go sightseeing in Aleppo, where I had been many times before, and I went on with Qayyad and Ahmad north of Aleppo towards the Turkish border. I soon discovered that Qayyad was prone to exaggeration – there was no gypsy encampment! We stopped to make enquiries in a village, where the people were all Turkomans, and were told that everyone was out hunting with their hounds and only a couple of puppies remained. One of them was a smooth almost black bitch and Ahmad was so enchanted with her that, after a great deal of haggling, he bought her and popped her in the boot of my car.

We continued north and in the next village heard a similar story – everyone was out hunting. I was beginning to feel it was pointless going on and was all for turning back but Qayyad, probably to save face, persuaded me that it would be different in the next village. Here a lad on a motorbike suddenly appeared from the hunt, with two hounds running beside him. These two hounds were coal-black and looked in terrific condition. A tractor then pulled up carrying a hare that they had just caught. With the sun beginning to set, more and more hunters were drifting back with an array of impressive hounds. Ahmad kept asking which ones I thought were best and I pointed out a couple that looked particularly good, but their owners were not interested in parting with them. However, a young man said he had two at home and took us to see them – a pretty feathered black and tan bitch and her sibling, a smooth bluish-grey grizzle bitch, both with intact ears. They were about 14 months old and looked well made, though on the small side. Ahmad went into another haggle and ended up buying them both. They went into the boot, and the puppy sat on Qayyad's lap as we drove back to the stables in Aleppo. I heard later that Ahmad went back to the village and bought the two hounds I had pointed out, plus another one, to form the nucleus of the hunting pack he intended to establish on his father's stud farm.

The next morning, Robert and I set out to take a meandering route across northern Syria, through small towns and villages along the Euphrates that were seized by the so-called Islamic State in more recent times. Our objective was Qamishli, close to the border with Iraq, where I had an introduction to the shaikh of the Tai tribe, who are famed throughout the Arab world for their hospitality and generosity. The shaikh maintained the high traditions of the tribe and, sending his son to bring us to his *majlis*, he saw to our every need. The Tai extend across a large area of north-eastern Syria and were once great hunters on their Arabians with falcons and Salukis. At the time of our visit they still bred Arabians, but times had changed and they had become farmers hunting on motorbikes and the only falcons they had were those they trapped to sell to the Gulf.

The shaikh summoned some of his men to take us out hunting the next morning. Two were already waiting for us at the *majlis* with two very athletic smooth hounds with cropped ears, a bluish-grey grizzle and a cream. Then two men rode up on a motorbike with the pillion rider holding a sack from which a Saluki head peeped out – a lightly feathered cream dog with hennaed feet. This was our team. They rode in a pickup and we drove some way behind from Qamishli near to one of the great archaeological mounds that dot the landscape, where they had caught three hares a few days before. They must have denuded the area for, though we walked up for a couple of hours, we had no luck. We could not continue as the shaikh had arranged a huge traditional meal for us and some of the tribal elders back at the *majlis*, and after that we began the long way back to Damascus via ancient Palmyra, stopping briefly en route at a wayside café, where the road branched towards Iraq. Here we found that the young owner was also a falconer and he showed us the skilfully made snares that he used to trap passager falcons on their first migration in the autumn.

Before leaving Syria, I had one more stud farm to visit near Damascus airport, where there were some Salukis whose DNA I wanted to collect. Here I found a heavily pregnant pretty little feathered black and tan bitch and her feathered red mate. They lacked proper attention and I managed to arrange some comfort for them so that the expected puppies would have a better chance of survival. The Syrian Arab Horse Association, through its Saluki sub-section, was then making great efforts to promote the preservation of the Saluki, but clearly some of the newer breeders were still in need of guidance.

Shortly after returning home, I had to seek attention for my own hounds. They were so pleased to have me back and to resume our long walks, but they ran into trouble almost immediately. There was a great commotion in a clump of bushes and I found them standing over a fox that had clearly put up quite a fight. Both my hounds were bleeding from bites and were hopping with fleas and, I suspected, mites too, as the fox had mange. I had to give them a quick disinfectant bath and take them to the vet for some antibiotic shots.

Before the opening of the SCC's modified winter season, I had some further exciting prospects abroad. Liese and I love all things Persian and have travelled quite widely in Iran, but we had not explored the north-west corner, especially the province of Kordestan, as it is called there. In September 2005, we managed to put that right. I already had a fair idea of the topography, and more particularly of the Kurds and their hounds, from my experience of the adjacent area of Kurdistan across the border in Iraq, from where I had acquired my first Salukis. I was curious to see whether the Kurds in Iran bred similar hounds.

But on the way from Tehran by road, we wanted first to visit the outstanding Sasanian bas-reliefs of hunting scenes at Taq-e Bostan, about seven kilometres north-east of Kermanshah, to see whether they might show Tazis. These large rock carvings probably date from the reign of Khosrow II (590–628 AD) and decorate the walls of a grotto above a pool of clear water. One wall is covered with the pictorial narrative of a royal stag hunt. In the upper layer the mounted king, under a parasol surrounded by his courtiers, surveys the stags as they are driven from three pens by beaters on elephants into a corridor leading into a large enclosure or deer park. In the middle layer, he is shown riding among the stags and shooting them with arrows. In the bottom layer, the dead animals are being taken away. A dog appears to be involved, but it is indistinct. The opposite wall is badly eroded but appears to show scenes of a boar hunt in a swamp. So, no Tazis there, but we were soon to see plenty.

Margret Tamp, an old friend living with her Tazis and horses in Tehran, and Ali Golshan, a wildlife writer and photographer, came to meet us in Sanandaj in the heart of Kordestan, and took us to see Jamil Tavana'i, a famous marathon runner, and his father Sherif, who had once been a member of Iran's Olympic equestrian team. Together they were also famous for their Tazis, as they called them in Persian, though in their Sorani Kurdish dialect they used the word *Tanji*, just as they do across the border in Iraq. Jamil said he had good contacts with the Kurdish breeders over there for his planned Tazi breeding centre. But first he wanted to show us his hounds.

I had never imagined the scene that opened up before us as we went through a rough wooden door set in a nondescript adobe wall. Tazis of all ages, sizes and colours bounded forward to greet us. There must have been about 20 in the dusty courtyard, though it was difficult to keep count as the hounds kept going in and out of the surrounding rooms and former stables. I would certainly not lack DNA samples here! The youngest were two eight-week-old puppies from a very nice feathered red bitch. She had had 12, of which one had died and the rest had been

Puppy in the bread basin.

farmed out to be raised by breeders in the villages. Jamil said he also had a number of other hounds that were out with shepherds in the countryside. This was a mutually beneficial arrangement, since they took over the raising of the puppies and got them into good hunting condition by chasing and turning wolves that attacked the flocks for the massive guard dogs to finish off.

In the courtyard were also two feathered puppies, about three months old, with their black and white dam, and two slightly older puppies that were smooth, confirming that smooth hounds did exist in Iran. Jamil said he used to run the small puppies on chickens, as this gave him a good idea of the ones that would be the best hunters. He also believed that, by picking them up by the tail soon after birth and looking at the way the skin wrinkled downwards, he could tell which were going to be the strongest. A mature black dog with a white bib looked particularly useful, and Jamil said he was his best hound, capable of hunting six to seven hares in a day. I also liked the look of an unusual smoky-grey and white dog. Some of the hounds had cropped ears, which Jamil said he did not like, but it was usually done when the puppies were in the villages. Sherif interjected that those with short-cropped ears usually died young because the rain got in! Two hounds stood out in the melee – a strongly built white dog with black patches, which Jamil said was not a purebred Tazi but was an excellent hunter, and a little white terrier, which was also useful at times. He promised we would see some of them run later in the day when it was cooler; but first they had to be fed. He had an arrangement with a local restaurant whereby they gave him all the leftovers from their tables and he walked around the yard doling out handfuls of mixed food. In a corner was a basin of hard pitta bread for those that still felt hungry.

Then we had to go to his house, as he had something special to show us. In a sitting-room decorated with cups, medals and certificates from his marathon days, he outlined his plans for the future of Tazis in Kordestan. He had obtained official authorisation, funds and a piece of land from the government for the construction of a Tazi breeding centre in Sanandaj. Building would start later that year, to his own design. He showed us the plans for the 800-square metre plot, which included, down one side of a central courtyard, a series of covered kennels with outside runs for bitches in season or in whelp; across the top end, store rooms and a kitchen; and, down the other side, a large covered winter enclosure. He had clearly prepared the project very carefully and had done remarkably well in persuading the authorities, who were generally antipathetic towards dogs, to be so generous; but then he was a national hero! The only doubt I had was whether there was a sufficient demand for Tazis to justify breeding on this scale. However, he seemed confident that, as he would be producing only the finest purebred specimens with appropriate documentation, he would find a market for them, both in Iran and abroad. I told him about the Arabian Saluki Center in Abu Dhabi, which had similar objectives and was flourishing.

Over an enormous meal in a restaurant that was almost entirely taken up with a Kurdish wedding party, Jamil spoke about his approach to Tazis. He said that he kept his hounds for hunting until they were about five years old, after which he sent them back to the villages, and preferred males for their strength and consistency. He once had one that lived to 15, but he admitted that they were often turned out to fend for themselves and died from lack of food or as a result of accidents or poisoning. Though he had some smooths, he had a general preference for feathered hounds as they withstood the winter better, when he would sometimes spend a month hunting in the Azerbaijan provinces of Iran. In fact, none of the hounds that I saw were particularly well feathered. He used henna to toughen their pads rather than for beautification. He believed in worming twice a year and had just dosed his hounds before the start of the hunting season. For ticks, he used a mixture of washing powder and washing-up liquid. For mange, he used a mixture of old engine oil and salt. He never stitched wounds that the hounds could reach by licking, only those on the head or neck. He let the hounds eat cooked chicken bones and, twice a week, gave them soft sheep bones to chew for cleaning their teeth. He hunted right through winter and the hounds had no problem with the snow, provided there was not a layer of ice underneath it.

We met again around 5.00 pm and followed his small car, in which were crammed four men with four Tazis in the boot, out of the town and into the hills. We arrived at a small farmstead, where the hounds were released and promptly flopped into the nearest water channel to cool off for, although it was mid-September, it was still quite hot and it must have been stifling in the boot. There was his favourite black dog, a red sable, a cream, and a cream particoloured that was coming out for the first time. We set off, walking over the surrounding hills covered with golden stubble but, though we walked for an hour, the only course was out of sight, when two of the hounds caught a fox. It was time to turn back, but two of the hounds were missing. Jamil showed his old skills by running straight up a hillside like a mountain goat to see where they were. He came back with one, but the particoloured novice refused to come to him and went off on its own. He left and said he would come back later for it.

We were supposed to meet early the next morning to do some serious hunting, but Jamil and his friends turned up late. They had been out in the evening and again early in the morning to recover the missing hound, but to no avail. They thought it would eventually make for the farmstead when it was hungry and could be caught. So we set off when it had already become quite hot and we had more than an hour's drive ahead of us to the villages where Jamil kept some of his hounds. At last, we turned off the asphalt onto a dirt track for several miles until we were far out into the countryside in the area of Bokan. We stopped at a place where a small stream ran under the track. The four hounds in the boot were let out and again made straight for the water. Jamil went off to collect a local guide and another Tazi and we finally began walking up when the sun was high overhead. Old Sherif went off at a cracking pace with the favourite black dog at his side. The others walked steadily in a wide arc over the undulating fields of stubble with another black Tazi with feathered ears and a smooth tail, the smoky-grey Tazi that I had admired, a crop-eared white male and a powerful cream male from the village. But it seemed to me to be too hot for anything to be stirring, and after an hour or so they agreed to call it a day. Back at the cars, the hounds collapsed into the water again as we said our farewells and headed north.

Our first objective was the nearby great Zoroastrian site called Takht-e Soleiman ('Solomon's Throne'), a partly restored series of fire temples and other religious buildings inside high walls encircling a lake of clear blue but highly mineralised water, but we were still on the edge of Kordestan and I kept my eyes peeled for Tazis. We were nearing the site through a well-watered valley when suddenly the driver, who was by then thoroughly indoctrinated, jammed on the brakes and pointed to something he

Cooling off.

had spotted in his rear-view mirror – a handsome smooth red Tazi with cropped ears had appeared briefly on the road before turning away into a field. This prompted me to ask of an artist painting copies of excavated pottery at the site whether there were any Tazis in the vicinity. His face lit up and he told me that he used to have Tazis and had been a keen hunter. He wrote down the name of a breeder in one of the nearby villages on our route where we would find some.

The entrance to the village presented a bucolic scene of girls in colourful costumes chatting and laughing as they washed clothes in the fast-running stream. One of them volunteered to guide us to the breeder's house through the narrow, dusty lanes. By then a crowd had gathered, and in the middle of them appeared a young lad with a pale red and white feathered male Tazi and a girl with an obvious crossbred, both dogs with cropped ears. I wished we had had more time to explore more of the surrounding Kurdish villages but, although we lingered for a while after an irresistible impromptu invitation to a Kurdish wedding, we had to press on.

We did stop en route to Tehran to admire the great domed mausoleum of the Mongol Sultan Oljeitu at Sultaniyeh, the magnificent mosques of Tabriz, the Assassins' former stronghold of Alamut and the former Safavid capital of Qazvin, where in living memory the Turkoman people once hunted foxes with Tazis for their fur. However, it was not until we reached Tehran and the relaxing garden of Margret Tamp that we were once again in the company of Tazis. She had six: *Toufan*, a big black with white male, and his black-fringed red sibling *Sam*, which I had last seen as puppies about eight years before; a fawn with white five-year-old male and his similar dam; a red with white bitch and another old fawn bitch that stayed asleep in her bed the whole time. Margret and Ali Golshan, who had been with us in Sanandaj, had arranged to take me on an expedition to Firuzkuh, a small town about 120 km north-east of Tehran, where they promised to show me something quite extraordinary.

From Firuzkuh we took a narrow, winding road through a valley called Tang-e Vashi, down which ran a fast-flowing stream. It was a Friday and the road was full of happy Tehranis heading for picnics by the cool waters of the stream. We were equipped with rubber boots because our objective was some way up the valley, where the path from the road was replaced by a torrent of water tumbling through a narrow cleft in the mountains. Trying not to fill my boots with the icy water as I clambered over the slippery boulders, I was glad when we arrived at last at a rocky platform from where, across the torrent, I could see a large bas-relief carved into the smooth rock face. It

Bas-relief at Tang-e Vashi, Firuzkuh.

showed the mounted figure of Baba Khan, recognisable by his famous long beard, out hunting deer with his companions and a whole pack of running and leaping Tazis. Baba Khan became the second Qajar Shah of Iran and took the name Fath Ali Shah on his coronation, ruling from 1797 to 1834. The sculpture is therefore about 200 years old, but much of the detail remains remarkably fresh, even to the feathering on the Tazis' ears. Remarkably little is known of its history, but it is believed that at Firuzkuh there may have been a Sasanian royal hunting enclosure, like the one depicted at Taq-e Bostan, and it is possible, therefore, that the Qajars continued the practice of hunting in a deer park, choosing to commemorate their exploits in the living rock. It was certainly a spectacular note on which to end our visit to Iran but, taken with our more prosaic hunting exploits in Kordestan, it was also a reminder of the continuity of the Tazi in the country.

I did not have much time to dwell on such thoughts as, two days after returning home, I was airborne again, back to the Middle East. After I had firmed up our plans for Iran, I had received an invitation from my friend Basil Jadaan, President of the Syrian Arabian Horse Association, to judge their first-ever Saluki show to be held in Damascus on 23–24 September 2005 in the context of their annual horse show.

The dates were somewhat inconvenient, but it was too good an opportunity to miss and I went. I had heard on my previous visit to Damascus in the spring about the association's establishment of a Saluki section and a registry, heavily influenced by their experience with the Arabians. It struck me as very ambitious to be organising so soon a Saluki show, but the Arabs are great at improvisation and I felt sure it would all come together in the end, though probably not without a few hitches – and so it proved to be.

I had travelled out in the company of the British horse judges, David Angold, with his wife, and David and Joanna Maxwell, and I was glad of their support and advice in making the arrangements at the venue, which was a huge covered horse arena. I discovered there that I was to be assisted by an old coursing friend from Hama, Abdulhamid, and Ahmad, a Syrian horse judge; neither had any experience of judging at a Saluki show, but Abdulhamid knew Salukis and Ahmad knew horses. I reminded myself that Arabic hunting and equestrian literature draws a close similarity between the conformation of the Saluki and the Arabian. One often-repeated story runs:

The Abbasid Caliph al-Ma'mun ordered one of his men to the desert to find him a good horse. The man replied, 'I know nothing of horses.' 'Are you not an expert on hounds?' 'Yes.' 'Then look for everything which you would aim for in a good well bred hound and look for the same in the horse.' (Allen and Smith, 1975). So I went forward to the show without too many qualms about my assistants' ability.

The horse show opened the next morning with a colourful pageant of Arab horsemanship, which delighted the large crowd of weekend spectators, and was followed by the British judges evaluating a series of classes of horse. Meanwhile, I found, tied up in the shade outside the arena, the poor Saluki contestants, mostly unattended, so I had a sneak preview of the hounds. However, I was totally unprepared for their eventual appearance in the ring. I had been told that we would judge just two classes – bitches of all ages first and dogs of all ages second. After the start of the Saluki show was announced to the public, the huge double doors into the arena were thrown open and in poured all the Salukis and their handlers, some of whom held up to three hounds, with the entry numbers dangling from the hounds' collars!

There was total chaos and confusion as the contestants ran in different directions around the arena. It took my assistants and me some time to gather them altogether in one place and to explain to them that there should be only one hound per handler; that they should first parade in the same direction around the ring; and that the dogs

A young hopeful with his crop-eared hound.

should then exit the arena to allow us to judge the bitches. It was too late to find numbered armbands for the handlers and we had to judge the entrants with their number hanging from their collar. The hounds were a mixed bunch. Most were unprepared for showing and in poor condition, with harsh coats from sleeping rough; most had cropped ears; one bitch was clearly just getting over a pregnancy; and they were of all ages, from puppies to veterans. In a way, this made the task of judging easier because the best three hounds really did stand out and my two assistants and I were quickly unanimous in our decisions. It was only afterwards that I learnt from Abdulhamid that the winning dog, a superbly built feathered red hound, belonged to my old friend Abu al-Ward from Hama, who had that very day been transferred to hospital in Damascus with leukaemia. I hoped the news of his hound's success would be some consolation.

Clearly, I had to set out some guidelines for the Syrian Horse Association's organisers on how to run a Saluki show, if they intended to make this an annual event. In fact, they wisely decided not to repeat the experiment, as the country's Saluki breeders needed first to be better informed about the purpose of showing. The association had managed to do this very successfully with the horse breeders since its establishment in 2002, and would, indeed, host the World Arabian Horse Organisation's conference in Damascus in 2006, but it had taken a lot of time and effort on the part of the association's small central staff, and they had not had the resources to invest similarly in the Saluki scene.

However, no such restrictions applied to my host, Basil Jadaan, the association's president. After the show was over, he took me to see his new kennels on a sort of farm outside Damascus. Here, a hillside was being terraced and planted out with olive and fruit trees and, at the bottom on a dusty flat area, brick-built kennels with outside pens provided accommodation for eight mature Salukis and two puppies. The hounds were released and raced around. I recognised among them the smooth black and tan bitch called *Tayra* that had easily won the first prize at the Saluki show. They were supervised by a farm worker who lived in an adjacent house, so I hoped they would have the social contact that Salukis needed, if they were not to become total pack animals. But, even as I flew home, my thoughts were already turning to a totally different canine scene in Europe.

Although I had studied the Russian language many years before, circumstances had always prevented me from visiting the country and, following *perestroika*, my first opportunity arose only in 2004, when I visited Moscow, St Petersburg and Novgorod. As already mentioned, while in St Petersburg I had met Natalia Leshchikova and her Tazys, which whetted my appetite to learn more about these hounds. As so often happens in life, a chance came out of the blue. In the summer of 2005, Natalia passed on an invitation from Lena Kojeva, also of St Petersburg, to attend the All-Russia Sighthound Breeds Wild Hare Hunting Competition near Tambov, some 620 km south-east of Moscow, on 21–27 October. I responded positively and then began a long exchange of emails as we worked on the details.

As I was to discover more directly as soon as I arrived in Moscow, Russia seems to function by means of networks. Lena met me at the airport, but the Moscow network of hunting sighthound enthusiasts had arranged for us to be collected by Vladimir Petrov, who drove us through appalling weekend traffic right across Moscow to his flat overlooking a vast wooded park. Here I was greeted by his wife Olga, who welcomed me to stay with them – and their three hunting Borzois – during that weekend. We were joined by Lada Ponamareva, a biologist, artist and expert on Russian sighthounds, of which she had indeed a large collection, as I was to discover later. In this company, I could not have wished for a better introduction to the hounds I was shortly to meet.

The next day was cold but bright and, after a long walk in the woods with Olga and the Borzois, I was taken by Lena and Lada at about noon to a display, improvised by Lada, of the gamut of sighthounds on a kind of heath in the woods. This was absolutely fascinating! Here I could see in one go the subtle connections between the breeds as they progressed from some desert-bred Salukis originally from Israel to the very similar Hortayas, distinguished by their roseate ears, to the South Russian Steppe Hounds, Tazys, Taigans, Kalagh Tazis and Bakhmuls, with only the Borzois looking noticeably different, but still easily identifiable with this general family.

Olga had prepared for us an enormous meal of Russian specialities, at which we were joined by Marina Kuzina, the Secretary of the Russian Branch of the Primitive and Aboriginal Dog Society (R-PADS) and a Laika expert. Together we all talked dogs and hunting until late and I was told about the arrangements for the following day – when, after an early visit to one of the Moscow hunting fraternity's great characters, Lena, Lada and I, plus their four hounds, two Tazys and two Steppe Hounds respectively, would drive to Tambov for the hunts. Or so we thought!

Vladimir drove us the next morning to the Moscow University complex where, in the botanical gardens, we were greeted by Tariel Varlamovich Gabidzashvili, a giant of a man with a flowing white beard and a mane of hair. Tarik, as he was

known, had been breeding Hortayas and Borzois – and handling bears and other wild animals – for years, and he was respected by everyone in hunting circles for his devotion to maintaining purebred hunting hounds. Certainly, the Hortayas that he let out of their kennels were built on very racy lines and, indeed, apart from their roseate ears, some of them looked very like the smooth Salukis I had seen only shortly before in Syria. His favourite was a black and tan puppy that actually had almost pendant ears. I was interested to see that the hounds were avidly eating up Rowan berries that had fallen from the trees – and, indeed, were leaping up

Tarik and Hortayas.

to snatch them from the lower branches. Tarik also had a couple of sporty-looking Borzois, not at all like the elegant, somewhat droopy creatures of the Western show ring. A friend of his brought along another couple of rather bigger Borzois to complete an impressive display of these two breeds.

Time slipped by, but our car for Tambov did not show up. In the end, we heard that the driver had been stopped by the police on his way to us with his three hounds – a Greyhound, a Whippet and a Borzoi – and had been hauled in for driving an allegedly stolen car! This would have fazed most people, but Lena and Lada worked the contacts and I was taken to Lena's brother's flat for the night, while Lada arranged with another hunter for him to drive us at 5.00 am the next day to Tambov.

Aleksei turned up dead on time in his family saloon car, into which we somehow squeezed four people, luggage and four hounds, and we cleared Moscow in the dark and in drizzling rain. It is at times like this that you realise that Russia is a big country. We drove without stopping for about 320 km through an almost flat and empty landscape broken only by swathes of silver birch woods. After refuelling, we drove on for another 200 km until we reached Tambov, where I tried unsuccessfully to register my visa, a serious requirement in Russia. A glamorous female police officer, looking as if she had just stepped out of *From Russia with Love*, told me firmly that I had to register where I was staying – and that was not in Tambov. So we had to go on for about another 95 km to a tiny village called Karian, which was where the hunters were accommodated.

This annual hunting competition was organised by the Russian Federation of Hunting Dogs (known as the RFOS in Russian) and was on a scale that, for most Westerners, is difficult to imagine. It seems that every town in Russia has a hunting club, and every year the RFOS sends out an invitation to all clubs to nominate a representative team of sighthounds to take part in the competition, which is held in a part of the Russian Federation that is determined by a number of factors, such as the accommodation for the hunters, sponsorship by local organisations, suitable hunting ground and availability of hares. That year the Tambov administration had made available a school, during the half-term holiday, where the hunters and their hounds were accommodated in makeshift dormitories in classrooms and local ladies ran a kind of soup kitchen to feed them. When I saw the conditions there, I was very glad that Lena and I were to share a very basic self-catering cottage with Yvonne McGehee from Wyoming, who had arrived at the weekend. No fewer than 18 teams had been entered for the competition, with altogether 53 packs consisting of one to three dogs of the same breed, making a total of well over 100 sighthounds! In fact, only Borzois and Hortayas had been entered. Teams had come from far and wide: locally from Tambov, as well as from Lipetsk, Moscow, St Petersburg, Stavropol, Volgograd, Yekaterinburg, Kazan, Voronezh and Chuvashia. The team leaders had gathered at the school on the Friday evening with the three officiating judges, led by Alexander Vasilyevich Shindelman, for the draw of between six and nine packs, depending on the number of dogs in each pack, to run each day, starting the next morning.

By the time of our delayed arrival on the Monday, some of the packs had already run and had gone home, because this was not a knockout competition but one in which individual dogs were evaluated according to a complicated system of scoring points and their results entered in their registration books. Points were awarded for speed in the run-up, sharp-sightedness in spotting the hare without the help of the owner, persistence in following the hare, the role of the individual dog if running in a pack, skill and coordination, conduct on the slip lead and attitude towards the caught hare (it should not tear or spoil the fur, and should preferably retrieve it or announce the catch). The scores were therefore a very serious matter for the judges as they determined whether the dog had earned enough points to be awarded one of four categories of diploma, which was, over time, added to the results of other competitions to give the dog a rating from 'elite' down to 'third class'. So a lot was riding on this competition for the dogs' owners, which probably explained their willingness to travel so far to take part.

The conduct of the competition was also unfamiliar, and worth explaining. The handlers of the dogs in each team's pack lined out on the field from left to right, in the order in which they were drawn, at a distance of about 4.5 metres from each other. The handler of each pack had the right to slip their dogs on any hare that got up immediately in front or in the sector to the right up to a notional line in front of the next unit. The exception was that the first in the line could also slip to the left. Clearly there was plenty of scope here for confusion, e.g. when it was not absolutely clear on which side of the notional line the hare got up, and sometimes mistakes happened on which the judges had to rule. As the line moved forward, the three mounted judges had to ride round in circles in order not to outpace the walkers. Each judge had one-third of the field to cover and rode after the running dogs, scoring as he went. If the pack consisted of three hounds, he clearly had his work cut out to score all of them.

The hounds were held on something like the poacher's slip lead used in Britain, but with the rope tied round the handler's waist and running through the ring on the hounds' collars back to the handler, who, when necessary, simply let go the free end to release all the hounds more or less simultaneously.

I now understood the system and had spent some time with the hunters, looking over their dogs. There were some very athletic Hortayas belonging to some Kazakhs from the Volgograd area that I liked the look of. They told me that, until about three years before, they had regularly sold their hounds to Chinese hunters, which might explain the appearance of some of the so-called Xigou. I also saw several Borzois that were more compact than what I had seen previously in Britain, and one Volga German told me that he expected his Borzois to be taut like a spring, to have a good breadth of chest and to be four fingers wide between the huckle bones. Two of the Borzois were also of an unusual colour – one brindle and one grizzle – and with something of the Steppe Hound about them; and another one had erect, instead of the usual folded-back, ears. There were also some Hortayas that looked to me suspiciously like Greyhound crosses, and indeed some of the hunters lodged a protest later about their participation.

I was keen now to see some action, but the omens were not good. On the first day, only two packs ran; on the second, although nine hares were seen, only four packs ran; and on the third day, again only two packs ran. This meant there was a growing backlog of units that had not run but were automatically being carried forward to the next day. So we set off on a cold grey morning with modest expectations, as it was already clear that the hares were not there. Some of the running hounds were loaded with their owners into a battered but very effective old bus for the drive out to the beautiful running ground, a vast field of stubble, and even before we began walking up a hare got up under the horses' feet and was away into some trees before anyone was ready. A good sign? Not a bit of it! After about an hour in a bitterly cold wind with nothing in sight, I took a lift in an accompanying vehicle.

That was a mistake! If I had stayed where I was, I would have seen coming straight at me the first course of the day. A hare got up on the right of the line at about 200 metres' distance, and the handler of the nearest pack of three Borzois decided to give the hounds a go. One very impressive young hound, owned appropriately enough by a Mr Zaitsev (Hare!) from Tambov, quickly drew away from the others and put in a very creditable run as the hare crossed a country lane and went over another field

Walking up, Russian style.

into a wood. I decided that I had better continue walking, and we went on and on for a couple of hours without seeing another thing.

We took a short break as the wind grew stronger and a little snow began ominously to fall. We walked up another field of stubble and, just as we were coming to the end and – annoyingly – I had switched off my camera, a hare got up, three Borzois were slipped and they all ran into some high hay. The hounds pressed the hare and it came out onto a dirt track, where it accelerated, but the hounds also moved up a gear and began to work it on a grassy patch. This was a very strong hare and it pulled away again in a curve, with the dogs trying hard to close again, but they were eventually slowed by a patch of soft ground, allowing the hare to escape into a wood. These were good hounds, belonging to a man who said he hunted with them 156 days a year. That's real dedication! After that, there was one false alarm as a hare got up in some high grass, but the slipped hounds were unsighted; and then nothing more until we called it a day at around 5.00 pm.

There was a frost overnight, and the sky was a threatening red as we said goodbye to Yvonne, who was returning to Moscow, and made our way over to the assembly point at the school. We had to hang around until 11.00 am to allow for the frost to thaw before we moved out to start walking up another endless field of stubble. But our luck was right out! We walked until about 1.00 pm without a sighting, and it was turning colder with a light snow gradually covering the ground and obscuring our vision. So, to general relief, the judges decided to call a halt and we all trooped off for some food and warmth.

The snow lasted for only a couple of hours, but by then the judges had called a meeting with the team captains and agreed with them not only to cancel the rest of the competition for lack of hares and the deteriorating weather, but also to annul the results up to that point. Russians are very stoical, and the hunters took all this very calmly. A group of enthusiasts invited Lena and me to go out with them for a spot of private coursing, and we piled into a couple of vehicles with an incredible number of dogs to some rough ground by a river, where I was assured the hares were hiding. We had Borzois, Steppe Hounds and Hortayas with us, and they were all let off the lead to work over the ground. With so many dogs, it would have been a pack hunt if a hare had got up but, though we walked for an hour or two, there was nothing. At least the dogs had a good run.

This was not, however, the end of everything, as Lada had invited Lena and me to visit her cottage 'near Kursk' for a couple of days for some sighthound field trials. Yuri, the driver of the 4x4 vehicle that had been wrongly detained by the police in Moscow, had arrived and he miraculously fitted all the luggage and three people with six dogs in the back, while he and I sat in front with his Whippet between us! But first, we still had to register my visa. The village police were very friendly but said they could not do it as I needed to go to a passport office, the nearest of which was about 40 km away – but it was closed that day for an inspection! However, they gave us a telephone number there that we could try. So off we went, found the police station and, after some telephoning, were exceptionally admitted. A very helpful police officer prepared some forms to fill in and then said the director wished to see us. We were ushered into a large office where a youthful lieutenant colonel sat frowning behind an enormous desk. He quickly relaxed and showed he was enjoying the novel experience of meeting an Englishman who had come all this way to hunt in his parish. He turned out to be, as he said, a passionate hunter, and proudly showed a photograph of himself with one of his trophies. He even gave me a cutting from the local newspaper about the competition. So we parted on excellent terms and with the precious stamp on my visa.

It was now after 1.00 pm and there was a long road ahead – not just to Kursk, but to the tiny hamlet of Bobrova, about 20 km from the border with Ukraine. Kursk was all in darkness when we arrived, yet Yuri said he needed to buy some supplies. To my amazement, he stopped outside a closed supermarket, hammered on the doors until someone opened them, and did his shopping. But the shop did not have any fresh bread, so we drove on to the only illuminated place in the town – a nightclub – where Yuri went to the bar and came back with a couple of loaves of bread! It was well after midnight when we finally turned off the asphalt and headed down a rough track into the pitch darkness, which was eventually broken by the lights in an isolated cottage. To all-round relief, we had arrived, and were greeted by loud barking from the surrounding kennels, especially from a Russian Ovcharka, which looked very like an Old English Sheepdog.

The next morning, Yuri and Lada went off to collect, from the Moscow train, two girls who were coming with their hounds to be trialled under Lada's expert supervision. They were both very small and seemed too young to be handling a big male Borzoi and a very lively Tazy. A bitterly cold wind was blowing as we headed out into the nearby fields of stubble with the two girls and their hounds plus Lena and her two Tazys, Lada and Yuri with his young Borzoi and his Whippet, which had been so determined to come that it had somehow squeezed through a tiny window and jumped out of the house and into the car. We walked up for two hours, with the Whippet working ceaselessly over the ground in a flushing capacity, but could find nothing; and then, when a hare did get up, it was just to my left and it ran backwards in the long grass so that none of the hounds was sighted. But at least I had seen a Russian hare, which looked the same as our European brown hare. (There are, in fact, several species: the rusak = *Lepus europaeus*; the tolai = *Lepus tolai*, which is a desert and dry steppe species; and the belyak = *Lepus timidus*, which is adapted to live in the forests.) We went on and on and finally, as we turned back towards the car, there was a movement in the long grass between us and a line of trees – it was a red fox. All the hounds were slipped as the fox made a quick dash to the trees and on into a thicket, where the hounds lost it. So there was no evaluation of the Moscow hounds that day and, sadly, the big Borzoi injured a front leg and was out of action for the next day.

The wind had dropped overnight and the sun shone from a cloudless sky, quickly thawing the light frost as we made our way to another endless field of stubble with the Tazy under trial, Lena's two Tazys, Yuri's Borzoi and two of Lada's Steppe Hounds. I found the latter interesting as they were from the same litter, but the black dog had a heavy coat and long pendant ears, while the red bitch had a much lighter coat and the more usual small ears. As Lada said, it has to be borne in mind that, across southern Russia, there has been a constant intermingling over centuries of closely related breeds, many of which were themselves broken down into a range of different types, often with distinctive names. So it is not at all strange that from time to time a throwback will come through. I was keen to see them run but, again, we had to walk for a long time before a hare got up away to my left at the end of the line. It was a mature light-grey hare of the rusak species, and took off like a rocket. Lena's Tazys were nearest and were slipped but, at eight and six years old and not in hard hunting condition, they could not make any ground on the hare. The other hounds were farther off, but all were slipped, and the black Steppe Hound went by at an impressive pace. But it was a hopeless chase as the hare had a long lead, which it maintained all the way across the stubble to a wood. The hounds took quite a while to return from the long loop they had run, and Yuri's young Borzoi and the black Steppe Hound laid down exhausted. They soon recovered and we went on until mid-afternoon, but we found nothing more. It was time to get back to an enormous late lunch of rabbit stew followed by a goose, before Yuri drove Lena and me back to Kursk to catch the night train back to Moscow.

Field trial near Kursk.

I had a day to spend in Moscow before my flight home, and Lena and I took up an invitation from Marina Kuzina to attend field trials of Laikas on boar and bear. We took a train to an area of dense fir woodland outside the city, where Marina met us and guided us to a huge fenced reservation in which the trials took place. All around the parking area were hunters with Laikas, a breed that is described as aboriginal and that I had never seen in the flesh before. According to Marina, in Russia there are in fact three breeds of Laikas: the Russo-European, which is always black and white, the East Siberian, and the West Siberian, which comes in two distinct types – the Hanty and the Mansi. Their role is to track wild animals by scent, to hold them at bay and to summon their handlers by barking. The trials here were designed to test their ability to perform this role.

One at a time, a Laika was released into the reservation to seek out where a wild boar was hidden in a hollow in a pile of logs. Having found the beast's lair, it had to show enough aggression to suggest holding it at bay, while barking loudly to attract its handler's attention. It then had to leave the boar and return to its handler on command. Three judges were on hand to evaluate the performance, as was the handler, who had the right to accept or challenge their score. On this occasion, the handler disagreed

Laika and bear trial.

and a lively discussion ensued. We watched another Laika perform, but it was a young dog and seemed to have no idea what to do about the boar.

As time was running out, we went over to see the trials on bear. A big black bear stood in a clearing secured by the neck with a long chain connected to a suspended steel wire, so that it could move about fairly freely. A Laika was released and made its way to the edge of the clearing, from where it could easily see as well as scent the bear, but it showed absolutely no interest, turned round and ran back into the forest! A more mature Laika appeared, located the bear and danced all around it just out of reach of the bear's claws, barking loudly all the while. But it seemed to tire of this activity and turned away to scent around the clearing. I was left with the impression that both dog and bear knew this was not serious and that they had done it many times before, but I suppose this simulated hunt is the only way for the judges to evaluate the dogs.

I cannot say this visit was a great success from the point of view of seeing hunting Russian style, but at least I made the acquaintance of some well-informed and extremely hospitable hunters and a wide range of unusual breeds in their natural surroundings. I was certainly given plenty of food for thought on the Hortaya, with its erect or roseate ears and at times curly tail, as the original sighthound portrayed in so many archaeological representations. I was also able to collect a lot of DNA samples for Dr Peter Savolainen's research into the origins of dogs, which may shed light on the Hortaya's place in history. I can only dream of how it might have been from a video I was shown in Moscow of Borzois dramatically coursing and spectacularly catching a hare on a snow-covered field.

I came back to the more relevant business of how the SCC was to adjust to the effects of the Hunting Act. We had had a further meeting with the Countryside Alliance and the other sighthound coursing clubs, when the various options were discussed. The SCC membership then met and agreed to suspend the Saluki Coursing Club and to establish the Saluki Conservation Club, with the objective of preserving the working capability of the Saluki within the parameters of the Hunting Act. We had established our strategy and it remained to work out the tactics, which we did over the Christmas period.

and when they see him and recognise him,

Chapter Fourteen

Adapt and Change

There was clearly no possibility under the Hunting Act that we could continue competitive coursing in the old way, but we could continue to preserve most of our hounds' working characteristics by going rabbiting, despatching shot and wounded hares, and flushing hares to guns or falcons, either as the SCC or in small groups of friends. We gave rabbiting a try in early 2005, with just a few of us early one cold morning on a farm in Wiltshire. There were plenty of rabbits and, although the runs were usually fairly short, all the hounds got some exercise. An unexpected bonus was a deer. A group of four suddenly broke cover in front of us and three of them raced away, but one was clearly in trouble – it had a broken back leg. So we had to shoot it and, as the farmer did not want the carcass, we went happily home with some venison. Over the rest of that winter we managed to meet from time to time to give the hounds a run and to maintain our relations with the landowners against the day when we hoped coursing might be possible again; but our last meeting of the season was cancelled because of snow.

What a contrast it was when, a couple of weeks later, Liese and I flew into Dubai for an interesting week among old friends in the Emirates. The weather was perfect and it was lovely to swim in the warm sea again. I had been in touch via the Internet for some time with Hamad al-Ghanem, Director of the Arabian Saluki Center in Abu Dhabi and, when he heard we were visiting, he very kindly invited us to dinner in one of the smart new hotels in Dubai. I could hardly believe my eyes when we entered the restaurant and found him sitting at a table with a hooded falcon on his wrist! The bird was put on a stand and occupied the place next to me at the table. As I discovered, Hamad liked to be at the centre of attention, and certainly the bird acted as a magnet for the eyes of all the diners there as Hamad regaled us with stories of his bedouin upbringing among camels, Salukis and falcons and made arrangements for us to visit his Arabian Saluki Center.

He came with his falcon to pick us up from where we were staying with Heli and Neville Allen, and this time it was Hamad's turn to listen. We had known the Allens since we lived in Dubai in the 1960s, but they had arrived there even earlier and had retired there after Neville's long career – first as the senior resident engineer of Sir William Halcrow and Partners and later as personal adviser to Shaikh Rashid bin Said Al Maktoum, the Ruler of Dubai. Neville had been responsible for the planning and oversight of much of the development on which Dubai's prosperity was founded. He fascinated Hamad with his stories about how it was in the old days, and it was hard to break away for the drive to Abu Dhabi.

The Arabian Saluki Center was opened in 2003 and occupies part of a large sandy compound, shared with the Falcon Hospital, not far from Abu Dhabi airport. It is well laid out, with a visitors' reception area, from which a corridor runs between a series of spacious Saluki rooms, with a raised platform on one side covered with a rug and access to outside pens and to a large kitchen. Here the hounds' food is cooked each day, consisting of a light meal of semolina, eggs, milk, etc. in the morning and meat with rice, herbs, spices, pulses, etc. in the evening, except in Ramadan when no food is served in daylight hours.

Hamad described his efforts to preserve the Arabian Saluki by selecting for breeding only local hounds of whose origins he was certain. He never inbred, but did try to preserve specific lines. He trained puppies with muzzles on live game, as hunting is not allowed in the UAE. Many of his hounds went to the shaikhs for hunting but some, with a pedigree, were sold to individuals all over the world. He had some beautiful hounds in the Center, both feathereds and smooths, which he and his staff used as models in expounding to the many visitors, especially school groups, the role of the Saluki in the history and culture of the Arabs.

We were joined on our tour of the establishment by Mike and Valerie Ratcliffe, old coursing friends of ours from England. They had previously lived with Salukis and falcons for many years in Saudi Arabia, and Mike was then working on a project in al-Ain to breed Arabian partridges and another in al-Dhaid to breed desert hare and stone curlews for conservation and sport. They took us with them to their home in al-Ain, from where we made a tour of another rather grand project of Hamad's to establish, within a fenced area of sand and scrub, a hunting reserve measuring seven square kilometres, in which it was proposed to allow hunting under licence with Salukis and falcons. Over dinner later, we met Patrick Paillat, a French expert in breeding game for conservation and sport. He gave me some very interesting photographs of a distinctive Saluki-like hunting hound from Baluchistan, where he had been in the late 1970s collecting houbara bustard eggs for conservation purposes.

On our way back to Dubai we ran into a sandstorm and at one point, near the Nad al-Shiba camel racetrack, looming out of the dust came the extraordinary sight of what I thought was a monkey riding a camel! Only on closer inspection did I realise that it was one of the new 'robojocks', which had been introduced to replace boy camel riders after a public outcry about the way they were treated.

In the summer, we took the hounds with us by car to revisit Liese's hometown of Kiel in northern Germany. The weather was glorious and we spent some idyllic days with the hounds on the miles of empty beaches and sand dunes, where they also managed to surprise a few hares. From there we made a short trip into Hamburg and went back to the Saluki racetrack at Hoisdorf, where we met the two Satterzadeh brothers, Iraj and Cyrus, who have made quite a name for themselves and their Salukis, imported from Iran, for their success on the track. Cyrus had a particularly nice black hound of the type I had seen in Sanandaj. He was interested to hear about our experiences in Kordestan, as it is an area from which his family originally came. We went on to see some more Salukis of Iranian origin at the home in Hamburg of Dr Monika Dahncke. She too has had a lot of success on the track and at lure coursing with her hounds, and they looked in excellent condition as they played in her garden, where we talked for hours about her time in Iran. She had known well our friends, Lev and Margret Tamp, in Tehran and had obtained her first Saluki from them.

We all had a lovely holiday in Germany, but it ended with a sleepless night for me. I had taken the hounds to a local vet to have them treated for worms and ticks before our return home, as required by law. The vet dosed the hounds and, fortunately as it turned out, completed the entries in their pet passports before checking their microchips. Once again, we hit a problem with *Sally*; this time, however, it was because the vet could not find the microchip. She passed the reader all over her but could not get a reading anywhere. I wondered whether the chip had somehow been forced out when *Sally* had had her accident with a car. The vet could offer no solution. The next 24 hours was a very worrying period as we contemplated all the possible difficulties we might have at the ferry terminal at Hook of Holland. When we arrived at the check-in, my heart was in my mouth as I took the microchip reader from an official. Then I noticed that it was of the same type used by my vet at home and was different from that used by the German vet. My spirits rose as I ran the reader over *Sally's* neck and it pinged. Whew – what a relief!

I faced another difficult decision the next month at the Festival of Hunting in Peterborough. For years it had been the practice of the SCC to have a stand there with information about Salukis and to take part in the grand parade of the different hunting hounds. It was always a good occasion to network with our counterparts and some of the landowners. We often combined our attendance with a formal meeting of the SCC membership, and I had decided I would use this occasion to announce my retirement from the SCC chair. I had helped to steer the club though some difficult times but, as I and my hounds were getting older, it was time to pass the reins on. Adrian Phillips kindly agreed to stand, and was unanimously voted in.

I was heavily involved in a whole range of other non-Saluki activities, and I could now enjoy the forthcoming winter season without the cares of that office. And what a season it was! We managed to exercise the hounds quite often in different parts of the countryside, including some new land, right through until March 2007.

In the summer, I was invited to a very different kind of festival – the Festival of Falconry, held on the Englefield Estate near Reading in Berkshire. It was advertised as the largest international falconry event ever held, hosted by the Hawk Board and sponsored by the Emirates Falconers' Club, during which there would be live displays of falconry from pre-history to the present time by falconers from all over the world. The organisers had asked me to give a talk on the Arab tradition of hunting with Saluki and falcon and to arrange for members of the SCC to bring their Salukis along to take part in an arena event on falconry in Arabia. So it was a great opportunity to present our breed to the wider public and, as the organisers wrote to me afterwards, it was most welcome for them to have something a little different from the usual, purely hawking-related seminars.

Hamad al-Ghanem was there with a well-presented display from the Emirates and it was good to have the opportunity to talk shop with him again. I was particularly pleased to be greeted by one of the large contingent of falconers from Kazakhstan, who had brought a message for me from Kostya Plakhov in Almaty. I would be seeing him there the following September at a conference on primitive and aboriginal dogs, and he wanted me to know that some hunting with Tazys would be arranged after the conference.

Before leaving for Almaty, I took up an invitation from the Northern Saluki Club (NSC) to give a talk at another festival – the Festival of the Saluki 2007, a week-long celebration of the breed organised by the SGHC. The NSC had arranged a symposium in the delightful setting of Hassop Hall near Bakewell in Derbyshire. My opening topic was the origins of the Eastern Saluki and its situation today, which was followed by a lively debate with members of the large audience. It was another useful occasion to network and to meet particularly the president of the Finnish Saluki Club, at whose festival I had been invited to speak a year later.

When I got home, I was greeted with the unpleasant confirmation that *Sally* needed an operation to remove three lipomas on her right side and armpit. I had to get that over with before my departure for Almaty less than a week later. Fortunately, it all went well and I could leave with a quiet mind.

Under the auspices of the Primitive and Aboriginal Dogs Society (PADS) and a variety of public and private institutions in Kazakhstan, the conference in Almaty was spread over the period 10–15 September 2007 and bore the grand title: 'Aboriginal Breeds as Elements of Biodiversity and the Cultural Heritage of Humankind'. Twenty-two specialists in the study of aboriginal dogs from five continents were there to present papers on a range of exotic topics from the Canaan dog of Israel to the dingo of Australia, culminating in a study elaborated by Kostya Plakhov to make the case for recognition of the Kazakh Tazy as a discrete national breed of hunting hound. I attended both as a member of the conference organising committee and as a speaker on the Saluki's origins, history and present situation, and recognised that some of my thesis might bring out differences with our Kazakh hosts. I was, however, quite pleased with the unexpected reaction of the president of the Veterinary College, who was in the chair during my session. I decided that, as most of the audience would understand Russian more easily than English even though there was simultaneous translation available, I would deliver my paper in Russian. At the end, the chairman jumped up and sought to ensure that the significance of what I had said about the position of the Saluki in Muslim society had been fully understood by giving a summary in Kazakh.

I had boned up on the Central Asian Tazy beforehand and had read a seminal study written in Russian by A A Sludsky in 1939 entitled 'The Central Asian Borzaya Taza and hunting with it' (*Borzaya* means here 'sighthound' and *Taza* is another way of writing Tazy). He maintained that Tazys appeared in Kazakhstan at the time of the Arab conquests in the 8th century and were crossed with some unspecified local mountain dogs to give a more robust hound capable of coping with the severe climate of Central Asia. These hounds became popular with the local dignitaries and in the Soviet era were used extensively in the fur (mainly fox) trade, so much so that Sludsky reckoned that in 1938 there were 4,300 registered Tazys working in Kazakhstan, though the real number was probably about 7,000, not all purebred. The Second World War had a devastating effect on the Kazakh economy, and commercial fur hunting with Tazys went into steep decline. This was compounded later by the dramatic fall in demand worldwide for fur from wild animals and the problems of restructuring the economy after the break-up of the Soviet Union and Kazakhstan's independence in 1991.

Against this background, I was interested to hear of the heroic efforts by Kostya and Ana Plakhov and a small dedicated group to rescue the breed, whose numbers had declined at the time of the conference to only 100–150 hounds regarded as purebred. After a painstaking programme to study over 1,000 individual hounds and to compare them with other sighthounds, they set about cleansing the Tazy of the effects of crossbreeding and establishing a breeding stock of hounds with a four-generation pedigree. They had also worked up a new standard and attempted to fix certain coat colours. While participants in the conference applauded these great efforts to restore the Tazy to something like its former state, many of us remained sceptical about their identification of the Tazy as a discrete breed. We were concerned about the consequences for these hounds of restricting their gene pool to the already depleted breed stock in the country and about the encouragement it would give to other countries with similar hounds to claim them as discrete national breeds, creating artificial division where none existed before.

In an unforeseen way, the case for the Kazakh Tazy was partly undermined by the sudden appearance in the conference hall of a local breeder with two cream hounds, which, to the chagrin of our hosts, all of us with long experience of Salukis immediately identified as such. They were small and sparsely feathered, like the Salukis to be found in the desert areas of the Middle East. They were, we were told, Kazakh Tazys of the Turkmen type, which hail from southern Kazakhstan, Turkmenistan and northern Uzbekistan, where the winters are appreciably milder and the terrain more desert-like, and the requirement is for a fast and manoeuvrable hound with stamina for the long chase.

Kazakh Tazy in Almaty.

Many of the foreign participants were accommodated in a hostel at the Šunkar kennels and aviary on the outskirts of Almaty, which I had visited on my previous trip. In green and pleasant surroundings, a dozen or more Tazys, some with puppies – the product of a careful selective breeding programme – were also accommodated there. My overall impression was, however, that these hounds looked even more like the kind of Salukis that I was accustomed to see in their more northerly ranges in the Middle East. The thought crossed my mind that the purification of the breed had been conducted so successfully that it had taken the local hounds right back to their Saluki ancestors! Some of these hounds were actively used for hunting, and therefore served as a good yardstick for what a Tazy should look like according to the standard.

After the conference, our hosts arranged for the foreign participants an excursion to the village of Nura, about 160 km north of Almaty. Here we would meet a famous hunter with eagles, known as a berkutchi from the Kazakh word *Berkut* meaning golden eagle, and Tazys. We were joined en route by a number of local hunters with their Tazys, and I actually drove with one of them and his little black and silver bitch and a West Siberian Laika (a hunting dog something like a small Husky). We were to see all these dogs running free later on, but our attention was concentrated for the time being on the spectacle at Nura.

We were greeted by Mukhamed Isabekov, known as 'Muluk', his wife and several children in front of a felt yurt in the yard of their property, where Muluk had established a small museum decorated with falconry paraphernalia and dramatic pictures of hunting with eagles and Tazys. Muluk was one of 14 berkutchis from the Nura area, out of total of 40 officially recognised in Kazakhstan. A couple of the local berkutchis came in, dressed in their colourful national costumes, to pose for us. My eyes were, however, more on an almost solid-black, beautifully proportioned Tazy that wandered loose among us, although the gates from the yard to the road outside were wide open. More constrained was a recently acquired smooth grizzle bitch of the Turkmen type from the Shymkent area that was chained to an eagle's perch to familiarise her with the bird. She was still rather shy, but she looked to me as if she had great potential and she would have been my choice of all those that I saw that day.

Muluk was keen, however, to show us his top dog, a dark-grey, sturdy hound called *Kogdalu*, who already had an awesome reputation, having killed 48 foxes the previous season and 36 the season before that. His sire had come from the far west beyond the Syr Darya (Jaxartes) river, where he was noted for killing jackals. *Kogdalu* had sired a litter from a rather taller light-grey bitch that was in a kennel with two puppies, one like her with dark eyes – 'like an eagle's', said Muluk – and the other identical in

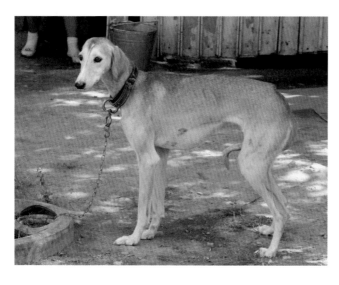

Puppy of the Turkmen Tazy type.

colour but with light-yellow eyes and ears that stood away from the head, which was sired by *Kogdalu* with a different dam that Muluk said was 'not quite pure'. *Kogdalu's* litter sister, a slightly smaller mahogany version of him, was also there. He reminded me strongly of a Kurdish hound that I had seen in Iran a couple of years previously, which was possibly a little longer in the leg. But the star of the show was Muluk's little daughter, who emerged carrying a six-week-old puppy with a strikingly patterned silvery-grey coat. With the screaming eagles in the background and Muluk's sons parading their hobby falcons on their wrists while enormous Tobets padded about, it was an unforgettable experience.

Muluk's children with their falcons and Tazy puppy in Nura.

I had hoped to stay with Muluk an extra day to go hunting with him but it was still far too hot. They prefer to go hunting from November to February, when the snow is on the ground and tracking the prey in these vast expanses of steppe is easier. Young hounds are trained either on foxes that have been caught alive by the eagles or simply run with the experienced hounds and learn on the job. Muluk said that not all Tazys were suited to taking fox, and he recounted an embarrassing story. An engineer had what he claimed was an outstanding Tazy and Muluk tried repeatedly to buy it. Eventually he succeeded and invited his friends round to see the hound perform on a fox that his son had shot and slightly wounded. The fox was released and the hound pursued it but, when it drew level, the fox turned on the hound and pursued it all the way back! The hound did not get a second chance.

However, we did at least have an opportunity to see the hounds run when we went on to visit the Charyn National Park. The Charyn Gorge is likened to the Grand Canyon in the USA, and it certainly is a spectacular sight. Although the area is a nature reserve, no one seemed bothered about the dogs running loose and we saw how easily they coped with the uneven stony ground. In addition to the two dogs in my car, there were two dark-grey hounds, a cream with a rather heavy head and a showy black-fringed sable. They were well trained and after a good run came obediently back to the cars for the long return journey. Apart from a lone falcon that flew up the gorge, the only sign of wildlife was a metre-long constrictor snake (*Eryx orientalis*) that we surprised as it warmed itself in the late afternoon sunshine.

We stopped again at Muluk's yurt on the way back and enjoyed supper set on low tables inside, while he showed video films of his hunting exploits with eagles and Tazys in the snow. The hunting is on horseback and it clearly requires a hound with plenty of stamina to keep up with the horses as they ride out to the hunting area, to course and catch the prey – which could even be wolf – and to trot back home afterwards.

Of course, such exploits were once common with Salukis in the days before 4x4s. Even in more recent times, I had known a hunter in Iraq who used to ride and hunt wolves with his pack of Salukis and I met a Kurd in Iran who hunted in similar winter conditions all manner of prey, including wolves, with his Tazis. Facts such as these seemed to surprise our Kazakh hosts, whose knowledge of Salukis appeared to be narrowly based on what they had seen and heard of the breed in the West rather than in the countries of origin. They were also surprised to hear that Salukis were perfectly capable of hunting with all their senses, given the opportunity to do so, and were not merely sighthounds. For them it was one of the distinctions between their Tazys and Salukis that their hounds could follow a scent and flush out game from the undergrowth. However, it is quite normal for Arab and Kurdish hunters to give their hounds the opportunity to search for game, though the ensuing chase would be largely by sight. One of the conference participants related that his Salukis used to hunt deer in dense forests in Scotland where sight, scent and hearing all played a role.

Did it matter that the Kazakhs had decided to establish a separate breed? As Kostya Plakhov said to the conference, 'to close the Tazy breed completely and focus on the Saluki, which already has international recognition as a breed' would be tantamount to

Kazakh hunter with Laika and Tazy.

'a double standards policy'. He recalled that in the West the number of differences between breeds was unimportant – so long as there was a single difference, that was justification enough. He believed there were sufficient differences for the Kazakh Tazy to constitute a separate breed and claimed the right of any country or people to determine their own breeds. Several speakers doubted the wisdom of this course. Leaving aside the question whether the claimed differences really exist, the first consideration must be the effect on the hounds themselves, and conference participants pointed to the harmful consequences experienced by other breeds of a restricted gene pool.

The situation in Kazakhstan was, in fact, even worse than we were led to believe, as I found later when I read the new breed standard, which further limits the breed stock by listing the following colours as a fault: 'brindle, piebald, tricolour'. In his presentation, Plakhov described such colours as 'clear signs of past interbreeding with other breeds'. Rather confusingly, he added 'solid black, brown and pure white' to this list, although the new standard gives the permitted colours as:

All shades of agouti, all shades of red, white, black; small patches of white are allowed on the muzzle, forehead, throat, paws and the end of the tail; ticking on the white patches must be of the same basic colour. A light or dark mask is also allowed. Black and tan and grizzle are allowed but not desired.

However, the visitors were generally of the view that, when starting from what was apparently a small number of hounds defined as purebreds, it was preferable to retain hounds that in all other respects were acceptable and to see through breeding how the offspring developed.

At the end of the conference, participants were involved in a long discussion of a resolution that finally we were happy to accept, as it kept to generalities. We could agree that every people and country should have the right to preserve their own populations of aboriginal dogs, as this was on the understanding that they could show that such dogs were exclusively their own. We could also agree on the need to draw international attention to their preservation, in view of the disappearance of such populations worldwide.

After leaving Kazakhstan, another paper by the Plakhovs and another colleague, M Eleusizov, which was not delivered at the conference, emerged. It covers much of the same ground as in their presented paper, but makes the specific suggestion that the Fédération Cynologique Internationale (FCI) should create an additional group of dogs – for example Group 11: Aboriginal breeds – that would initially include those recommended by canine organisations or specialists. For such breeds, bodies would be appointed to oversee their management as regards drafting standards, showing and trialling, etc. until such time as the requirements of the FCI were met for their registration as new breeds. However, we had already made clear at the conference that, if the Kazakhs wished to seek recognition for their breeds, they were already at liberty to make representations through their breed clubs to the FCI. In the case of the Tazy, they would need to show how it differed significantly from the Saluki. If a comparison were made of the Kazakh hounds with the images of some of Brigadier General Lance's Saluki imports of the 1920s, the resemblance would be striking.

The ball was left therefore very much in the Kazakh court. They had established unilaterally the Tazy as a breed of Kazakhstan, and now they had to prove it to the satisfaction of the outside world. I never discovered how this move was viewed in neighbouring countries with Tazy populations, though I gather that it ran into opposition in Russia. It is a pity that the Kazakhs took up a fixed position in advance of the (unfortunately overlong awaited) publication of the results of the research being undertaken in Sweden by Dr Peter Savolainen and his team into the origins of dogs, for which DNA and mtDNA samples from Tazys have been submitted. The outcome could spare them embarrassment or, conversely, strengthen their case. As it is, I have heard from other contacts in Kazakhstan that not everyone is happy with the new standard and that some hunters are ignoring it and continuing to breed Tazys according to their own long-established traditions.

Mike and Valerie Ratcliffe attended the conference and I was very glad of their company, especially on the excursions around Almaty. Mike almost acquired a Tazy puppy, but the price was rather steep and we contented ourselves with just admiring these attractive hounds. We ended our stay by inviting the Plakhovs and Almaz Kurmankulov from Kyrgyzstan to a lively dinner in town, where we discussed all the issues of the conference far into the night. I was fascinated to hear from Almaz that wolves had become a major problem in Kyrgyzstan, taking some 25% of all livestock per year, and that this had led to a resurgence of interest in Taigans for stock protection. Kostya said that there was a similar problem in Kazakhstan since the old Soviet measures of control had been abandoned, but here the interest was more in acquiring Tobets as guard dogs.

A few weeks later, in October I was once again in an entirely different hunting scene – Iberia. The SCC embarked on its most ambitious group trip, to course in Portugal and Spain over two weeks; and this time there were no mishaps for me with my hounds' passports. An old friend, Arzhic Basirov – a native of Azerbaijan raised in Iran and settled in London – came along to help me with my hounds. We foregathered on the beautiful sporting estate of Comenda Grande in central Portugal, which is known for its partridge shooting as well as its excellent wines. We were the first group to course there and our hosts were a little concerned that we might not find enough hares; but they need have had no fear. We found plenty, and all our hounds had some good exercise chasing the small but swift local hare, which is not averse to taking refuge down holes in a landscape that does not generally provide the security of English hedges and coverts.

The next day we moved onto another sporting estate at Quinta do Duque, where we had another brilliant day's rough coursing, in which all the hounds had a good workout. We then tried yet another sporting estate at Bala, where they also had a large kennels of Galgos. After all our hounds had had an initial run, we organised a competition with them by way of preparation for what lay ahead of us in Spain.

Members of the SCC at Comenda Grande, Portugal.

These were powerful animals with an explosive burst of speed, but our hounds kept up well, especially when it came to twisting and turning among the trees and rocky outcrops. Sadly, *Sally* showed signs of distress and the next day I had to take her to a vet in Carmona, across the border in Andalusia, where we had moved to stay on the El Triguero farm. She diagnosed a blockage in *Sally's* colon and kept her on a drip for the next 48 hours, while we engaged in some stiff competition from the local Galgos.

These hounds were amazing. In our encounter with Galgos in Portugal the preceding year, our Salukis had won every course b

ar one – and that was a draw. We therefore went confidently into the field with these Andalusian hounds, but they were a revelation. They were supremely fit and athletic, with pumped-up leg muscles that made our hounds look puny. We consoled ourselves with the thought that they would probably not have the endurance of our hounds in the long chase, but we could not have been more mistaken. These Galgos may have looked like coursing Greyhounds and, indeed, may have *been* largely coursing Greyhounds, but whatever else was in their makeup clearly gave them the stamina to course over long distances – at least on the flat.

At the beginning of our tour, our hounds were nowhere near the level of fitness needed, though they improved visibly almost daily, so that by the end they were going very well. Both we and the Galgos' owners soon spotted that our hounds could get on terms with the Galgos when the course went uphill and over varied terrain. As Adrian remarked succinctly in motoring terms, the comparison was like that between a Ferrari and a Range Rover! This meant that the Spaniards tried to keep to the flat land, whereas we favoured running on the more rugged terrain. At all events, we all had a lot of good-natured fun and some grand performances from the hounds. After a much-needed day off to see the local sights and to give *Sally* time to recover, we had another day out with the Galgos and were again impressed by their perfect adaptation to the local flat and dusty landscape.

The last stage of our tour took us north to Tembleque, near Toledo in La Mancha, where a contact made at the Festival of Falconry in July had offered to arrange some coursing for us on his huge estate. He had also arranged for Spanish television to come and film us to project an image of the economic benefits of coursing conducted in a disciplined manner. On a brilliant morning, we set off with a gamekeeper to an area where one cameraman with a mounted camera could film us from a hillcrest, while another with a hand-held camera could take close-up shots in the field. It all went very well, especially when two of our hounds got onto a hare that ran up the

Spanish Galgos.

hill, leapt spectacularly over a fence followed closely by the hounds, and continued straight at the camera.

Our final day was extraordinary! Although we planned an early start with the film crew, we woke up to thick fog. Eventually we groped our way to the fields as the sun slowly broke through to give another fine day. Again, we were able to site the fixed camera in a good vantage point, while our hounds put in some great runs below. Finally, I gave a long interview on the coursing Saluki, which was woven into a nicely produced film, broadcast later on Spanish television.

The adventure was not yet over. Our host happened to have an Iranian guest engaged in preparing a book on falconry, which was eventually published under the title of *Sky Hunters: The Passion of Falconry.* I already knew Hossein Amirsadeghi well from London, where I had agreed to contribute a chapter to his book on Salukis and falconry. Hossein and my friend Arzhic Basirov obviously got on famously. Hossein had brought a professional wildlife photographer with him to take pictures of our host's peregrine falcons hunting for partridge, and we spent a memorable late afternoon together with the peregrines putting on an amazing display of speed and tenacity in the clear blue sky.

Back home, I had my vet check *Sally* thoroughly with the results of the blood tests she had had done in Spain. They showed that she had had a build-up of lactic acid in her muscles, which was not exceptional given her age and the warm running conditions. Anyway, she made a full recovery and we were able to take part in another busy season with the SCC. We even spent Christmas in Klosters, Switzerland with one of our sons, who had taken up residence there. Once again, the hounds showed their remarkable adaptability by revelling in the snow.

Once the season was over, Liese and I were ready to pay a further visit to Turkey, more particularly to western Anatolia. We started, as always, in the old town of Istanbul but then crossed over the Bosphorus to the Asian side to stay for a few days exploring around Bursa and Iznik, where the glorious ceramic tiles are made. However, our main focus was to be Konya, which, in addition to its long and fascinating history, is also an important centre for all kinds of hunting, not least with sighthounds.

A Turkish friend I had made at the conference in Almaty took me to see the extensive kennels at Selçuk University in Konya, where a carefully regulated programme of breeding Kangal (Karabash and Akbash) shepherd dogs is run with the object of preserving the breeds and distributing them among shepherds and households as guard dogs. Among dozens of these magnificent statuesque beasts, one dog stood out from the rest – a very nervous black and tan hound with a mane of hair flowing from its head and long hair hanging from its shoulders and legs. It was described as a Tazi and had come from the 'old town' of Konya, where I was to meet some of the breeders later. The explanation for its strange appearance may lie in the fact that this hound had been living all winter in an unheated outdoor kennel and had simply grown a thicker, longer coat to protect itself. As I was soon to see, all the other Tazis, despite the warm spring weather, had not yet abandoned their warm winter coats.

We set off to drive from the university about 80 km north to the large village of Kolukisa, set in a vast fertile plain – ideal coursing country. Osman, a cheerful villager, showed us around, banging on the iron doors to walled compounds for admittance into the courtyards, each with a Tazi or two. He said there were about 60 Tazis in the village, but it was already midday and we had time to see only about ten or so before and after a protracted lunch in his house. The first hound was his own six-year-old grizzle bitch, which had rather small, folded-back ears. This proved to be fairly common among Tazis in the area. Next door was a young feathered particoloured dog, who was a remarkably compact 61 cm tall by 56 cm long, and a beautiful nine-month-old smooth cream bitch, still wearing her winter coat.

Osman and his three-generation family then entertained us to an impromptu meal on the floor of the main living room, with the most delicious sheep's yoghurt, a dish of hot burghul (cracked wheat), boiled eggs, freshly baked pitta bread and salad, washed down with strong black sweet tea. Osman recounted that they never

Hairy Tazi in Konya.

fed the hounds meat, as this only encouraged them to eat their prey. They gave them hard bread and cooked barley meal. The hounds lived typically for 10–12 years. They started to train them with older hounds at about nine months and they continued hunting until they were about seven years old. I showed him a photo of a brindle, but he had never seen this colour in Tazis. The villagers here did not crop the ears, and applied henna to the hounds' feet to protect them. Depending on the availability of hares, it was not unusual for a hound to run four courses in a morning.

After lunch, we went on through the dusty alleys to a nearby house, where we were greeted by a delightfully bouncy feathered tricolour puppy that took some time to settle down for a photograph. There was also a young smooth black-masked red, with folded-back ears. Next door was a black and tan feathered dog that measured a surprising 68.5 cm by 61 and was the sire of the puppy. He was a good hunter and I thought he looked very nice, but Osman said he would show me an even more beautiful dog. We went to a house in a large garden where, on a raised veranda, a handsome feathered two-and-a-half-year-old black and white particoloured dog was chained up, barking defiantly at us. Like all the other Tazis, he had sparkling teeth from a diet consisting mainly of hard pitta bread. Finally, after trying several houses where the doors were locked and getting tangled up with flocks of sheep guarded by enormous Kangals wearing spiked collars against wolves, we met a feathered black and white particoloured dog with a lot of black ticking called *Boncuk*. I had been taking DNA swabs from some of the other hounds, but this one took off as soon as I approached with the swabs in my hand.

The next day another contact of mine, who runs a travel agency for hunters, rang and proposed a visit that afternoon to the 'old

Kangals with spiked collars against wolves in Konya.

city' of Konya. He said there were some gypsies there who had Tazis, and I knew that this was where the long-haired mystery hound had come from. The 'old city' proved to be quite close to our hotel and this quarter consisted of compound houses backing onto an open grassy area. As we approached the house of Shaban, the iron doors opened and three or four Tazis bounded into the roadway to welcome us. For their safety, we got them back into the compound and out of a back door so that they and some other Tazis could run on the field behind.

Shaban had a variety of hounds: two short-coupled smooth black and tans; two tiny smooth puppies, one copper-red and the other black and tan; and a very agile feathered black and white dog. They were joined in the field by a feathered grizzle. Shaban said he fed his dogs on leftovers from the table and did not mind giving them meat, so long as it was cooked. He hunted throughout the winter season, but preferred it when there was snow on the ground as this made tracking easier. I commented on the folded-back ears that I had seen and he said that previously all the Konya Tazis had pendulous ears but more recently people had started bringing in Tazis from other parts; indeed, he said his Tazis had some Syrian blood in them.

Then his brother, Serdal, appeared and we had to go and see his Tazis. Behind the usual compound doors, he showed us with pride his favourite hunting hound – a feathered black and tan bitch with cropped ears. Although already eight years old and the dam of a beautiful pair of two-year-old smooth grizzles, she was pregnant again. He also had a one-and-a-half-year-old smooth black and tan dog, a six-month-old feathered black and white dog and a crop-eared grizzle – quite a houseful! The hounds all looked in good condition and entirely relaxed with strangers in their midst, so that I could take DNA swabs without any fuss at all.

Serdal and his favourite bitch in Konya.

We had to move on to Ankara the next day, but on the road north I made a small diversion to the village of Dedeler. I had an introduction to another hunter, living in a house backing onto the endless Anatolian plain. He produced a pair of very different hounds. The dog was a powerfully built two-and-a-half-year-old smooth black and tan with nice pendulous ears. He measured exactly 63.5 cm square. The bitch was a terribly emaciated three-and-a-half-year-old feathered black and white, measuring 65 cm by 61. Communication with the hunter was difficult, but I gathered that they were both good hunters. It is possible that the bitch had not yet recovered from a litter, but I could not confirm the reason for her condition.

Although this was a very short visit, I had heard and seen enough to indicate that hunting with Tazis was holding up well in this part of Turkey. Rural life was improving all the time and there were enough incentives for people to stay on the land, which was ideal for hunting with sighthounds. I was surprised that the majority of the hounds were smooth, but this follows the tendency across much of the Saluki's range. I was equally surprised by the incidence of small, folded-back ears, but I neither saw nor heard of any evidence of crossbreeding with other sighthounds and assume that this was a local phenomenon, which does of course occur occasionally in other parts of the countries of origin. In the main, the hounds looked fit and well looked after.

Back home again, our dog sitters had kept our hounds in great condition and I was able to resume our long walks as before. The urban foxes seemed more numerous than ever, and my hounds were kept very active. It came, therefore, as a complete surprise when, one day in the middle of May, *Sally* suddenly went off her food and started eating grass avidly. My vet felt some distension in her stomach and gave some treatment for a possible infection. *Sally* perked up but, two weeks later, she went off her food again and just stared vacantly in distress. This time my vet did a scan, which revealed a large mass around her stomach and spleen, which was inoperable. I could not bear to see her suffer and agreed that the kindest solution was to put her to rest. It was a heart-wrenching time when she slipped away, as I recalled how she had always been so close to me for more than 11 years, since the day she was born. She was not only a coursing phenomenon but also a really loveable character that brought so much pleasure into our lives. We buried her ashes under a tree in the garden with the help of some of our grandchildren, with whom she had always been so gentle from the time they were babies.

They deliver him with their wagging tails.

Chapter Fifteen

The Last One?

With the death of *Sally*, I was faced with a serious dilemma. We had always had at least two Salukis in the house in the belief that they kept each other company. Now we had only *Filfil*, and she was already a veteran. Should we acquire another puppy? I had already had a number of offers from friends in the Middle East and I had a number of trips abroad planned for the coming period, when I could bring one back, though this would mean a period of quarantine. I could even have had a puppy from a litter sired in Italy by *Sally's* 11-year-old brother without the problem of quarantine. But as I contemplated my imminent 74th birthday, I wondered whether it would be the right thing to do, taking into account that a Saluki lives on average 10–12 years. Regretfully, Liese and I concluded that we would enjoy *Filfil* for the rest of her days but that she would be our last Saluki, unless she was very unhappy on her own.

Over the next week or two, *Filfil* was completely unsure of herself. She had always taken her lead from *Sally*, and she could not make out that *Sally* was no longer there. On our walks, she would keep stopping and looking back, and once she even turned round and ran back home. But then she seemed somehow reconciled to having to do things for and by herself – and a very strange thing happened. Without our being aware of it, *Filfil* killed a vixen out of sight at the back of our garden; Liese discovered it by accident the next morning. I put the corpse in a black bin liner, which I put at the side of the house ready for the rubbish collection the next day. However, the next morning, some workmen at our house found the bag shredded to pieces and the corpse dragged into the garden. They were digging the foundations of a new wall and buried the corpse in the trench. I concluded the culprit must have been the vixen's mate; but how strange! Anyway, Filfil had clearly come into her own and was capable of acting independently.

I then had to switch my mind onto another plane – the Saluki World Congress in Mustiala near Helsinki, Finland from 26 June to 2 July 2008, only the second time in the history of the Saluki that such an event has been held, the previous one being in Santa Barbara, California in 1995. I had been invited by the Finnish Saluki Club to give a talk on the history and development of the eastern Saluki. Finland is not a country most people would associate with the Saluki of the desert and the Club has been recognised as a breed association only since 2005, but at the time of the Congress there were some 900 Salukis registered in Finland and I looked forward to seeing how Salukis coped in such a different climate and to exchanging views with our hosts and fellow guest speakers. I was driven almost immediately on my first day to Micaela Lehtonen's place deep in the countryside, where I was glad to meet up again with Hamad al-Ghanem from Abu Dhabi and John Burchard, with whom I had corresponded for years but had never met before. Micaela's hounds were clearly flourishing, including her import Khattaf that I had last seen in Damascus. Our Finnish hosts looked after us very well and had made excellent arrangements for the visitors from eighteen countries from all over Europe and as far afield as the USA, Canada, Brazil, Australia, Japan, the UAE and Tanzania to attend a varied programme of shows, lure coursing, racing and a series of talks over a wide range of Saluki topics. I was particularly interested to meet for the first time Brian Duggan from the USA, for whose then forthcoming book, *Saluki: the Desert Hound and the English Travelers who brought it to the West,* I had written the introduction. His talk was based on the book and illustrated with some of the wonderful old photographs he had uncovered in his research. Hamad al-Ghanem's presentation on the Arabian Saluki Center in Abu Dhabi made me feel quite nostalgic, as did John Burchard's on coursing in the desert in the USA. But it was a talk by Dr Hannes Lohi of Helsinki University that I really applauded, as he spoke clearly and professionally on the importance of diversification for the avoidance of disease in our breed. I was less interested in the other talks on aspects of Western Salukis but, as always on these occasions, it was the discussions in smaller circles over a meal or a drink that were most stimulating. I also showed the television film made in Spain on coursing there the previous year, which seemed to go down well.

A couple of weeks later, I was involved in making another television film, this time for a BBC programme that was to prove very controversial. It was to be called *Pedigree Dogs Exposed* and would reveal in graphic detail some of the horrible results of the degeneration of some breeds through inbreeding. The director, Jemima Harrison, was interested in the comparison with our Salukis from a diversified background. We met on a farm in Wiltshire, where she interviewed John Burchard, who was passing through on his way back to the USA, and Paul Sagar from the SCC, who had brought along two of his Salukis, related to mine, and a falcon. We all gave her a comprehensive briefing on the Saluki, and her cameraman took some shots of Paul's Salukis working with the falcon and my *Filfil* running free. Sadly, in the end they had so much material that only *Filfil* made a fleeting appearance. But the programme really shook up the breeders and the Kennel Club. The BBC stopped covering Crufts after 42 years, the Dog Advisory Council was established and the Kennel Club amended 78 breed standards, which led to some changes in breeding practices. The impact rebounded, however, on Jemima Harrison, who was sent hate mail, abused on social media and banned from filming at other dog shows.

Then, out of the blue, came an invitation of a different kind, which caused me some heart-searching. Hamad al-Ghanem called to invite me to judge the 3rd Arabian Saluki Beauty Contest, as part of the Abu Dhabi International Hunting Exhibition (ADIHEX), on 8–11 October 2008. Saluki beauty shows are not really my scene, as I am more interested in performance, but Hamad assured me that these Salukis would be hunting hounds and my familiarity with them in their native habitat and with the Arab hunting culture would give me a more than adequate basis for assessing them. So, as soon as Ramadan and the following holiday were over, Liese and I flew from the cold and wet of London to the sunshine and pleasant heat of Dubai, and from there we headed for the Arabian Saluki Center in Abu Dhabi. Hamad showed us his present complement of hounds, with lots of lovely puppies growing up together in harmony with both their dam and their sire in their airy, purpose-built kennels. There must have been about 40 hounds there, many of them of an age to go to their new homes, mainly to hunters in the region but some to overseas destinations. It was a most useful preparation for the task ahead, as I was reminded of the prevalent local types.

ADIHEX started in Dubai in 2001, not only as a showplace for all kinds of hunting equipment and facilities but also as an auction house for camels, Arabian horses and falcons. Salukis were also paraded as part of the traditional hunting scene. The exhibition was originally planned to rotate annually between Dubai and Abu Dhabi, so the following year it was held in Abu Dhabi, but it has stayed there ever since. Thus, it was to the state-of-the-art National Exhibition Centre in Abu Dhabi that I made my way to judge an event that was transformed in 2006 from a mere parade to a full-blown show, entering by the door labelled 'Salukis only'! The Arabian Saluki Center occupied a spacious stand near the huge show arena and offered a traditional Arab welcome of cardamom-flavoured coffee and dates, consumed in a setting of bedouin rugs and cushions, with the odd Saluki curled up here and there oblivious to the movement all around. In an adjacent office, Hamad's staff checked the registrations of the eighty or so confirmed entries.

The hounds had been divided into batches of about 25 to be judged on each of the first three days, with the first and second finalists in each of the two categories of

The author with Hamad al-Ghanem at ADIHEX 2008 in Abu Dhabi.

feathered and smooth hounds going through to the Best in Show (BIS) contest on the last day. A quick look at the judging rating cards, giving the hounds' registration details, made me realise that this arrangement would present some particular difficulties – dogs and bitches would be together, and their ages ranged from eight months to seven years!

Time in the Arab world is fairly elastic and the 11.00 am start came and went with Salukis and their handlers, some of whom had travelled far, trickling unconcernedly in. Eventually I was given the signal to enter the arena – a vast, sandy oblong designed more with showing horses and camels in mind than Salukis. I agreed with Hamad and Sumaya, the hard-working ring steward, to use about one-third of the space, divided from the rest by potted plants. Thirteen feathered and ten smooth hounds had shown up, and were called forward one at a time by number and name to run one circuit before forming a line opposite me, with the feathereds to the left and the smooths to the right.

Some of the handlers and most of the hounds had never been in the ring before – indeed some of the hounds had never worn a collar – and needed some gentle guidance on what to do, but all credit to them as they all managed to finish where I needed them. The lack of ring experience did, however, make examining them individually quite tricky. It was not a question of the hounds' temperament, which was exemplary under my hands, but rather the unpredictability of their movement around the ring.

Nearly all the hounds were smaller in stature than is commonly seen in the West. Two distinct types were in evidence – at one end quite majestic, athletic hounds, many bearing the scars of the chase, and at the other dainty little creatures no bigger than Whippets. They all seemed to float around the ring with a beautiful, light, flowing gait that was hard to fault. A few carried their tail high, a few had shorter ears than usual, one had an uneven bite, some were overweight (common at the end of summer and the lay-off for Ramadan before the hunting season starts), but others were, by Western standards, underweight (which suggested that some were already in training). Within this wide variation, picking the winners in each category was no easy matter. In the end, I selected for the final the hounds that stood out from the rest: from the feathereds, first *Walla'*, a rangy one-and-a-half-year-old black and tan bitch, and second *Basma*, a delightful little three-year-old red and white particoloured bitch; and from the smooths, first *Tarrah*, a superb five-year-old sandy dog, and second *Qannas*, a powerfully built three-year-old grizzle dog.

On the second day, we had an evening slot after a camel auction and were due to start at 7.00 pm, but the auction went on until 9.30 pm, so that by the time the second batch of ten feathered and eight smooth hounds entered the ring we were all looking a bit jaded. However, I soon felt uplifted when I saw that I had a far more homogeneous batch, with fewer of the petite hounds, which Hamad said were specialised for hunting hare and not other game – a distinction I had never come across before in the region. This time it was quite easy to pick the overall feathered winner: *Lahhaq*, a four-year-old beautifully built black and tan dog that would grace any Western ring, with a very assured cream four-year-old dog called *Salaam* in second place. Among the smooths, I went for first *Antar*, an almost copper-red, black-masked four-year-old dog and second *Ruby*, an attractive little two-and-a-half-year-old red bitch. I worked as fast as I could as it was so late, but it was still after 11.00 pm by the time we trooped off exhausted from the glare and heat of the ring – and the hotel was 90 minutes away!

The third session was the following morning. It was a Friday and the local weekend, so the crowds of enquiring visitors from all over the Gulf grew as the day wore on. Again we started well after the advertised time, with a batch of ten feathered and 17 smooth hounds, from which I selected for the final first *Shatoob*, a stylish feathered one-and-a-half-year-old black, tan and white tricoloured dog and second *Khattaf*, a two-year-old grey grizzle dog with hennaed ears. Walking to the restaurant afterwards for a late lunch at around 3.30 pm was like navigating an obstacle course, as Hamad stopped every few minutes to greet relatives, friends and contacts curious to know how the show was going and what I thought of the participating hounds.

The last session, to pick the BIS feathered and the BIS smooth from the 12 finalists, was held in the late morning of the last day of ADIHEX, still the local weekend and even more crowded with visitors. The ring looked like a battlefield, as it had been churned up by the preceding horse show and had not been raked smooth. It was too late to do anything about this and I felt sorry for the handlers and their hounds, as they would have to negotiate the pockmarks, and concerned for myself, as I would have to judge their movement on such uneven ground. However, I had seen them all before and had my rating card on each of them as a guide. We began with individual circuits, followed by group circuits to give the spectators something to see. I then gave each a more cursory examination, more to confirm the mental image I had already formed of the likely winners. My choice for BIS feathered fell easily on *Lahhaq*, the showy black and tan dog that had impressed me earlier. The smooth selection was more difficult, and lay between the beautifully proportioned cream *Tarrah* and the striking black-masked copper-red *Antar*. After another look at the two of them, I gave BIS to *Tarrah*, as such an excellent specimen of the typical Salukis of the region.

Lahhaq, BIS feathered.

Overall, I think the show was a great success, particularly in meeting the organisers' main objectives – to attract the attention of the wider public, to encourage Arab pride in their breed and, above all, to stimulate the interest of the youth of the Gulf in their natural heritage in an era of limitless distractions. On a personal level, it was a great opportunity to see in a relatively short time the diversity of the Saluki in part of its native habitat, as well as all those special characteristics that make the breed so endearing – grace, symmetry, elegance, equable temperament and affection. My only regret was that I could not see them do the business for which they are so perfectly made!

However, on our return home I made up for this by taking *Filfil* to a friendly farm in Oxfordshire, where a group of us met on a beautiful day to exercise our hounds on the rabbits there and she had a really good run. She then had her season, and in early 2009, on a routine visit to the vet for her booster shots, some small lumps were spotted in her teats. The vet suggested a biopsy to start with and, if necessary, the surgical removal of all the lumps. I did not like the sound of all that trauma, so he suggested a homeopathic treatment that had proved quite successful. We began a three-week course and it seemed to work. The lumps diminished and *Filfil* was full of bounce, so much so that by the end of April I decided it was safe to leave her with our dog-sitters and take off for a memorable visit to another part of Turkey.

South-eastern Anatolia is really an extension into Turkey of Ancient Mesopotamia – or *Bilad al-Rafidain* (the Land between the Two Rivers – the Tigris and the Euphrates) as it is known in Arabic – and it shared in ancient times a common history with what we now call Iraq and Syria. I thought it probable, therefore, that I might find there similar hunting hounds to those across the border in northern Iraq and Syria, and I was not disappointed.

Liese and I began by taking a road from Gaziantep that led towards the Syrian border, now virtually a no-go area because of the fighting to close it off as a route taken by would-be combatants of the so-called Islamic State, whose 'capital' lay just across the border at Raqqa. At this time, however, all was peaceful as we turned off in a small village, where some friends had reported seeing Tazis about three years before. Sure enough, I quickly spotted a Tazi (or rather 'Tazhi', as the word is pronounced in the local Kurmanji Kurdish dialect) in a coat between two mud-brick houses. As I stopped to take pictures, the owner appeared and welcomed us to see his handsome three-year-old brown and white particoloured dog *Toufan* without its coat. He was a substantial dog, about 68.5 cm at the shoulder. He was soon joined by a very nice grizzle bitch and a bouncy young black and fawn bitch. All the hounds were smooth with crudely cropped ears, as are most of the Tazis in that part of Turkey. They were guarded by a fierce-looking Kangal (Akbash), fortunately restrained by a chain. The people were all Kurds and, as communication proved difficult, we moved on along a road almost parallel with the border to Harran, reputed to be one of the oldest continuously inhabited towns – since the days of the biblical Abraham in 1900 BC. The people speak Arabic, but I could elicit no information about Salukis there. This was strange because it appeared ideal flat hunting country. In fact, I was told later by some Kurds that they did indeed hunt there! But it was getting late and we needed to reach Şanliurfa by nightfall.

I had an introduction to a member of the Şanliurfa Veterinary Faculty, who led me unexpectedly into the director's office. He proved very helpful and arranged for me to be taken to the *Muhtar*, or headman, of a nearby village who would show me the Tazis

Qassab, who later turned up in Hama, Syria.

in his area. The *Muhtar* deputed his son to guide us and at the first call *Qassab*, a two-year-old strongly-built smooth red dog with a white blaze, was led out. The owner said that two of his brothers had been sold in Dubai. A neighbour then brought in a smooth cream dog with upstanding cropped ears that was a half-brother. *Bela*, a handsomely hennaed two-year-old feathered dog with intact ears – a rarity – was also brought out. The owner said that he usually started hunting in September, when the puppies were five to seven months old and he would continue using them until they were seven to eight years old, when they might be used for breeding.

We went on to another village, where I took a DNA sample from *Douman*, a one-and-a-half-year-old smooth grizzle in the presence of *Tayra*, a two-year-old smooth black and tan bitch, whose sister had been given as a present to 'the shaikh of Dubai', and a smooth tricoloured dog. They were guarded by an 11-year-old Kangal (Karabash) with a spiked collar against wolves. I was happy to let his owner take the DNA swab, as even an elderly Kangal is still a fearsome beast! Another young Kangal was doing its best to pull down the tree to which it was chained to get at the foreigner!

With my guides, I then set off on a drive across dirt roads to a small group of houses perched above the vast azure-blue artificial lake behind the Ataturk Dam on the Euphrates. We were warmly welcomed by a group of men, who were partly fishermen and partly cotton farmers; they were also hunters with Tazis. Two large Kangal (Karabash) hovered in the background.

Chichek and her puppies.

Once I had explained my purpose, they installed us on rugs and cushions in the sunshine and served strong tea in glasses. They produced a smooth tricoloured dog, a smooth grizzle dog and a similar bitch. The bitch was clearly lactating and one of the men went off to a shed from which he emerged with an armful of puppies. They were just 15 days old, but already their ears had been cropped and had healed. The dam, called *Chichek*, was a great coursing hound and regularly caught four hares a day. There were three female and two male puppies and the owner said that the first-, third- and fifth-born would be the best, in that order. All their dogs were vaccinated with imported vaccines against rabies, distemper and parvovirus. I showed them some of my photographs of coursing hounds, which they promptly copied with their mobile phones! I showed an Iranian brindle, but they were unfamiliar with this colour in Tazis. I also showed some Greyhounds, but they did not recognise them and did not even know the word for them.

On our way back to town, we made one more stop to see another couple of hounds: *Kina*, a four-year-old smooth grizzle bitch carrying puppies due two days later by *Gushtu*, a two-year-old slightly feathered grizzle dog. Both hounds were very affectionate with their master and looked in very good condition.

From Şanliurfa we wended our way via a series of historic towns and fortified monasteries, made all the more colourful by the riot of yellow, red and purple spring flowers that covered the ground, towards the ancient walled city of Diyarbakir that stands somewhat menacingly on a hill above the Tigris. A local guide said he would take us to a nearby town to see his aunt, who would know who owned Tazis there. The next morning we set off with the guide for the small town of Çinar and his aunt, a splendid Kurd with a tattoo on her chin. As we were drinking tea in her courtyard, a local gypsy passed by and he was immediately engaged to take us to see the breeders. But we were out of luck; at the first house we learnt that the man had gone 'to the mountains' with his three Tazis; at the next the man said he had just sold his two Tazis, and at the third no one was at home. However, at a fourth house we were given directions to a nearby village where Hajji Hasan definitely had Tazis. Somewhat doubtful, we arrived at a substantial three-storey house, typically unfinished for reasons of municipal tax. The door to the courtyard was flung open and out shot a beautiful smooth grizzle dog, followed by a very nasty-looking Kangal. Someone grabbed the Kangal and locked him away in a storeroom so that we could enter the house safely and get a proper look at *Sha'ar*, a 63.5-cm three-year-old of very gentle

Hajji Hasan's beautifully proportioned hound near Diyarbakir.

disposition. He was in excellent condition and, like all the other hounds I saw, was fed mainly on leftovers from the table.

But Hajji Hasan, a beaming cotton farmer, and his large family, insisted we come in and partake of a delicious impromptu lunch spread out on the floor of his comfortably installed sitting room. Over the meal, he related that his family had hunted with Tazis for generations. His wife chipped in that she had to take second place in the house to his Tazi – so Liese felt an instant bond with her! He liked to start the females hunting at six months and the males at nine to twelve months, as they matured slower. He preferred females as they could continue hunting longer than the males – he claimed for up to ten years! Sadly, his bitch had recently been stolen. I commented that I had seen only young hounds and asked what happened to the older ones. He denied vehemently that they would ever put down a healthy Tazi, but said that when they got old 'usually the guard dogs kill them'. The hunting season started as soon as the cotton crop was harvested in September. He liked it best after rain, when the tracks of the *kiroshk* (hare) could more easily be found. We were interrupted by one of his sons, who wanted us to identify our house in London on Google Earth! When we returned, Hajji Hasan said he would take us to his brother's to see his Tazi. As we drove along a dirt track through the fields, we could see two men walking towards us with a hound running free. This was his brother's Tazi, *Havees*, a litter brother of Hajji Hasan's dog. He too was in superb condition and was alert for the chase.

Our host said goodbye with directions to another village on the way back to Diyarbakir. We turned off the main road towards some warehouses for storing the picked cotton, where about a dozen men sat under a tree drinking tea and chatting in the late afternoon sunshine. In answer to our enquiry, a young man went over to one of the warehouses and let out two quite different Tazis. One was a tall (about 68.5 cm) black and white particoloured two-year-old dog, again called *Havees*, with henna liberally applied to the feathering on his cropped ears and to his well-feathered tail. The other was a rather short (about 61 cm), compact one-year-old smooth red bitch with a black line down the topside of the tail, called *Howre*. The owner of *Havees* said he was an excellent courser and had caught on his own 12 hares in a month.

After Diyarbakir, we had a long drive back to Adana via the snow-covered mountain of Nemrut Dağ, and heard of other places along the way where Tazis were to be found, but we did not have the time to seek them out. However, although I had only scratched the surface of this very large area, I felt confident that the Tazi or Saluki was thriving in these ideal conditions of a largely rural economy on the northern edge of the great Mesopotamian plains.

Turkey is a candidate for membership of the European Union and, if it succeeds, it could become the first Country of Origin with free movement for Salukis into Europe. Turkey therefore holds out the prospect of a supply of new blood for the established Western Saluki gene pool. Turkish hounds have already made their mark, particularly in Germany and the USA, and on the evidence that I saw both in Britain and in south-western Anatolia the previous year they could undoubtedly make a significant contribution to the long-term health and diversity of the Saluki in the West. A problem looming over the horizon is, however, that the Turks appear divided over the breed, with some seeking to have it identified internationally as a uniquely Turkish breed called the Anadolu Sultan Tazi, which, it is claimed, is feathered and different from the commonly smooth Tazi of the Şanliurfa area that so closely resembles the Saluki across the border in Syria as to be indistinguishable. With the present turmoil in the region, it seems unlikely that this problem will be resolved soon.

On our return, *Filfil* was in very good shape and was soon busily chasing the early morning foxes again. Later in the autumn she pulled off a feat that left me marvelling at the faculties of the Saluki. We were visiting, with Adrian and Lucinda Phillips, a

Havees.

country fair near Winchester that was very well attended on a fine day. We had to park in a field adjacent to the fair ground and wend our way through the crowds to see the various displays. I kept *Filfil* on the leash all the while, but she started to become nervous near a display of clay pigeon shooting. Someone let off a gun very close to us and she spooked, slipping out of her collar and making a dash for it. I went after her but quickly lost her in the crowds and, although I asked everywhere whether anyone had seen her, I could find no trace of her. In the end, I played a hunch and made my way back to where we had parked. To my great relief, there sitting by the side of the car was *Filfil*, equally happy to see me. How she had managed to navigate her way back – presumably by scent – through all those people and hundreds of parked cars, was incredible. And who says Salukis are only sighthounds? But perhaps I should not have been so surprised because, as a recent article in *The Times* reported:

> Experiments on butyric acid, the chemical that gives feet their odour, suggest that a dog could easily smell a sweaty sock in an auditorium the size of the Royal Albert Hall. (Tom Whipple, Science Editor, 'How the dog knows you're coming home', *The Times*, 19 November 2016)

If this is so, then finding her way back to her blanket in our car must have been a doddle!

But I was getting itchy feet again and, when a friend said he was keen to make a tour in Syria, I gladly agreed to go along and show him some of the lesser known byways. What I liked about Syria most was that, until the last few turbulent years of civil war and insurrection, it has changed very slowly compared with many of the surrounding countries. Wherever you went, the landscape was immediately recognisable as Syria as it was half a century ago. What changed most was the size of the population, and this had led to the cities and towns expanding inexorably outwards. However, until comparatively recently, one did not have to go far to reach the countryside, where life went on more or less as before. Usually I tried to time my visits to coincide with the end of the coursing season in March, when the weather is still relatively cool and the wild flowers colour the ground, but autumn could be beautiful too – and off we went at the beginning of November.

Damascus is always a pleasure as the gateway to Syria, especially when my Syrian friends are so welcoming and hospitable, though sometimes this can be somewhat overwhelming and the time passes too quickly in a blur of historic buildings, sumptuous meals in exotic restaurants and hours of discussion. This time I deliberately kept the period in Damascus to the minimum, but this still allowed for a visit to an Arabian horse farm and a Saluki kennels.

The horse farm was reached through a maze of narrow lanes on the outskirts of the city. My host was keen to show me his latest acquisitions – not only Arabians but also some massive Kangal guard dogs imported from Turkey, all living amicably with about 30 cats. First there was a parade of that year's foals, then some yearlings undergoing training for showing in the ring and finally some of the breed stock. They all looked beautiful but, just as with the local Salukis, they seemed to have a more rugged quality about them than what we are used to seeing in the West.

From there my friend Basil Jadaan took us on to see his new kennels, which I had seen under construction four years before. These were set in a large compound and the hounds were allowed out to run as much as they wanted. I easily recognised one black and tan bitch called *Tayra* that I had seen on my previous visit, but Basil said that he had lost a number through disease and one had run away after being attacked by some of the others. There were just five left.

My real objective was, however, to move on to Hama, where the coursing fraternity were waiting to take us on a day out in the desert with the hounds. Hama is an easy drive from Damascus and we arrived with ample time for a quick tour around some of the breeders in the town and the surrounding area. My dentist friend, Ghanem al-Barazi, took us first to see someone I had not met before, though his late cousin had been one of my regular coursing companions. Abu Ibrahim had a compound that was kept especially for his hounds. There were six of them, all in their *kouban* or winter coats, but he quickly took these off and they looked in excellent condition. First came *Doughan*, a powerful three-year-old black and tan dog, then a two-year-old grey grizzle called *Sarukh*; the names of the others came too quickly for me to note down. Most had cropped ears, though Abu Ibrahim said he never cut those of his own breeding, and only one was feathered, a wild-looking black-masked red dog recently imported from Turkey. When I thought I had seen them all, Abu Ibrahim said he had some more in the neighbouring compound as they did not get on with this pack. Next door were three more, including a remarkable (for these parts) feathered dog of six years called *Abu Nab* that had been a great hunter and was now at stud. Abu Ibrahim had, however, another secret weapon, which I was not to see until the next day at the hunt.

Over a glass or two of tea in a little reception room off the compound, I commented to Abu Ibrahim on his hounds' beautiful collars, decorated with beads, cowry shells or brass studs. He said that they were made to order by the prisoners in the local gaol. He added that the distinctive metal fastenings were designed to give off a jingling noise to alert the hare, as it was believed that the hare should never be taken by surprise but only after a fair contest. I asked how he kept his hounds in such good condition, if he fed them only on dry pitta bread, as was the local custom. He said that he did in fact give his hounds Eukanuba kibble (the first I had ever seen in Syria) in addition to the pitta bread, and once a week he gave them cooked chicken necks. He also showed me a range of Western food supplements that he used. Here, at least, there were some signs of change.

We needed to move on, as I wanted to see some breeders in the nearby villages of Khan Shaikhoon and Sawran, but on the way we stopped by a dusty square off the main road where – exceptionally, as the hounds were usually hidden away – a group of young hounds was playing and fighting over an old sandal.

In the first village, an old friend called Abdulrazzaq produced a series of hounds from under a crude shelter made of old tractor tyres and plastic sheeting. He seemed very thin and a bit down on his luck, and his hounds were not as well cared for as before. It was the same in the next village, where another old friend called Ahmad had only a few unexceptional hounds. Abu Ibrahim told me later that there was a growing problem with some of the breeders selling all their hounds, even their breed stock, to rich Saudis, Qataris and Emiratis. This was very short-sighted, and could have harmful consequences for the future. I told him about stories emanating from the Gulf that Syrians were selling Greyhound-Saluki crosses there. He ridiculed the notion as he said there were no Greyhounds in Syria! Then, after a moment's reflection, he said that he had heard of an Emirati who had brought a Greyhound to Syria and mated it to a Syrian Saluki bitch on the understanding that he would return for the puppies. He went away with the Greyhound and returned later to take the crossbred puppies back to the Emirates. I also asked him about rumours of a kind of marketplace where Salukis were sold to visitors from the Gulf. He said he had never heard of such a thing. Sales were usually on an individual basis, though it was possible that such visitors had been to gypsy encampments. The gypsies are great breeders of Salukis and their tents might give the impression of a marketplace.

Before leaving the village, we went to another famous breeder, but he too had aged and his hounds seemed to lack the quality of old. Finally, we went to a nearby farm where Ghanem was keeping his hounds overnight before the next day's hunt. His hounds were all youngsters of less than 18 months. They were let loose, and promptly gave chase to a very large guard dog, belonging to a gypsy encampment, which backed off very slowly and warily. An Arabian was also brought out for exercise on a lunge and one of the hounds pursued it crazily round and round in circles, keeping just out of range of the hooves. The hounds seemed very keen for the hunt.

The next day we set off before dawn in fog, which slowed our progress until the rising sun burnt it off as we reached the edge of the cultivated land and the desert. I had to drive our hire car, as the hunter who was to give us a lift had cried off in the night due to unexpected visitors. So we were in a convoy of three, led by Abu Ibrahim in a huge pickup with four hunters and three hounds inside and followed by Ghanem with his father in a small van with four hounds. The place where we stopped looked very unpromising – hard and very stony – but there were reputedly hares there.

We walked for about an hour without so much as a sign of one. By then Abu Ibrahim had decided to follow the hunt in his pickup and invited me to join him to take pictures. I was more than glad to do so. Then the four hounds that were running free, as was the custom when walking up there, put up a hare and, to Abu Ibrahim's and my consternation, the other three hounds were slipped too. The hare gave them a good long run but the outcome was a foregone conclusion. The hounds caught it and fought over it. By the time we drove up, there was little of it left. Abu Ibrahim took the remains and buried them, cursing his companions for running all the hounds at once. They answered unabashedly that this was the hounds' first time out and they needed a run. But at least they agreed to

Overshooting the hare.

put two of the worst offenders from the novices back in the van. We went on with five hounds, one of which had cut the stop on its foreleg and was limping slightly. About half an hour later, another hare got up and the course proved a carbon copy of the first. All five hounds were slipped and, after a long chase, caught the hare and tore it to pieces. Abu Ibrahim once again railed against the others, saying they should never run more than two or three hounds, but their enthusiasm was hard to control.

We tried some different ground with directions from a passing bedouin, and put up a third hare. This time there were only four hounds running, two of which were experienced and kept ahead of the novices. The hare gave them a magnificent run, which I followed with my camera from the pickup. I managed to get one shot in which one of the hounds seemed to overshoot the hare. Eventually they wore it down and caught it intact. There would be at least one for the pot. It proved to be the only one for, although we continued until 1.00 pm, we put up only one more hare, which managed to disappear in some dense bush.

Over a delicious barbecue in the lee of a drystone wall, I asked Abu Ibrahim about the dog that seemed to be leading the pack. It was not one I had seen the day before. The dog, called *Qassab*, was red and white with cropped ears. Abu Ibrahim then recounted an extraordinary story. I had given him a DVD I had made featuring some Salukis I had filmed near Şanliurfa in Turkey the previous April. He had watched it overnight and had recognised *Qassab* and the man from whom he had recently bought it – what an amazing coincidence! It was certainly an exceptional hound. Abu Ibrahim had earlier owned another exceptional two-year-old grey grizzle hound that he had sold to Turkey, where it had caught two gazelle on its own. As a result, he had bought it back and it was now running beautifully on its home soil. These stories serve to illustrate the close relationship between the breeders and hunters and their hounds on either side of the border.

The hunters went off to discuss the day's events in their sort of club, but we needed to prepare ourselves for the onward journey. It started the next morning when Ghanem called to guide us to his new farm, which happened to lie on our route to see the Crusader castle at Shaizar. The farm was approached by a narrow muddy track and we were greeted at the entrance by an extraordinary sight – a pair of Kangals (one recently imported from Turkey) and, beside them, a harlequin Great Dane! The latter was a descendant of a pair Ghanem had brought back from Romania years before. Also running around loose was a mischievous Saluki, which was kept separate from the main kennels where, to my astonishment, I counted another 13 hounds! They were all young, many of them siblings from recent litters. Ghanem said that he had just retired and was now able to devote himself more to building up his kennels and to going hunting. He certainly had plenty of material to work on! Whatever some Syrian breeders were doing with selling off their hounds, clearly there were others who continued to maintain the old traditions in Hama.

We drove on north to see the vast archaeological site at Apamea, which was one of the great cities of the Seleucid Empire founded by Alexander the Great's general Seleucus I Nicator, before crossing east to the small town of Ma'arrat al-Nu'man, which held a treasure of particular interest to hunters. In a magnificently restored Ottoman caravanserai, there was at the time an amazing collection of Byzantine mosaics, lifted from ruined villas in the surrounding area and mounted there on the walls. The richness of the colours and the artistry of the designs are an attraction in themselves, but the subjects depicted are largely of hunting scenes, showing a range of predators, including some Saluki-like hounds, and prey, indicating how this area was formerly – as it is today – good hunting country. Sadly, the town has been severely damaged in the civil war and I wonder whether these masterpieces have survived. At least they have all been indelibly marked, which would make them harder to sell if they were plundered.

We went on to stay in Aleppo, from where friends were going to take us out to some of the surrounding villages in which I had seen many Salukis in the past. However, I was hit suddenly by a bug and had to keep to the confines of Aleppo itself for a couple of days, which at least allowed us the opportunity to explore the labyrinth of almost medieval bazaars in the old town below the Citadel, most of which, sadly, have since been obliterated by the fighting.

On returning to Damascus – probably for the last time, as things have turned out – I was saddened to hear that the efforts by the Syrian Arab Horse Association to establish a Saluki registry had foundered, largely for lack of human resources to run it. In any case, it probably would not have survived the present civil war, which broke out the year after our visit, since the people are more concerned about their own survival in a country where in many places law and order have broken down completely. It will probably take years for a situation to come about in which people will have the means and the leisure to restore some semblance of the old way of life; and it remains to be seen whether there will still be place for the Saluki in it.

Back in England, we had a good winter season with *Fifil*, with lots of outings with her into the countryside after rabbits, and she seemed to have recovered completely. As spring came, the Middle East beckoned again, though first an echo of it came to London in the shape of Basil Jadaan from Damascus. He happened to be over for a meeting of the World Arabian Horse Association, so we invited him round for lunch. Liese laid on a superb oriental meal over which Basil philosophised, recited Arabic poetry and generally charmed. He had had a litter of three puppies and offered us one, but we had to harden our hearts and decline. We discovered that his family was originally from the Na'im tribe, whose shaikh Liese and I had been invited to meet in Ajman the following week. What a coincidence!

The very next day we flew to Doha in Qatar, where we were keen to see the new Museum of Islamic Art and meet some Saluki friends. The museum is stunning and we spent hours in the beautifully presented galleries before having dinner with a vet who had been very helpful to me in Morocco over the National Geographic film. She happened to be the daughter of a former colleague of mine, and was married to a doctor working in the main Doha hospital. She had brought with her from Rabat a Sloughi, and had adopted a Saluki in Doha – and I could not resist the temptation to take samples of their DNA for comparison. We also visited a member of the ruling family, whom I had known before as a great hunter with falcons and Salukis, and I hoped to see again the farm where they were kept; but I learnt to my chagrin that the pressures of his business life had forced him to give up hunting and he no longer had any hounds. He had, however, established a huge private museum in a reconstructed fort, which he arranged for us to see before we flew on to Dubai.

We stayed in Dubai with some old friends and were picked up from there by Dr Saif al-Bidwawi, a local historian and adviser to the Ruler of Ajman. He took us to call on the Ruler, whom I had known well in the late 1960s when he was the heir apparent. Shaikh Humaid bin Rashid al-Na'imi received us in his *majlis* and we swapped stories from the old days. We also met his eldest son, who was a falconer and had recently returned from a hunting trip to Iraq but without Salukis.

The next day I met another shaikh who had lots of them – by his own estimate, in the region of three hundred! Shaikh Rashid bin Ahmed Al Maktoum picked me up

Saluki show jumping.

and took me to the Al Maktoum family compound in Za'bil, Dubai, where he had his purpose-built kennels for about 30 of his Salukis and several Greyhounds and Saluki-Greyhound crosses. He concentrated on breeding for Saluki racing, at which he had been extremely successful. He also indulged in crossbreeding hounds for shorter races up to two kilometres, for which he found a female Greyhound mated with a male Saluki produced the best results. I noticed that some of his Salukis had cropped ears, which was not a local custom. However, he said that he did this on some of his hounds before the age of two months if they had very long ears that got in the way.

Over lunch on the floor in a bedouin tent, he talked about his other passion, show jumping, in which he had also had considerable success as a member of the Dubai team – though juggling all these commitments with his university studies was clearly a challenge. Afterwards he took me into a large hangar to show me how he exercised some of his Salukis using show-jumping techniques. Two kennelmen were walking round two Salukis: *Haddad*, an amazingly fit 16-year-old smooth red dog, and *Lam'ah*, a one-year-old smooth Irish-marked red bitch. Two other kennelmen held aloft two poles used as barriers in show jumping and Shaikh Rashid ran at them with the Salukis one at a time on a long leash and they jumped over like show horses. It was amazing!

He invited me to see their training methods with live gazelle in the desert, but I could not find the time before returning to London. However, it sounded pretty hair-raising, as it involved following the Salukis chasing a gazelle over several kilometres before a vehicle was driven between the leading Salukis and the gazelle, thus obscuring the hounds' view, whereupon someone leant out of the vehicle, caught the gazelle by the horns and pulled it to safety.

I was very busy over the next few months working on a new book on Oman, which involved a couple of trips there, and I was involved in a museum project that took me to Basra in Iraq. During this time, *Filfil* started to behave strangely. There were days when she did not want to walk and others when she did not eat. Eventually, in July, I took her to see my vet, as her stomach looked very swollen. He confirmed my worst fears that, like *Sally* before her, she had a massive tumour in her stomach that would become increasingly painful for her and that it would be best to end her suffering. It was a terrible moment, but there was no alternative and we had to say goodbye to our last Saluki.

Puppy at home in Meknes.

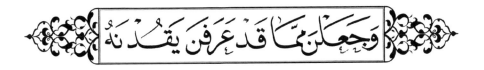

When they recognise him, they lead him in,

Chapter Sixteen

The Lure of the East

The passing of *Filfil* was an occasion for reflection on my life with Salukis over the previous 25 years or so. Clearly, they had added an extra dimension to a diplomatic career spent in large part in the countries of the Saluki's origin, and had brought great pleasure – as well as more than a little pain with each parting. The question that kept arising was, however – what next? Liese believed that I should devote more time to my other pursuits, professional, cultural and artistic, and so I did, but the lure of the Eastern Saluki remained strong – and from time to time I indulged, now without the problem of arranging dog-sitters.

I could not resist the invitation of Mohammed Soujaa, President of the Royal Moroccan Federation for Traditional Hunting, to spend a few days in Meknes to attend the federation's first international festival on 25–26 September 2010. It was a courageous and colourful occasion, which had as its main objective the preservation of traditional hunting with Sloughis and falcons as part of Morocco's national patrimony.

Despite promises of support from the authorities and sponsors, it largely fell to Mohammed Soujaa and his helpers to fund and organise the event. Right up until the last moment, it was clearly only by a superhuman effort that it happened at all, and the fact that it took place reflects well on the organisers as well as on the Jami'at Al-Gannas (Hunters' Society) of Qatar, which sent a delegation of about a dozen hunters, led by the society's president, with some of their Salukis and falcons, and helped overcome some of the difficulties on the spot. Among the visitors were also some from France with their Sloughis.

The festival was held in the spacious grounds of the Military Riding Academy, which provided a covered stand for the spectators to view the events. On two sides of a large field facing the stand, the federation erected three large black tribal tents to accommodate the official visitors and guests, and to provide a forum for the Qataris to screen a beautifully produced film about traditional hunting with Salukis and falcons and to show a range of their publications. An adjacent, even larger field was reserved for live and lure coursing and a display of falconry.

Mohammed Soujaa in Meknes.

By mid-morning on the first day, a crowd of hunters with about 60–70 Sloughis and four peregrine falcons were milling around on the main field, while a group of gaily caparisoned horses, with their riders carrying old muzzle-loading rifles, capered around to the music of a colourful band of folkloric musicians from the Atlas Mountains and another from the Meknes area. The intention had been to hold a Sloughi show, but the invited qualified judge did not come, so instead there was a parade of hounds with their owners in front of the stand. This provided an excellent opportunity to compare the hounds. As was to be expected, they showed a diverse range of types, from those that the Qataris identified as most like their Salukis to those that were rather larger and more robust, often with broader heads and thicker necks.

In the afternoon, there was keen competition between Sloughis and visiting Salukis in the live coursing events, in which captured foxes were released about 50 metres in front of the competitors for the hounds to chase. It was interesting to contrast their different running styles, with the Sloughis generally faster on the straight but less manoeuvrable than the Salukis on the turns. One of the Qatari Salukis clearly puzzled the spectators as it was a smooth black-masked sable of a type they did not associate with the Saluki, which was beautifully represented by another Qatari feathered cream hound, made all the more striking by its henna colouring on ears and paws.

The next day started with some lure coursing, with four to six hounds chasing a lure over a straight course only about 150 metres long, which did not test the hounds as much as the real thing but gave them some exercise and the spectators some pleasure to see them run. This was followed by some further live coursing on foxes. Then it was the turn of the falconers, who put on an excellent display of flying their peregrines to a lure.

One of the Qatari Salukis coursing a fox.

By this time, we were all ready for the magnificent lunch of Moroccan specialities that was served under the tents. The afternoon continued with more live coursing, rounded off by a 'Fantasia' by the horsemen, who charged at the spectators and wheeled their horses around at the last moment.

The festival was brought to an end with speeches of thanks by Mohammed Soujaa and the Qatari delegation in front of the Pasha of Meknes and other dignitaries. Prizes were awarded to the owners of some of the best performers among the coursers.

Only then was there time to sit and reflect on the whole affair. Mohammed Soujaa was plainly pleased that the festival had achieved its objective of increasing public awareness of the the need to preserve these traditions, through both the attendance of the crowds of spectators and the extensive media coverage. At the same time, there was some disappointment that the organisers had not been able to offer the full range of activities that had been foreseen. However, they emerged with the strong conviction that the festival had set a firm basis for future such events and, with the declared support of Qatar's Hunters' Society, it seemed likely that the following year would see a more comprehensive celebration of traditional hunting to encourage those determined to keep it alive as part of the nation's heritage. This is under threat not only from the pressures of the modern way of life but also from within the hunting community itself, as local hunters are tempted to experiment with imports of foreign sighthounds such as Galgos, to the detriment of the local hound.

A month later, I was off again in the opposite direction on a different quest – the mysterious Chinese Xigou. Hope and David Waters' book *The Saluki in History, Art and Sport* (1984) includes a beautiful painting of Salukis from the 10th century, attributed to the Tatar artist Hu Huai, in which three hunters are depicted returning from the chase on horseback, two with their Salukis carried in front of them and one with his hound behind him. The Waters describe the artist as originally a Tatar tribesman who was familiar with nomadic life and with Salukis. They also opine that the Saluki reached China from Persia via the Kyrgyz nomads on the steppes of Central and Southern Siberia and Turkestan.

But were the hounds depicted by Hu Huai really Salukis? The Waters clearly had no doubts, describing the hounds as 'of absolutely typical appearance', but this is a question that had troubled me for a long time, not least for its implications for the extent of the area, which we tend to refer to these days as the Saluki's Countries of

Origin. If they really were Salukis and they were sufficiently common in Asia for a China-based artist to paint them as an aspect of everyday life a thousand years ago, what were their origins and how did they relate to the other sighthounds to the west in Central and Western Asia?

A search of published material and the Internet revealed little information in English, though a Chinese website showed some pictures of a Saluki-like hound called Xigou (pronounced 'See-gow'), meaning 'Slender Dog'. Then, out of the blue, a Chinese hunter contacted me after having seen my own website, and so began a process that eventually led me, in October 2010, to Xi'an in Shaanxi Province of north-central China, one of the main centres of the Xigou today.

Xi'an was formerly known as Chang'an and was the terminal point on the Silk Road, along which from the 1st century BC until well into the 17th century AD traders, soldiers, missionaries, nomads and pastoralists of a variety of nationalities and ethnicities moved with greater or lesser ease, depending on who was in control of the land mass through which the routes passed. Trade along the Silk Road reached its peak in the 7th century under the Tang dynasty, with its capital in Chang'an, when China was the richest and most powerful country in the world and Persians, Arabs, Uighurs and Jews flocked in with their different languages, customs and religions to create a most cosmopolitan society. The first Arabs are recorded as having reached Chang'an in 651 AD, but Islam made its major impact on the area in 751 when Muslim Arabs defeated the Tang army at the Talas River (now in Kazakhstan). The Arabs at that time were prodigious hunters with both hawk and hound and it is probable that they brought with them their Salukis, most likely of the feathered variety from northern Iran, which they had already conquered. This is the variety portrayed in the Waters' book and the earlier representations that I found in the Xi'an museums.

However, there is evidence of earlier types of hunting hound in the region. As Xavier Przezdziecki records in *Our Levriers* (2001), images of a graceful sighthound appear on Chinese funerary bricks from the 3rd century BC. Of perhaps even greater relevance to the Xigou of today is a remarkably explicit painting of a foreigner holding a hawk on his wrist while a Xigou with a distinctive 'banana-shaped' nose looks up at him, which is to be found as a mural in the tomb of Prince Zhanghuai, who died in 684 AD and was buried near present-day Xi'an. Later paintings, such as the one used as the masthead on the Xigou website from the Ming dynasty dated to 1427, show a similar hound with what contemporary Xigou breeders refer to as a 'sheep's nose', a

The author with a Xigou near Xian.

high ridge something like that of a Bull Terrier.

Xi'an today is a big, bustling modern city of some eight million people, but traces of its glorious past are to be found at its centre in its massive, 25-km long old city walls, its Grand Mosque founded in 742 with its beautiful Arabic calligraphy, and several towering pagodas from the 14th century. However, most impressive of all is the 'Eighth Wonder of the World', the terracotta warriors and horses of the Qin dynasty's first emperor, Shi Huangdi, from around 204 AD, located at a site a short drive east of the city. Xi'an did not seem the place to see hunting hounds, but I was wrong!

My Chinese guide and mentor, Sun Hui, took me to an estate of towering tenement blocks, on the sixth floor of one of which I met probably the most Saluki-like Xigou I was to see throughout my visit. Her name was *Xianni* and she was a sleepy 15-year-old. I took her rough measurements and she proved much taller than long: 71cm at the shoulder by 64 cm in length. This made her a large hound by Saluki standards but, as I found out later, she was truly representative of the Xigou in this respect. She was accompanied by *Ying Cai*, a three-year-old grey bitch measuring 70 cm x 66. They were both kept as pets and were fully adapted to a life of ease in a flat, while their owners were out at work all day. This was not at all what I had expected to find, but it was in one respect typical – it showed the close bond that the Chinese have with their Xigou. As one hunter told me, Xigou are counted as members of the family. Sometimes they live inside the house, though more often they live in kennels in the courtyard typical of Chinese houses outside the cities and protect the house. During the Cultural Revolution (1966–76) – when keeping dogs was banned and many were destroyed because of outbreaks of rabies – rather than lose their precious Xigou, owners would hide them in the house and

Xigou puppy in a doorway.

even keep puppies out of sight inside their shirts!

But I was keen to see these hounds in their more natural environment in the countryside, so Sun Hui took me east from Xi'an on a circuitous journey to the Hua Mountains. On the way, he used his laptop to show the Xigou in all its aspects, so I was quite well prepared by the time of our first stop at the typically ornamented portals of a house in a small town. An attractive, mini-skirted young woman opened the massive gates into a courtyard, where a self black male Xigou of 17 months was bounding about. The prosperous owner was happy for me to take DNA samples from this hound and another pure white year-old male attached to a kennel. Both had a slightly 'banana-shaped' nose, which is common but by no means general among the Xigou; and I recall hearing about Salukis with such a nose on the West Coast of the USA at one time. It was quite difficult to measure these two, as they were nervous of me as a stranger, but both were around the average at over 70 cm tall and about 7–8 cm shorter in length. Their coat was also representative, silky with quite long ear furnishings but only wispy feathering on the tail. In this respect, they were similar to the Tazys of Central Asia. Their coat colours proved also to be the most common – black, often with a tiny patch of white on the chest, or pure white – but I also saw cream, grey, and red sable, some with brindle. The black dog was popped into the boot of our car and we sped off across country along narrow roads, made even narrower by patches of maize grain spread out to dry.

We reached another small town and stopped before the even more imposing portals of a house where a black Xigou puppy greeted us amid the drying maize. He was accompanied by a brindle Greyhound puppy, the first of a number of Greyhounds I was to see. The hound we had brought in the boot was handed over to its new owner

A striking red male Xigou.

and we set off again to another small town. It was dark by the time we arrived at another substantial house, where two Xigou ran out to greet us. They were two-year-old brothers; one was black but with chocolate overtones, particularly on the ear feathering, and the other, called appropriately *Laohu*, meaning tiger, was an unusual dark brindle with a coat pattern I have only seen before on some North African Sloughis. The first measured 72 cm by 65 and the other 69 by 61. After some heated discussion, a deal was done and the black-chocolate dog was put in the boot. I was told that the going rate for a mature hound like this was $700, whereas a puppy might go for $300. As elsewhere in the Saluki's countries of origin, Xigou are exchanged or bought and sold purely on trust, as they have no written pedigrees, though births and parentage are sometimes recorded on the Xigou website. At the end of a very long day, I was glad when we finally checked into an hotel in Huayin, while the car returned to Xian, with the dog uncomplainingly still in the boot.

The next day we set off to meet two of the principal breeders of Xigou in Huayin. The first call started unpromisingly in what was a metal-working yard, with men welding together sections of chain-link fencing! However, as soon as I got out of the car I could hear a familiar howling in the background. Sure enough, at the rear of the yard behind a mountain of steel pipes was a purpose-built kennels with about 30 Xigou and an assortment of other hunting and guard dogs. The Xigou were all two to a kennel, with an outside run and an inside sleeping compartment on a raised wooden floor. The hounds were hardy, as they slept there without bedding or coat, even in winter. I had clearly come to the right place to see a range of these hounds.

The first hound brought out for my inspection was really striking – a year-old male, he was big, measuring 80 cm at the shoulder, and he was a black-masked red sable with honey-coloured ear feathering. But it was the shape of his head that was most remarkable – a most pronounced sheep's nose. None of the many other hounds that I saw had such a pronounced nose. Over the next hour or so, one hound after another was brought out for me to see, photograph, measure and take DNA samples, if they were unrelated.

It was time to move on to another breeder and, once again, I was surprised to be shown into a large yard, in the centre of which this time was a mountain of old shoes! However, all around the yard were kennels with lots of Xigou, where the hounds at least had straw as bedding on the bare boards. One caught my eye immediately – a bouncy little four-month-old puppy of the same smoky-grey colour that I had seen at Nura in Kazakhstan a few years before. Another rarity for me was brought out – a black and tan Tibetan Mastiff, a breed extensively used in the area for guarding. He was only nine months old, but already very large. I was a bit nervous about taking his DNA, but he proved to be as gentle as a lamb and no problem at all. Time flew by, and reluctantly we had to call it a day to prepare ourselves for the forthcoming hunting expedition.

We foregathered the next cold but sunny morning in the metal-working yard. About 15 Xigou with about 20 hunters piled into an assortment of vehicles and we set off in convoy. I had expected we would head into the deep countryside, but we stopped after about 20 minutes, still in sight of the massive smokestacks of the town's

The hunters at the start.

power station. The land all around was flat and cultivated with alternate strips of cotton bushes and sprouting winter wheat. A river meandered through the fields and provided some rough cover along its banks. The hunters broke up into small groups and began beating out one of the cotton strips.

Within minutes a hare got up, though far from me, and quickly evaded the five or six Xigou slipped on it by running into a tangle of undergrowth alongside a busy road. Sadly, it was the only hare of the day! We walked up field after field and beat out the river banks, all to no avail. We were joined along the way by other hunters with a motley collection of hounds: Greyhounds, the import of which had been allowed from the USA and Australia since 1998, lurchers, a Borzoi from Russia, and more Xigou. Altogether there were about 30 hounds in the field, any or all of which would be slipped at the sight of a hare.

Hunting here is not just a sport; it is all about giving your hound a run and catching the hare, which rarely escapes. I was shown a number of videos of previous hunts and they all followed the same pattern, with as many as a dozen hounds being slipped at the same time. One hunt at the previous New Year consisted of around 150 hounds, so it is not so surprising that so many hounds are slipped together, as running them in pairs would mean that many would never have a run all day. In such circumstances, it surprised me that the hare was not usually demolished by the pack, but there always seemed to be someone on hand miraculously to grab the hare the moment it was caught. For this is China, and even in the fields there is always someone about, ready to intercept the pack if the hare is pulled down nearby. At the end of these hunts, I saw how the hunters returned with the bag suspended from poles looking remarkably undamaged. The hare is similar to our European brown hare, though somewhat smaller, weighing typically up to about 2 kg.

It was also clear from the videos taken over the last 15 years or so that, as elsewhere, times are changing. In the earlier years, the hunters would pool their resources and hire a bus to take them and their hounds to the hunt. Today, as a sign of China's growing affluence, many have their own cars. I also saw one hunter arrive on a motor scooter with a Greyhound perched between his knees. What a contrast with a glazed terracotta figurine that I saw in the Xi'an Museum of the Tang period, dated to 701 AD, carrying his Xigou on the pommel of his saddle! The earlier hounds also looked smaller, and I was told that today the hounds, like their owners, eat more and better. The arrival of Greyhounds also represents a change, which is not necessarily a good one, as it will be a temptation for some Xigou hunters, with the game being scarce, to prefer a faster hound that may have only one chance of a course in a day; or to crossbreed to Greyhounds for greater speed at the expense of endurance. Although I saw a few lurchers, I was told that the serious Xigou breeders kept their hounds pure.

However, as in most of the Saluki's countries of origin, there is no official Chinese Xigou breed standard, though I was given a draft of one that is under discussion. The draft says that there is both a smooth and a feathered variety, but I did not see any smooths and my companions did not know of them either. There is also a smaller, lighter variety on the plains and a larger, heavier variety in the hills. Interestingly, the draft condemns the sheep's nose as 'a long way from normal development', but prefers a 'pliers' or square bite to a scissors bite, though it accepts that the latter is prevalent. Otherwise it contains many of the characteristics that would apply to the Saluki, such as a deep and moderately broad chest, a pronounced tuck, and prominent huckle bones. It does not list brindle among the common colours but, as I saw, it is present in the breed.

It is reckoned that there are around 600 Xigou in Shaanxi Province and about another 300 elsewhere in China, principally in Hebei and Shandong, which represents a small population for sustaining the breed. I took a lot of DNA samples for laboratories in Sweden and the USA, and it will be interesting to see what the analysis shows about the relationships between these hounds and with other similar hounds in Western and Central Asia. I saw no evidence of health problems – on the contrary, the hounds looked well cared for and long-lived. However, as elsewhere, the Xigou is under pressure from modern development on its traditional hunting areas. The pressure on the hare population is also increasing, as greater affluence means that there are more people more able to indulge in hunting, not only with Xigou but also with exotic breeds. Certainly the hunters I met were great enthusiasts of the breed and were justifiably proud of maintaining the long tradition of hunting with these hounds in this part of China.

The following spring, Liese and I with two friends decided to explore the south-eastern corner of Turkey, which had been a no-go area for years due to the ongoing conflict with Kurdish rebels seeking greater autonomy but had been reopened following a ceasefire. The landscape is spectacular, with the immense Lake Van reflecting the snow-capped mountains surrounding it. I reckoned that where there were Kurds we might also see a few Tazis. What I had not realised was the devastating effect the conflict had had on Kurdish rural life, leading to the relocation of the inhabitants of the villages to towns like Van, where there was no place for Tazis. So, though we thoroughly enjoyed the cultural sights and genuine Turkish hospitality in all sorts of colourful places, we saw only one very old grizzle Tazi near the medieval Armenian capital of Ani, where villagers told us that Tazis had become too expensive – no doubt a reflection of the drain of hounds to the Gulf for racing.

For Liese's birthday in September, we planned to take up another invitation from Mohammed Soujaa to attend the Second International Festival of Traditional Hunting in Meknes with Adrian and Lucinda Phillips, who would come over from their second home in Portugal with their two Salukis. However, after we had made all the arrangements for our travel and accommodation, I heard a few days before our departure that the festival had been postponed indefinitely for various administrative reasons. Our dilemma was: to go or not to go? That question was quickly resolved by Mohammed Soujaa, who kindly offered to arrange a programme in Meknes with some hunting with Sloughis instead. So off we went, and it proved a rewarding experience.

We took in some culture first, with a few days in and around Fes, staying in a beautifully converted traditional house on the edge of Fez al-Bali – the fascinating Old City – which was owned by the appropriately named Mr Tazi! While there, we had to go back to the nearby early Roman outpost at Volubilis, where in 1992 on a circular tour of Morocco to study the Sloughi population I had been greeted at the entrance by a delightful Sloughi puppy owned by the souvenir vendor. The vendor's shop was still there and everyone remembered the man and his Sloughis, but he had retired and sadly there were no longer any Sloughis.

In Meknes, we called at Mohammed Soujaa's home and were entertained by the antics of two puppies from his latest litter and the tortoises that wandered in his garden. He explained that he had arranged a hunt for us on an estate outside Meknes, for which he had permission to hunt for predators only, as the hare coursing season opened only in October. In this case predators meant foxes, which do a lot of damage to livestock on the surrounding farms – in that area they had recently accounted for 18 foxes in a single day! As an Englishman, I had the momentary thought of mounted hunters in red coats following a pack of Foxhounds, but having hunted in Morocco before I knew that this would be rather different.

The hunt started long before dawn. A small party of hunters foregathered in a well-known café that was just opening up as we arrived at 5.00 am. Fortified with coffee and Danish pastries, we set off to collect some of the Sloughis before rendezvousing with more hunters on the road outside Meknes. We set off in convoy, but had hardly left the town when we ran into thick mist. We crawled along, with visibility in places down to less than 50 metres. So, although we drove only about 25 km, it was about 7.00 am when we all assembled for the hunt and it was still very misty.

There were Sloughis off leash everywhere, as well as a couple of Pointers, and there must have been around 20 hounds altogether as more and more hunters arrived, including Susan Bamford from England, Eliane and André Cadosch from France and Mariana Raposo, resident in Morocco, whom I already knew, with their Sloughis. I could not believe that all the hounds would run free, but soon saw the reason as we began walking up. The wadis were full of clumps of thorn bushes and dead thistles, and the practice was to surround the clumps and beat them out in the hope that, if a fox broke cover, at least one or two hounds would be near enough to give chase. It would simply not have worked to slip only two or three hounds on sight of the prey.

The first wadi produced nothing – but then it was hard to see anything at all in the mist. But by around 8.30 am the sun had slowly burnt off the remaining patches and we could see more clearly just how difficult it was for the beaters, a pair of black and white Pointer-like hounds and the Sloughis to make their way through the coverts. Suddenly, a large red fox appeared briefly but, before the hounds could get on to it, it turned back into the covert and quickly disappeared. It was the size of a European red fox and not the small, bat-eared desert fennec.

Sloughi in the mist.

We walked on and I was attracted by a dark brindle Sloughi called *Ghalies*, about 14 months old, belonging to one of the beaters. He was of a small compact type that is often best for coursing hare. His cream litter sister, *Jdiya*, was also there and she was of the same type – no show winners in the Western world, but good working hounds in Morocco. As I discovered later, they were of Mohammed Soujaa's breeding.

For the next hour, we continued drawing through a long wadi. Then another big red fox broke cover and unwisely attempted to run up the wadi side pursued by one of the Pointers into the path of several Sloughis, who quickly brought it down. It proved to be the one and only kill of the day, though we were not to know that and continued up the wadi. Shortly afterwards, an even bigger red fox appeared, hotly pursued by a group of Sloughis, but they could not catch up with it in the scrub and it went to ground in a foxhole. For the next hour in the heat of the midday sun, the beaters took turns to dig out the fox. This was a tricky business as there were several entrances and they were not sure where it had gone in. Then, as the excitement grew, one of the diggers prodded with a long stick down one end of the hole and out of the other popped the fox. Although there were people and Sloughis all around the hole, the fox cleverly evaded them all and flew down the wadi in great bounds like a gazelle. The pursuing hounds simply could not keep up in the patchy scrub and it was soon lost to sight. What an anticlimax!

We continued walking for another half-hour and I was alone on the rim of one side of the wadi when a small fox sneaked out in front of me and disappeared down into a side wadi. I shouted to the Sloughis but they were unsighted. The hunters rushed in the direction the fox had gone and found another group of foxholes. They were happy to start digging again, but Adrian and I and his Salukis had had

The fox makes his escape.

enough. It was fiercely hot, well over 30° C, and we still had at least a half-hour slog back to the vehicles. It was time to call it a day – an exciting and unusual day of fox-hunting Moroccan style.

In December, we enjoyed a different kind of day – at the races – that proved equally exciting and unusual. It all came about in the context of the Second International Festival of Falconry, under the auspices of the Abu Dhabi Authority for Culture and Heritage in the oasis town of al-Ain, close to Abu Dhabi's border with Oman, where falconers from some 70 countries foregathered. It was a rich and colourful occasion, with a mix of academic and practical lectures and workshops as well as opportunities for the participating national delegations to demonstrate their skills in the arena and in the desert with a variety of birds of prey, sometimes together with Salukis.

The United Arab Emirates and other states in the Arabian Peninsula have a long tradition of hunting, not only with falcons but also with Salukis. This tradition is also practised in some of the other participating countries, notably in Central Asia. The falcons and Salukis need to grow up together and be completely accustomed to each other to avoid any accidents in the hunting field. They will then work happily together in a mutually beneficial partnership. The Salukis drive the game from the undergrowth into the open for the falcons to stoop on or, where the Salukis become

The start.

unsighted by obstacles, the falcon acts as spotter, following the movement of the game and showing the direction it takes to the pursuing Salukis.

To demonstrate this partnership, the festival organisers laid on a traditional hunt in the desert. Sadly, it was frustrated by the unexpected fog that blanketed the nature reserve some 50 km south of al-Ain, where, for the first time in 30 years, a hunt had been approved as an exception to the nationwide ban. Despite conditions more reminiscent of Europe, the mounted hunters set off with their falcons and a brace of Salukis in the hope that the fog would lift. They soon put up a hare but only the Salukis could be slipped, as the falcons would not have been able to see the prey and, if released, the falconers could not see them. The hare gave the Salukis a good run, but was finally caught. Later they chased another hare, but it managed to evade them to run another day. They at least had hunted, whereas the falconers had had a fruitless morning, though the falcons were given a taste of the hare as a consolation.

To show the wider public how Salukis perform in a more controlled environment, the festival organisers also laid on two days of Saluki racing on part of a sand track at Remah normally used for racing camels and horses. Well over 100 Salukis competed in five races on each day, with the first four hounds in each race going on to compete at the al-Dhafra Camel Festival a week later. Only purebred Arabian Salukis were eligible, and competitors came from the UAE and other countries of the Gulf Cooperation Council, many of them with crop-eared Salukis bred in Syria and Turkey. Every owner was given a Certificate of Appreciation for participating in the festival races, and those lucky enough to win at the finals in al-Dhafra collected handsome trophies and other prizes.

The course was over 1.5 km on a slightly curved section of the track, on either side of which ran asphalt roads. As the hounds and their handlers lined up the Salukis for the start of each race, a blindfolded live gazelle was presented to them at a safe distance of some 20 metres to excite their interest. Then it was discreetly removed from their sight and replaced by a stuffed gazelle suspended over the track from a boom mounted on a pickup truck on one of the side roads. As the pickup set off, the Salukis were released and the race was on. I enjoyed the privilege of riding in a vehicle immediately behind the pickup and so had a wonderful view of the competitors on the move. The Salukis' admirably suited feet easily coped with the soft sand of the track and, such is their sound temperament, they ran without muzzles. The excitement was intense as the hounds flew along the track, throwing up puffs of sand behind them,

The winner.

while their owners raced along the side road, yelling encouragement, to be at the end to pick them up. Amid all the turmoil of people and cars, it was amazing how easily owners and hounds found each other.

Although it is in the Saluki's instinct to chase a moving object on sight, some of the hounds did not take to this form of exercise. In each race a few of them stopped running, turned round and came back to their handlers. One of them asked me what he could do to make his two young Salukis race; they were both efficient hunters on live game, but were not interested in the artificial lure on the track. I could only suggest frequent practice and a reward at the end. But such is the nature of the intelligent Saluki – some quickly recognise the difference between the lure and live game, and decline to play.

With a hunting ban in place in much of the region, it is not easy to maintain enthusiasm for preserving the tradition of hunting Salukis. Those who can afford it go on hunting trips with their falcons and Salukis to other countries where hunting is allowed, but clearly this is a pastime not open to all. In any case, the foreign hunting trips can fill only a limited part of the hunting season. People in the Gulf are therefore turning increasingly to track racing and live gazelle chasing as a means of encouraging popular interest in the hounds while maintaining their physical fitness for hunting.

Track racing was started as long ago as the early 1990s in al-Ain, Abu Dhabi, but somehow it did not catch on and lapsed for some years until it was revived recently. Live gazelle chasing is newer and has been taken up only in more recent times, but has quickly gathered a large following. This takes the form of releasing a captive gazelle, of which many are kept on some of the recreational farms in the region, on a flat expanse of desert well ahead of a line of Salukis, whose numbers may vary from event to event. The Salukis give chase and are allowed to pursue the gazelle over a pre-established distance, usually of between 1.5 and 2.5 km. With great excitement, the owners follow the chase in their vehicles, and that is part of the fun! As the limit of the distance is approached, a vehicle is driven in front of the hounds so that they can no longer see the gazelle, giving a handler the opportunity to recapture it in safety. Some of these chases are now organised at the national and even Gulf-wide level, with the owners of the winners collecting generous prizes.

Some people have expressed concern at these developments on various grounds. With regard to track racing, they fear that it will lead to the breeding of a different kind of Saluki and encourage crossbreeding with Greyhounds. Such fears are largely due to an incomplete understanding of the kind of track racing involved. First, the intention is to extend the distance to four kilometres on a straight sand track, which would admirably test the speed and stamina of the Saluki but would discourage crossbreds. Second, most Westerners are more familiar with Salukis for hare coursing, with the hare taking a varied route and compelling the hounds to think intelligently. However, in its traditional role in the Middle East the Saluki was used as much for gazelle coursing, and the gazelle tends to run in a straight line until it becomes exhausted and starts to zigzag. Hence, a track race after a stuffed gazelle is not too unlike the real thing. Moreover, many of the Salukis also have the chance of free coursing at other times and so enjoy a more varied experience.

In an interview before the races in Remah, Hamad al-Ghanem, Director of the Arabian Saluki Center and Head of the Race Organising Committee, said that the races gave an opportunity to demonstrate the beauty and incredible speed of the Saluki. He also said that the races aimed to create awareness of traditional values and ethics of local life and to preserve and celebrate the Saluki in its homeland. Judging by the enthusiastic response of the large number of Emiratis present at the track, it would seem that these aims were largely achieved. The races were also fully covered on local television for the wider public.

At the festival proper, we were able to make some good contacts with falconers from Central Asia, who were to prove very helpful to us on our next trip, the following spring, to Turkmenistan and Uzbekistan.

I was already acquainted with the exciting history of Russian expansionism into Central Asia in the 19th century and the literature of travellers who provided a wealth of information on the culture and customs of the region, including hunting with falcons and some extremely Saluki-like hounds. Some of the Central Asian falconers we had met confirmed that, while comparatively rare, they were still used for hunting in the desert areas. So we hoped we might see some.

Although I had read how Ashgabat, the capital of Turkmenistan, had been completely destroyed by an earthquake in 1948, rebuilt during the Soviet era and rebuilt again since independence in 1991, nothing had prepared me for the amazing sight of the sweeping wide boulevards, bounded by lush gardens and backed by monumental buildings faced uniformly with white marble. At times, I was reminded of parts of Arabia. Turkmenistan is similar, a mainly desert country with a relatively small population and huge hydrocarbon resources that have been employed to develop the centres of population to a very high standard.

The Turkmen History Museum and the Carpet Museum were close by our hotel and they provided a graphic introduction to the colourful nomadic origins of the Turkmen people. The area of modern Turkmenistan has been settled since early Neolithic times and has seen wave after wave of peoples attracted by the abundant waters of its two great rivers – the Amu Darya (Oxus) and the Morgab – and its access to the Caspian Sea. The Turkmen of today descend from the Oghuz Turks, who moved westwards from the Altai Mountains of Mongolia in the 7th century AD, came across the Siberian steppes and settled in what used to be called Transoxiania ('the land beyond the Oxus'). Here they are believed to have intermixed with such ancient tribes as the Scythians, Sogdians, Parthians and others. They were supplemented in the 11th century by the Seljuk Turks, whose two major centres of population were at Merv and Konye-Urgench, which were razed to the ground during the Mongol period of devastation (1219–21 under Genghis Khan) and never recovered, though some idea of their former magnificence can still be gained from their extensive ruins. Merv was known as Merv-i Shahjehan – Merv, Queen of the World – and in its heyday stood alongside Damascus and Baghdad as one of the great cities along the Silk Road.

That the Turkmen managed to survive so many upheavals is largely due to their nomadic lifestyle and their ability to move quickly from place to place across the great Kara Kum Desert. But they could not withstand the might of the Russian Empire under Czar Peter the Great and they were forced into submission at the battle

Turkmen Tazy.

of Geok Tepe in 1881. They remained within the empire, and later the Soviet Union, until independence in 1991.

The Soviet era was a period in which the Turkmen were obliged to abandon much of their customary way of life, but since independence there has been a great drive to reaffirm their traditions and culture. Not least in this renaissance is the reestablishment of hunting with falcon and Tazy, with the encouragement of the National Falconers' Association, which was founded in 1998, with a special section for the Tazy. According to its president, Ata Eyeberdiyev, the origins of the Tazy go back far into the history of the Turkmen. Evidence of this is to be found in the Turkmen language, in popular proverbs and sayings, and in Turkmen rugs, in which its hooked tail appears among the designs that have been employed by rugmakers for centuries. A modern hand-made rug in the Carpet Museum actually depicted a Tazy inside a typical Turkmen border.

The National Falconers' Association promotes the revival of interest in hunting with the falcon and Tazy through presentations and demonstrations at national festivals and exhibitions. At the present time, the association has information about only 86 Tazys, but it is known that in many settlements in the Central Kara Kum region there are many fine working Tazys that are not registered. From time to time, the Tazy section of the association receives some of the best examples of these hounds for breeding purposes, and in return distributes among the hunters from this region some of the best hounds that it has bred. By 'best' is meant those hounds showing the best hunting characteristics during the hunting season, but account is also taken of their conformation, character and colour. The season for hunting with falcons and Tazys is regulated by a law of 1998 and runs from 1 October to 1 February, though it is possible to obtain special permission to hunt with hounds in certain designated areas at other times.

It was therefore clear that our visit was too late for the hunting season, but our Turkmen friends were keen nevertheless to show us their hounds in their natural habitat – the desert. It had rained heavily during the night, which made the trip much easier than usual as it laid the dust and made the loose sand firmer. The desert was blooming after a wet winter, and tamarisk bushes and wild flowers dotted the sand dunes as we left the asphalt and headed out to a shepherds' camp some 40 km away. As we approached our destination, two Tazys ran out to greet us. There was *Garash*, a well-proportioned two-year-old chocolate male in good hunting condition, and *Uchar*, an eight-month-old cream female. But first we had to follow custom and, after introductions to the shepherds, we drank from a foaming bowl of fresh camel's milk and we were honoured with the slaughter of a goat for lunch.

Only then could I have a proper look at the Tazys. In addition to the two that greeted us, there was *Melegush*, a rather shy bronze-coloured three-year-old female, who needed to be coaxed out of her kennel. The shepherds explained that there would usually be more at that time of year but, because the desert pasture was so abundant after the rains, many shepherds had gone off with their flocks to take advantage of this. The falcons were already in their summer quarters in the villages, but I was shown some pictures of them in their most distinctive embroidered hoods.

According to Ata Eyeberdiyev, the Turkmen Tazy is formed by its desert environment and differs from the Kazakh Tazy by being finer, lighter and less stocky. It is also used mainly for hunting the tolai hare in tandem with a falcon, rather than

Turkmen entertainers.

for hunting fox. In the Turkmen language, it is known as 'the assistant', because from the age of about six months it learns to assist the falcon in the hunt through the scrub over the undulating dunes. First, it learns to spring into action when it sees or even only hears the falconer launch the bird, and then it follows the falcon's flight to pick up the route taken by the hare until it has it in sight. Once it has adapted to this style of hunting, a Tazy is capable of continuing until it is eight or nine years old. During the hunting season, the hounds are fed on a soup made out of hare offal and bread made with a special kind of flour. At other times, they eat boiled meat and drink camel's milk, which the Turkmen believe improves the hounds' speed. Bitches with puppies are given milk, eggs and bread soaked in sheep fat.

The three Tazys looked in good condition on such a diet. They were all quite small – the tallest was *Garash*, who was only 63.5 cm at the shoulder. Like Tazys elsewhere in Central Asia, they had quite well-feathered ears but only very sparse feathering on the tail, which was a little short and carried with a pronounced ring at the end. The puppy had a woollier coat than the mature hounds. Their chocolate and bronze colours are quite common and derive from black. I did not see any black hounds but Ata Eyeberdiyev provided a picture of one. Later I saw another Tazy in Ashgabat that was in the same range of colours. This young bitch, called *Achar*, had just been fed and was so sleepy she would not move!

The shepherds also keep Turkmenistan's other national breed – the Alabai – for protecting their flocks against predators and for guarding the house. Some also breed them for fighting, but I was assured that such fights were never to the death. As soon as one dog or the other showed any sign of submission, it was withdrawn. I heard this from a Kurd out exercising his dog whom I met by chance when visiting the ancient Parthian capital at Nissa. He was from the nearby Kurdish village of Bagir, where he said they bred fighting Alabais. I also visited the home of the president of the Alabai Association, where I saw a number of these magnificent mastiffs, including some delightful puppies. Interestingly, these dogs all had a rear dew claw, which is common to some other mastiff breeds across Europe.

Of course, no visit to Turkmenistan would be complete without seeing the national horse breed – the Akhal Teke. At one of the stud farms we saw some of these amazingly slender-looking horses, which are, however, noted for their endurance as well as their golden colour. The Turkmen believe that the Akhal Teke is the progenitor of all other racehorses. Turkmenistan has a national holiday to celebrate the breed, which happened to coincide with our visit, and among other manifestations there was an all-day endurance race over a huge circular course with stations along the way where people in their colourful national costumes danced and sang and generally had a good time.

With the renewed interest in these different aspects of Turkmenistan's natural heritage, which has the full backing and encouragement of the state, it seemed to me that the Tazy has a brighter future here in a country where it is still possible to hunt with it in the traditional way than in some other parts of Central Asia, as I was soon to be reminded.

We crossed over the border into neighbouring Uzbekistan, where I knew from a previous visit in September 2001 that the task of finding Tazys now would be difficult. (On that occasion, a member of the dog breeders' club in Tashkent told me that the majority of its members who hunted with Tazys were ethnic Russians and many of them had returned to Russia following Uzbekistan's independence.) Nevertheless, I began to make enquiries through various contacts, which produced some surprising results. I was told that because of the exceptionally wet weather most of the nomadic Kazakh shepherds were scattered in the desert with their Tazys. However, there was one household in a place called Nurata where there was a Tazy, and I knew from experience that very often one Tazy would lead to others – it was a matter of making a start.

On the long drive from Bukhara, I was particularly keen to make a short detour to the Sarmysh Gorge, which offers a rich selection of some 3,000 petroglyphs depicting various animals, including dogs with men in hunting scenes, from the Bronze Age to the Early Middle Ages, on a background of dark shale rock. At first we wound our way along a narrow road beside a stream through the verdant gorge, but then we reached a point where the stream crossed the road and the driver was not willing to risk his minibus. I began taking pictures of the petroglyphs high up among the rocks using a 300-millimetre lens. Soon I found myself wandering alone along a narrow sandy path with dense undergrowth on either side. Just as I was thinking what a natural place this was for snakes, there was a loud hiss and the swaying but immediately identifiable shape of a hooded cobra rose up before me! I stepped back smartly and raised my camera to capture the scene; but my huge telephoto lens could not focus on such a near object! Possibly because of the whirring noise of the lens as it tried to focus, the cobra gave another angry hiss but then turned tail and slid into the undergrowth. I made off smartly in the opposite direction! Only on my return home did I discover what a lucky escape I had had. The snake was a Caspian cobra (*Naja oxiana*) and its bite can be fatal unless an antidote is given within 40 minutes! There was no way I would have found the serum in that remote location.

Finally we reached Nurata for my prearranged meeting with the owner of the Tazy. With growing excitement, I was led by my guide to the iron gates to the courtyard of the house. I had hardly stepped over the threshold when a dark shape leapt forward out of a corner. I almost collapsed – with laughter. It was a Cocker Spaniel! My perplexed guide said: 'But you said the Tazy has long silky ears …!' After we had explained to the owner what it was all about, she said that it was true that she had had a Tazy but it had died in the previous ferocious winter, when the temperature stayed below minus 25° C for a whole month and many of their livestock had died. Her little daughters then produced two tiny Spaniel puppies for us to admire and we all had a good laugh together. At least she confirmed that there were Tazys in the area but, sadly for me, they were too far away with the shepherds in the desert.

In February 2013, we escaped the British winter for a week with friends in Dubai. While there, I was in touch with an Internet contact, Muhammad al-Saedi in Abu Dhabi, who invited us over to see Salukis being trained with live gazelle not far from al-Ain. We set off early one morning, only to run into a blanket of dense fog, which reduced our speed to a crawl. We finally reached the rendezvous, but Muhammad said that the exercise had been called off because of the fog. However, he volunteered to take us around some of the hunting kennels outside al-Ain that afternoon. This gave me a valuable insight into the way in which the breeding of Salukis, largely for racing, has mushroomed in the Gulf.

We went to three spacious compounds, each with about 25–30 Salukis, enclosed by an outer perimeter of chain-link fencing, covered with jute sacking to keep the wind and sand out.

Peninsular type of Saluki.

Around an inner sandy exercise square were kennels, consisting of a covered sleeping area and an outside pen, in which there were one or two Salukis. They were almost all smooths of Turkish or Syrian origin, many with cropped ears, though Muhammad said that increasingly people were breeding on from the imports, and I saw evidence of this in litters of puppies without cropped ears.

I also saw one beautiful cream Saluki of the old Arabian Peninsular type that has become quite rare among all the imports. Previously people had not wanted the trouble of finding a suitable breeding pair, mating them and raising and training the offspring – it was easier to import mature hunting-hardened hounds. But the purchase price and transport costs had gone up and, with all the political turmoil in Syria, people were adopting a more professional approach towards breeding and training their own stock. I saw, indeed, an Australian-made treadmill used for training Greyhounds; and Muhammad said that he regularly exercised his hounds by running them behind his car, either on the beach in Abu Dhabi or in the desert round about. They also ran them in muzzles on live gazelle, and Muhammad showed another compound where the gazelle were kept. The hounds were fed exclusively on imported dry food.

It was already near the end of the racing season and the hounds looked in tip-top condition. Muhammad had only one crossbred Greyhound-Saluki, and one of the other hunters said he had also tried crossbreeding but had given up as the offspring were not good enough for the major races, which were typically over 2–2.5 km. It would have been fun to see them run, but that would be for another time – and before then I took part in a different kind of renaissance.

I was invited back to Morocco by Mohammed Soujaa for the postponed second International Festival of Traditional Hunting in the small town of Sidi Mokhtar, about 110 km west of Marrakesh, on 5–7 September 2013. (I had attended the first such festival, in Meknes, in 2010 – see page 275 *et seq.*)

This was a big event for this small rural town, and the first time it had seen anything quite like it. As a result, the crowds of spectators were huge. I knew from previous visits to the area that the rural communities round about had plenty of Sloughis. It came as no surprise, therefore, that for the opening parade well over 100 hounds took part. I soon found out, however, that some of the participants had come from far and wide across Morocco; and there were also some old French friends with their hounds, either resident in Morocco or visiting especially for the festival. Many more local breeders and hunters would undoubtedly have come if the event had been supported

Entrants awaiting their turn.

by the Moroccan Kennel Club with a qualified FCI judge and the possibility of owners obtaining official registration of their hounds. As it was, the Royal Moroccan Federation for Traditional Hunting (ANMOCT) and the local authorities put on a remarkably successful display of Sloughis, falconry and horsemanship. The owners were also encouraged to present their hounds for free anti-rabies vaccinations.

The opening parade was held in a small, dusty square, with a long tent down one side for the seated spectators and participants. Barriers on another side kept the crowds at bay. High walls closed off the rest of the square. With such a captive audience, it was too a good opportunity to miss for sending a message, especially

Fantasia.

to the younger generation, to take an active interest in the Sloughi, and in falconry too, as part of their natural heritage. Mohammed Soujaa, president of ANMOCT, therefore spoke in Moroccan dialect, André Cadosch spoke in French, and I followed in modern literary Arabic; between us, we left the spectators in no doubt of the importance of preserving their ancient traditions. I also put the same message across in interviews with Moroccan and Qatari television.

The parade also gave the opportunity to see in one sweep a kind of panorama of the diversity of the Moroccan Sloughi (as well as a couple of Pointer puppies that sneaked in somehow!). At first, I saw nothing exceptional in the range of colours, with the usual predominance of black-masked sand or cream-coloured hounds or sand with black overlay or sand with brindle, but then I started to notice some less usual hounds.

Most striking was a dog with a chocolate mantle, a colour I had never seen before in a Sloughi, though it occurs in the Saluki. It was standing by a pair of hounds that would have been called tricoloureds if they were Salukis, and my guess was that they were probably crossed with Galgos. Another pair of hounds caught my eye that, had they been Salukis, I would have described as red and white particoloureds. Another one nearby looked to me as if it might have been crossbred, and I suspected a touch of Galgo blood there somewhere. Another hound stood out from the rest, but for a different reason – it was at the top end of the range for height at about 68.5 cm

Coursing over the harsh terrain.

(whereas most of the other male hounds were closer to 63.5 cm and below), and it had a dark overlay over a sand coat, with a white patch on its chest. The owner came from Oujda in the north of Morocco and he told me the dam came from Tlemcen in Algeria, while the sire was from Mariana Raposo, a well-known expatriate breeder living in Morocco. In view of the sometimes heated discussion on white patches, which are viewed in the West as a fault, I asked the owner whether he attached any importance to it. The answer was not quite what I expected: yes, he did attach importance to it – as a sign of Allah's blessing! He added that he and his family had bred Sloughis for generations and had always taken this view of white patches.

The festival was not only about Sloughis but also about falconry, and some young falconers talked to the crowd about the historic practice of capturing wild falcons, known as *Shahin Bahri* or sea peregrines, along the coast on their passage south in winter, training them to be flown from the fist and returning them to the wild the following season. On a nearby open square, they also put on an impressive display of their control over their falcons by flying them to live pigeon lures.

They were followed by an even more spectacular display of a Fantasia. Five groups of 15–20 horsemen each charged across the open square straight at the spectators sitting under a huge tent, and at the last moment they stood in their stirrups, twirled their long, silver-decorated muzzle-loading rifles and fired – blanks, fortunately – with a deafening noise and at the same time managed somehow to rein in their splendidly caparisoned mounts in a cloud of dust. Fantastic – *Fantasia*!

Among the many other hounds at the festival were some good specimens that looked as if they could perform well in the field but perhaps not in the show ring, as they were generally rather small and more compact than is commonly seen in the ring. Some of them would have the chance to demonstrate what they could do the following day, when a competitive fox hunt was to be held. It meant driving out to a dry, barren plain, littered with rough stones, enough to damage or even break the feet of hounds unaccustomed to it. After a long discussion between the president and the large group of owners, three hounds were selected for the first course and were held by their collars facing up the field. At about 80 metres from them, a handler took a live fox from a cage and released it. It ran up the field and the three hounds were slipped. In such open, unfamiliar ground, the fox had no chance and it was soon caught and despatched by the three competitors plus another hound that appeared out of nowhere, which was later to prove the subject of a controversy. Another fox was produced before three more hounds, but this one was amazingly fast and agile. It took the hounds on a long, looping run but again, in such circumstances with no refuges, the outcome was inevitable.

That was all for that day, but it provided the substance for some serious discussion afterwards. First, there was the matter of the loose dog in the first course. The owner was summoned to a meeting presided over by Mohammed Soujaa to explain himself. His dog had been confiscated, but was returned to him after he explained that it had broken free accidentally. I had a good look at the hound, a solid black dog, and concluded that it was probably a Galgo cross. The owner had another hound with him, a red brindle with a bushy tail that also looked like a Galgo cross. However, the more important discussion ran more generally over the suitability of such competitions for testing coursing ability. The feeling was that in future the hounds should be muzzled and the terrain should be such as to provide the fox with refuges.

Another amazing Fantasia in the twilight brought the festival to an end and, as the crowds dispersed and the television crews finished their round-ups of interviews and stories, it was time for some reflection on the outcome. On the basis of the large numbers of Sloughis attending the festival, the breed seemed on the surface to be surviving remarkably well, but the true picture is probably somewhat different. First, the hunting field is not a level one for Sloughis. The French law of 1844 banning the use of hounds for hunting game is still in force, favouring hunters with guns, who do far more damage to wildlife. As it is, anyone found contravening the law risks the hound being shot and the payment of a fine. This law ought to be relaxed to allow the Sloughi to be used legally in its traditional role. Second, ANMOCT and the Moroccan Kennel Club need to work together to put a stop to the present anomalous situation whereby a dozen or so Sloughis may be judged under FCI rules at a limited number of shows, while ANMOCT's events may be attended by ten times as many hounds that have no chance of recognition and are therefore excluded from contributing to the pedigree gene pool. ANMOCT also needs official support for its events, which not only work to preserve Morocco's cultural heritage but also serve as potential tourist attractions, as the annual festival at Douz in Tunisia has proved.

A couple of weeks later – after many months of discussions with a small group of friends with a mainly archaeological interest in Iraq, and with advice and assistance from Kurdish contacts – in September 2013 Liese and I were at last able to undertake an adventurous journey that had been a dream for many years. This was to return to

Kalar, a small town in eastern Iraqi Kurdistan within sight of the mountains of Iran. Kalar was where we were given our first Saluki, *Tayra*, and we often wondered how our friends and their hounds there had fared in the intervening two turbulent decades. So it was with a great sense of anticipation that we flew into Erbil, the regional capital, in time for Liese's birthday, as well as with some trepidation because of the unsettled security situation in Iraq. However, Kurdistan had remained generally peaceful in recent years and travel there was no longer discouraged by the British authorities. In fact, we were able to travel right across Kurdistan without any concerns for our safety.

This turned out to be a journey full of surprises, when things seemed to happen without any warning – fortunately mostly for the better. The visit to Kalar was an exception, though it started most auspiciously. I had made the acquaintance years before of the then Mir (prince) of the Yazidis, an obscure religious sect, whose main shrine was at Lalish in Iraqi Kurdistan. Their religion is a complex mixture of beliefs that contains Zoroastrian elements and Islamic Sufi doctrine introduced to the area in the 12th century. I had arranged to meet the new Mir, Tahseen, not least because I had previously seen Salukis in the vicinity of the shrine. Sadly, the day before the meeting, the Mir told me that one of his sons had died and that he would be holding a wake in the small town of Shaikhan, if we wished to pay our condolences. I had been to Shaikhan before and knew there were Salukis there, so there was every reason to go. The huge reception hall was lined with hundreds of mourners but the Mir invited me to sit next to him for a while and to join him later for lunch. This meant rather a long wait, but there was no escape and in the interval things turned to my advantage as I moved to sit opposite the Mir and my two neighbours proved to be very interesting.

On my right sat a man in the distinctive clothes of an Arab shaikh. After I had introduced myself in Arabic as the former British Ambassador to Iraq, he said that he thought his uncle knew me and had been talking about me only recently. His uncle turned out to be my old friend and Saluki mentor, Subhi Yasin Agha, who in my time in Iraq used to hunt on horseback with a pack of Salukis from his farm west of Mosul, Iraq's second city. What an amazing coincidence! Within minutes, my neighbour had his uncle on his mobile phone and we had an emotional conversation together for the first time in over 23 years. Subhi told me that he had had to give up hunting and his Salukis because the situation in his area was so dangerous that if he went out into the fields someone was likely to take a shot at him. However, he gave me the name of a breeder in Shaikhan; but because of the wake, lunch and our subsequent visit to the magical Yazidi shrine at Lalish, there was no opportunity to meet him – this time!

An equally amazing coincidence was the identity of the man sitting on my left – Dr Hassan Jaff, a Kurdish academic from the renowned Jaff clan, whose family seat was in Kalar. I told him my story about Kalar and our intention to return there. He insisted that the family look after me and my companions when we reached there. He was, however, discouraging about my chances of seeing my old friends or any Salukis there. Kalar was, when we lived in Iraq in 1985–90, a ramshackle town, surrounded on the western outskirts by groups of small, breeze-block courtyard houses, built by Kurds who had been uprooted from their homes near the border with Iran by Saddam Hussein's repressive regime during the Iran–Iraq war, as they were considered 'unreliable' because of their kinship with the Kurds across the border in Iran. These displaced people had brought with them whatever they could, including not least their Salukis. However, Kalar had expanded rapidly since the establishment of Kurdish regional autonomy over 20 years before, and now even boasted a university. The refugees had either gone back to their former homes or had been settled in new housing estates with the generous support of the Kurdish Regional Government. Moreover, the government had introduced a ban on all forms of hunting to preserve Kurdistan's wildlife, so people no longer had an incentive to keep Salukis (which he referred to in our conversation in Arabic by the Sorani Kurdish dialect word '*Tanji*').

Sadly, he appeared to be right. A week or so later, we drove to Kalar and were met by his brother, Ali Jaff. He had prepared a huge lunch for us, over which he confirmed what his brother had said – there were no Salukis left in Kalar! I had to accept his word, and I could not go off exploring to see for myself without giving offence. However, the visit was not entirely in vain, as our host instructed one of his sons, Hawry, to give us a guided tour of the Jaff family seat, a castle now turned into a folklore museum, standing imposingly on an archaeological mound at the entrance to the town. But I would clearly not see another *Tayra* in Kalar! Or should I have probed deeper? Only after my return home did I have reason to doubt what I had been told. I was sent by another contact a series of YouTube videos of hunters with Salukis in the vicinity of Kalar as recently as 2009. I concluded that our hosts had been reluctant to let us explore the outskirts of the town as it lay quite near to an area where there had been some security incidents.

We continued on our circular tour around Iraqi Kurdistan and paid a visit to the Syrian Orthodox monastery of Rabban Hormizd, which clings to the rock face high in the mountains behind the largely Christian town of al-Qosh. The monastery is deserted now, but is undergoing restoration as a national monument. As we rested in the shade from our climb, we were joined by a local man and two emigrés on a return visit from their home in Denmark. I asked about Salukis there, and the local man said there used to be many but because of the hunting ban there was only one breeder left in al-Qosh, Sa'id Sallou. He gave me directions to the latter's house and, while the others went to have lunch, I set off to find him. It was not difficult, as everyone seemed to know Sa'id. He turned out to be a larger-than-life character, who talked rapidly in Arabic with hardly a pause for breath about his life with and affection for Salukis. He eventually led me to a nearby walled garden, where I was greeted by *Lasti*, a smooth, grey grizzle of 14 months. She was small at about 61 cm but well-made, and with a nice temperament. Sa'id said that he had always kept about four or five Salukis for hunting in the vicinity but he had got rid of the others because of the ban. He appeared quite keen to sell

Lasti in al-Qosh.

me his last one, too, for a mere $20 but, tempted as I was, there was no way I could take her with me.

By then I was beginning to think that the prospects for the Saluki in the Kurdistan region were looking decidedly bleak, if the hunting ban was as discouraging as I was being told. However, things are not always as they seem and, once again, matters took a surprising turn. I was resting my hopes on a Kurdish acquaintance I had made recently in London, who had promised to show me some Salukis when I was in the capital, Erbil. He kindly sent a car to take us out to a farm less than an hour's drive away.

We arrived at a newly fenced plot where a house was being built. As we drove through the gates, a number of canine shapes emerged from the deep shadows where they had been resting from the still hot sun. The first two were a couple of very aggressive and noisy Kurdish shepherd puppies. Behind them moved, more warily and silently, three Salukis: a big (68.5 cm), powerfully built, smooth 'seal'-black dog, a smooth grey grizzle dog and a much smaller, feathered tricoloured bitch of a quite different type, though she and the grey grizzle were siblings about two years old. Their ears were intact, which I thought unusual for Kurdistan, and I was told that they all came from a different area near Mosul, which lies on the edge of the Kurdistan region. I liked the little bitch, called *Manou*, and was immediately offered her by Yasin, a smartly dressed man in Kurdish costume, who was obviously in charge. He proved to be a colonel in the Kurdish Peshmerga militia, and was accompanied everywhere by two heavily armed guards. He said that his clan owned all the extensive agricultural land round about and he invited us to see some hunting with Salukis on a nearby farm.

We set off in convoy and overtook a pickup with two more feathered Salukis in the back. Things were clearly looking up! Then, as we drove along a dusty dirt road, I could see, galloping across a vast field of stubble, three horsemen with a couple of Salukis (or 'Tazhis' in the local dialect). The riders looked splendid in their Kurdish costumes, without boots or protective headgear. One of them told me he was 67 years old, but he leapt off his Arabian mare like a young man. He said he was a lifelong hunter with Tazhis.

The hounds with him were a sandy cream, one smooth and the other lightly feathered, and both had their ears cropped 'to prevent them from being damaged'. They were very lean and muscular and he said he fed them mainly on bread and table scraps but not meat, as it was not good for them! One of the other hunters interjected that they were good for hunting for only about five years, which I thought unsurprising on such a meagre diet. They invited me to join them in the hunt but, though a tempting prospect, I did not think I could manage the very lively horse! I asked the elderly hunter if he had any puppies. He replied that he had one I could have, but it would have meant a long trek back to his village and we did not have the time. All the while we were chatting, the two hounds were being held gently on rope leads by the young son of one of the hunters. Here was the next generation completely at ease with the hounds. He was also learning the ways of the mounted hunt as he was lifted up into the saddle to ride with his father. So, as the hunters rode on with the elderly man leading one of the Tazhis on a long rope lead, I was left with a memorable image of this unchanging aspect of their way of life while, far away on the horizon, the flare from a gas vent on an oilfield was a reminder of the new pressures on their world.

However, at least in this part of Kurdistan not only were there Salukis but they were being used for hunting in the traditional manner, despite the ban. Colonel Yasin maintained that hunting hare on private land was allowed – so there was no problem there. Later enquiries, however, presented a mixed picture of the Saluki's future in Kurdistan. In one area between the region's second-largest city, Sulaimaniya, and the Iranian border, some British archaeologist friends working there told me that they had seen a Saluki on their

Leading the next generation.

previous visit and had made some enquiries on my behalf through their local workers over a wide area, but had drawn a complete blank. Everywhere their workers were told that this was because of the hunting ban. Yet while visiting an old Ottoman fortress in Koi Sinjak, a small town further north set in some incredibly wild and beautiful country, I chatted in Arabic with a group of local Kurds, who told me that there were still Salukis in the surrounding villages. I went into one such hamlet, which looked a picture of rural tradition, but was told firmly by a man leading a cow by the roadside that there were no Salukis there, and a very large guard dog discouraged any further enquiry in the hamlet itself.

I conclude, on the basis of this limited survey, that the hunting ban has had a profound effect in some areas but that elsewhere the Saluki still survives. The question is: for how much longer? Nature Iraq – an Iraqi environmental NGO created in 2004 to protect, restore and preserve Iraq's natural environment and the rich cultural heritage it nourishes – told me that the hunting ban is proving difficult to monitor; and it is likely, therefore, that some local hunters will continue to find ways of maintaining their traditions. On the other hand, Iraqi Kurdistan is developing at a phenomenal rate, as it is now exploiting its oil and gas resources independently of the central government in Baghdad. The land is being gobbled up by vast commercial estates, private and public housing, and large university campuses, as well as new infrastructural projects such as highways, dams and airports, while the rural population is declining rapidly, as people leave for the easier life of the towns. In addition, over 1.5 million people have been displaced to Kurdistan to escape the fighting against the so-called Islamic State. In these conditions, there will be enormous pressures on all aspects of life, not least on such traditional pastimes as breeding and hunting with Salukis, unless new ways of keeping such old traditions alive can be developed, as has been achieved in the Gulf. At the same time, public awareness of the potential loss of the Saluki as part of Kurdistan's natural heritage needs to be promoted.

The leaders of the United Arab Emirates have in the last decade or so acknowledged the rapid rate of change in their society and have been making strenuous efforts to preserve for the younger generation the traditions of the past before it is too late. At the forefront of these efforts today are the sons of the late Ruler of Abu Dhabi, His Highness Shaikh Zayed bin Sultan Al Nahyan, who set the example himself by successfully employing the hydrocarbon riches of an obscure desert shaikhdom to transform it into an ultramodern state, while continuing to hold fast to his natural heritage. I was fortunate enough to have known Shaikh Zayed when he was the governor of the inland oasis of al-Ain in the mid-1960s and a renowned hunter with Saluki and falcon. I had also visited the area many times since then, including a memorable tour of his large Saluki kennels in the early 1990s, as described in Chapter Five. So, when the Emirates Heritage Club invited me to return in February 2014, I had no hesitation in accepting.

The occasion was the annual Heritage Festival of His Highness Shaikh Sultan bin Zayed in a desert setting at Sweihan in Abu Dhabi. For most of the year, Sweihan is a desolate place with little to suggest that it might be a centre of attraction. In February, however, it comes alive as thousands of people congregate there to enjoy a series of spectacles to remind them of the recent past, when they enjoyed a largely nomadic way of life. At the centre of it all is the camel, which once was the mainstay of their life, but the Saluki is also there as another essential provider. My role in the festival, with two British colleagues – Chris Lewis of the Knightellington Kennel and Adrian Phillips, Chairman of the Saluki Conservation Club – was to judge the quality of the contemporary Salukis.

We had about four days to wait until the Saluki show, so there was plenty of time to explore the local scene from our hotel in al-Ain. First, as an introduction for my colleagues to the area and its recent past, I took them to Fort Jahili, which houses a permanent exhibition of some of the superb photographs taken of the area by Wilfred Thesiger in the late 1940s, when, after his second crossing of the Empty Quarter by camel, he spent some time hunting in the desert around al-Ain with Shaikh Zayed and his Salukis and falcons, as he describes so evocatively in *Arabian Sands.* Those fabulous exploits of 60-odd years ago still resonate in the area today. We also toured some of the large kennels, where we reckoned to have seen more than 150 Salukis of all ages. Among them we saw only one visibly crossbred and, we were told, none was imported from the West. There were no Greyhounds around, either.

However, as I knew from past experience of judging in Abu Dhabi, ours would be no straightforward task, for a variety of reasons. First, these would not be show Salukis in the conventional sense. The Salukis of the area are bred exclusively for hunting, in all its forms. Moreover, we were told that many of the best would be excluded from the show as they were incomplete with cropped ears – which, as noted earlier, is a common practice in the Kurdish parts of Turkey and Syria, from where many of the local hounds are imported. It is only in comparatively recent times that shows have started to be organised for the purpose of judging Salukis for their beauty, and the hunters have not yet become accustomed to them.

Furthermore, there is no central registry for Salukis and no written standard against which to judge their conformation. There is none of the show culture as it is known in the West, and neither the hounds nor their handlers are practised in being on show in the unusual surroundings of something like a fair ground. My colleagues and I were all experienced in coursing hounds and we decided we should try to bring that experience to apply to the evaluation of these hounds, while recognising that it would be impractical to give them the ultimate test of coursing.

To make things easier for us, the organisers of the 'Beauty Contest', as it was described, had prepared copies of a template bearing the details of the hound and its owner and a series of criteria which we should score on a scale up to 10, ranging from behaviour to general appearance and hunting skills (though we obviously could not assess these!) to make a total out of a maximum of 100 points. We were told that about 60 hounds had been entered and would be divided between males and females and between feathered and smooth, but would not be grouped according to age.

The ring was a rather cramped sandy area to one side of the spectators' stand for the camel beauty show. We started with the feathered females, from which, after discussion between us, we selected those that merited detailed evaluation, which we then scored individually for the organisers to tally. Next, we worked through the feathered males, followed by the smooth females and finally the smooth males, the largest entry. At the end, the organisers identified from their individual scores the first three hounds as the winners in each group, but there was no further selection for Best in Show.

My colleagues and I were unanimous in admiring the good standard of health and fitness of the hounds, though few of them would have gone far in a Western show ring. They were for the most part moderate and well-balanced and their movement was light, without any overreaching or crabbing. However, they looked different from the average Western show Saluki in their smaller size, the sparseness of their feathering, the amount of rib showing and their general muscularity, as becomes active hunting hounds. There was a considerable range of types from the lightly built, smooth hounds from the Arabian Peninsula to the slightly larger, more heavily built, often lightly feathered hounds imported from Syria and Turkey.

Where they were nearly all less than satisfactory was in their ring behaviour. They were clearly unused to being walked or trotted on the lead and were inclined to shy away from their handlers. They were also

A feathered contestant.

somewhat nervous of being handled by us, but not aggressively so, and we had no problem with laying hands on them or examining their dentition. Considering all the distractions outside the ring of the adjacent camel beauty show and inside it of pushy television journalists and cameramen and photographers, with loud music blaring in the background, the hounds stood up remarkably well to the test.

As the afternoon drew on, the top three Salukis in each group queued up with their handlers to receive their prizes from HH Shaikh Sultan and an engraved glass plaque marking their participation, but first the winners of the camel beauty competition were announced to loud applause from the crowd of spectators gathered under a vast tent. All the owners and supporters had every reason to be delighted, as the prizes were very generous.

Part of the festival that attracted a much larger participation of Salukis was the racing. Ten heats of roughly ten entrants each, divided between males and females, competed over a 2.5-km straight sand track. The Salukis were held by their handlers along a chalked line. A blindfolded gazelle was produced from behind a sacking screen and shown to the hounds, close enough for them to smell it. The gazelle was then returned behind the screen, whence a stuffed gazelle appeared over the track, suspended from a boom mounted on a pickup, which set off driving parallel to the fenced track. The race marshal lowered his flag and the hounds were released to a cacophony of hooting and shouting as the hounds' owners drove alongside the track urging their hounds on. In each heat, the first three hounds were selected to run a week later at the same festival, when extremely valuable prizes would go to the winners' owners.

We could not leave Abu Dhabi without a visit to the Arabian Saluki Center, where the hounds led a much more cosseted existence in their spacious rooms, with outside runs and a special diet of home-cooked food. We saw some beautiful mature hounds there and puppies, most of them destined in due course to join the hunting kennels of the local shaikhs. Once again I was sorely tempted but …

We were all agreed that it was most encouraging to see the enthusiastic response of young and old to the festival's practical demonstration of the relevance to contemporary life of the old traditions of their desert forebears. As a direct link with the past, some of the greybeards regaled anyone who cared to drop in at their hospitality tents with stories of their youth – and their Salukis. However, the sheer number of actively working Salukis in the area today is in itself an eloquent statement of the renaissance of the breed in the Gulf region, enthusiastically promoted mainly

The author inside a hospitality tent.

by members of the younger generation, who have taken to racing in a big way. At a time when the Saluki seems to be in decline in the West, I am glad for the long-term good of this ancient breed to have had the opportunity to see it enjoying such a revival in the lands of its origins.

However, concern has been expressed in some quarters over the danger of the extinction of the indigenous Saluki of Arabia as a result of crossbreeding, and in 2013 the International Aseel Arabian Saluki Center (IAASC) was established in Riyadh with the declared objective of preserving the breed as part of the natural heritage of the Kingdom of Saudi Arabia, not least by maintaining a purebred Saluki registry. It is still too early to say how much influence the IAASC will have over the activities of local Saluki breeders with their own individual ideas as well as tribal traditions about breeding Salukis to suit their purposes.

I had cause to ponder again the historical origins of the Saluki at the opening of an extraordinary exhibition at the British Museum in May 2015, entitled *From Arabia to Ascot*. It was obviously devoted to the horse, but one of the organisers had alerted me to the inclusion of some new finds of Neolithic worked stone artefacts from al-Magar in Saudi Arabia, purporting to show a horse in harness, a falcon and the head of a Saluki. The objects were dated to about 7000 BC, long before domesticated horses are known to have existed anywhere, and this would be the earliest known representation of a Saluki. Their discovery was, however, not straightforward and further work is ongoing to establish their background more precisely. But, if the dating and the sourcing are confirmed, what a find! It would mean rewriting the history books.

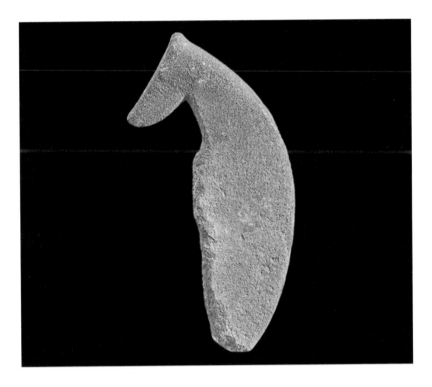

Neolithic carving from al-Magar.

almost speaking their welcome!

Tailpiece

After *Filfil*, I had not expected to have a dog of any description again, not least because Liese was so firmly set against it; but, by a strange constellation of circumstances, our resolution began to crumble – in Azerbaijan, of all places!

In the spring of 2015, we planned to explore this part of the Silk Road with a small group of friends, inspired in part by a kind of Romeo and Juliet love story between an Azeri Muslim and a Georgian Christian, called *Ali and Nino*, by Kurban Said. We were delighted by the exotic beauty of Baku and some of the other smaller towns and the rugged wildness of the Caucusus, which form the backcloth to the book. I also had hopes of finding traces of the once flourishing hunting scene, but did not see a single Tazy except in some hunting murals in a former khan's palace at Sheki, although I did at least manage to take some DNA swabs from some huge Ovcharka shepherd dogs.

However, along the way Liese discovered that one of our company, Gaye Drysdale, whom we knew less well than the others, was a devotee of Whippets. In the course of some of the long bus journeys, Gaye gradually convinced Liese that what she really needed at this stage of life was a Whippet. She was about to acquire a puppy for herself and could put us in touch with the breeder if we were interested. When Liese revealed to me her discussions with Gaye and began to speak of how much she missed having a dog in the house, I was quietly amazed but said nothing to discourage this new line of thought.

By the time we were back home, we had overcome all our scruples and doubts about taking on the responsibility of another dog at our advanced age. However, though we considered some Whippet puppies, we decided that a mature hound might make more sense. We began making enquiries and searching the rescue websites, but without any luck. I also enquired at the SGHC's own Saluki Rescue but they had nothing either. Then one day, on the spur of the moment, we went to Battersea Dogs and Cats Home, which is near where we live.

The home is very well appointed, with dogs two to a (spacious) room off long, airy corridors. We saw many appealing dogs, but only one came over to me and licked my hand – a blue with white female Greyhound called *Milly.* She was described as an ex-racer, about 2½ years old. We both liked the look of

Milly.

her, but we went away to think it over for 48 hours before making the commitment. It was just before my 81st birthday when we went back, had another look at *Milly* and decided that she was the one.

She came very quietly and walked easily on the lead to our car. She hopped in without any fuss and we drove her home. Everything was of course strange, as she had lived only in kennels before. She was wary of doors and stairs but, after a good meal, she was happy to snuggle down in one of our old Saluki beds. She was a little upset for the first two nights, but quickly settled down thereafter and was absolutely no trouble at all – except that she would give a few short sharp barks at 6.30 am to remind me that it was time to go for a walk. I walked her on the lead for the first two weeks and then, somewhat apprehensively, let her run free. I need have had no qualms, as she proved to be the most obedient hound I have ever had and responded immediately when I called her. In the open field she ran circuits out of pure joy but, when she had done, she ran quietly back and trotted after me as if on the lead. She was comfortable with other dogs of all sizes, but she did show early on that she was a hunter. She ran off one day into a clump of trees and bushes and returned with a squirrel in her mouth, which she dropped neatly at my feet. Her greatest ambition each day is to repeat that feat, and she has done so from time to time.

I was, of course, curious to know more about *Milly's* background, as most Greyhounds in rescue are around five to six years old at the end of their racing career and she was clearly much younger. Battersea had given me only an approximate date of birth, and no other details. However, like all Greyhounds, she had a registration number tattooed in both ears, which indicated that she was Irish, as British hounds are tattooed in only one ear. I sent an email to the Irish Coursing Club to see if the number could be traced, and within 24 hours I had back her five-generation racing pedigree. She was registered as *Fiona's Blau* and was only 22 months old. What the Irish could not tell me was how she had ended up in rescue. I made some deductions myself over the following year.

At first, I treated her just like a Saluki, but I soon discovered how different she was. I had, of course, seen many Greyhounds run and had even coursed with them, but I had never studied one closely before. The big difference was her lack of stamina. She would run a few circuits and would be breathing like a steam engine. I thought initially that this was simply because she was out of condition. I even took her to see my vet after a run, but he said everything was in good order, though her temperature was elevated. This was normal in Greyhounds after exercise, but it confirmed that she would not be able to cope with prolonged running. I used to cycle with my Salukis for miles, but *Milly* clearly would not be capable of that. Then I noted how fragile her feet and legs were by comparison with my Salukis. In the course of her first year with us, she has twice sustained badly cut pads needing stitches under full anaesthetic, as well as painful injuries to her legs and shoulders. So, my guess is that she never made the grade as a racer.

However, we got her as a companion and in this she excels. She has learnt our ways very quickly and has adapted smoothly to her very different surroundings. She protects the garden from some of the depredations of the foxes and squirrels and is a good watchdog in the house. She keeps us active with a regular exercise regime and always responds appreciatively to a little care and attention. We are lucky; and so is she!

Glossary of names in the text

Abu Nab – Father of the fang
Amina – Faithful
Amira – Princess
Antar – Name of a celebrated hero and poet
Barhush – Lurcher (Morocco)
Basma – Smile
Battah – Thrower down
Bora – Typhoon (Turkish)
Brjaa' – Beautiful eyes
Dabbouh – Slaughterer
Dhiba – She-wolf
Doughan – Falcon (Kurdish)
Douman – Everlasting
Fahda – Lioness
Farhud – Lion cub
Fazza – Darter
Filfil – Pepper
Fitna – Trouble
Ghalies – Tiger (Morocco)
Ghazal – Gazelle
Guru – Wolf (Kurdish)
Haddad – Blacksmith
Hamra – Red
Hawa – Wind
Hizza – Lively
Jazzar – Butcher
Jdiya – Active
Jinah – Wing
Kalb – Dog
Khamleh – Scent of the garden
Khattaf – Snatcher
Khowla – Dancer
La'aban – Playful
Lahhaq – Overtaker
Laila – Night

La'iq – Worthy
Lam'ah – Shining
Luqi – Lurcher (colloquial)
Maha – Dark eyes, or oryx
Mani'a – Forbidding
Mirya – Bellwether
Moda – Merry (?)
Najma or Najmah – Star
Naseem – Desert breeze (m.)
Nisma – Desert breeze (f.)
Qais – Name of a tribe
Qannas – Hunter
Qassab – Butcher
Qaysar – Caesar
Raddad – Retriever
Raddeh – Steadfast
Rakkala – Kicker
Rihan – Sweet basil
Rishan – Feathered
Rogo – Kurdish name
Saddah – Killer
Sa'ida – Happy
Salam – Peace
Sami – High, superior
Sarukh – Rocket
Saqlawiya – Polished or burnished
Shahin – Falcon
Shatoob – Fine stature
Showha – Kite (bird)
Tarrah – Flinger
Tayra – Bird
Toufan – Typhoon (Persian)
Warda – Rose
Walla' – Ardent
Ziwa – Silver (Kurdish)

Annex

Texts used as chapter headings

Chapters One to Eleven:
I will sing the praises of a hound whose owners'
Good fortune is assured by his strenuous efforts.
All the good things they have come from him;
His master is always his slave.
At night the master brings him nearest to his bed;
If he is uncovered, his master puts on him his own coat.
He has a blaze and his legs are white;
His excellent conformation is pleasing to the eye.
What fine jaws he has! What a fine muzzle!
Gazelles are really in trouble when he is hunting!
What a fine hound you are, without equal!

Abu Nuwas

Chapters Twelve to Sixteen and Tailpiece:
My guest is guided through the perils of the night
By my brightly burning fire or the barking of my dogs,
And when they see him and recognise him,
They deliver him with their wagging tails.
When they recognise him, they lead him in,
Almost speaking their welcome!

Abu 'l-Fadl Ahmad bin Abi Tahir

وقال أبو نواس

أنعت كلبا أهله من كده

قد سعدت جدودهم بجده

فكل خير عندهم من عنده

يظل مولاه له كعبده

يبيت أدنى صاحب من مهده

و ان عرى جلله ببرده

غرة محجلا بزنده

تلذ منه العين حسن قده

يا حسن شدقيه و طول خده

تلقى الظباء عنتا من طرده

يا لك من كلب نسيج وحده

و قال أبو الفضل أحمد بن أبي طاهر

و يدل ضيفي في الظلام اذا سوى

ايقاد ناري أو نباح كلاب

حتى اذا واجهنه و عرفنه

فدينه ببصابص الأذناب

وجعلن مما قد عرفن يقدنه

ويكدن ان ينطقن بالترحاب

Bibliography

Ahrens, Kristen D. 'Deciphering the genetic history of an ancient dog breed, the Saluki, using Y chromosome autosomal microsatellites, and mitochondrial DNA'. Thesis presented to the faculty of the Department of Biological Sciences, California State University, Sacramento, Summer 2016.

Ahsan, M.M. *Social Life Under the Abbasids*. Longman, London, 1979.

Allan, Diana & Allan, Ken. *The complete Saluki*. Ringpress Books, Letchworth, 1991.

Allen, Mark. *Falconry in Arabia*. Orbis Publishing Ltd., London, 1980.

Allen, Mark & Smith, G. Rex. 'Some notes on hunting techniques and practices in the Arabian Peninsula'. In Serjeant, R.B. & Bidwell, R.L. (eds) *Arabian Studies*, Vol. II. Hurst & Co. London, 1975.

Amherst, Florence. 'Oriental Greyhounds'. In *Cassell's New Book of the Dog*, 1907.

Amirsadeghi, Hossein. *Sky Hunters: The Passion of Falconry*. TransGlobe Publishing Ltd., London, 2008.

Bell, Florence (ed.). *The Letters of Gertrude Bell*, Vol. II. Ernest Ben Ltd., London, 1927.

Bell, Gertrude. *Amurath to Amurath*. Heinemann, London, 1911.

Blunt, Anne. *A Pilgrimage to Nejd*. John Murray, London, 1881.

Blunt, Anne & Blunt, Wilfred Scawen. *The seven golden odes of pagan Arabia, known also as the Moallakat*. Chiswick Press, 1903.

Brewer, Douglas, Clark, Terence and Phillips, Adrian. *Dogs in Antiquity: Anubis to Cerberus – The Origins of the Domestic Dog*. Aris & Phillips, Warminster, 2001.

Clark, Terence. 'Saluqis in Oman and the Lower Gulf', in Goodman, Gail (ed.) *The Saluqi: Coursing Hound of the East*. Midbar Inc., Apache Junction, AZ, 1995.

Clark, Terence. 'The Eastern Saluki: past and present'. *Asian Affairs*, Vol. XXX, Issue 1, 1999, 65–72.

Clark, Terence & Derhalli, Muawiya. *Al-Mansur's Book On Hunting*. Aris & Phillips, Warminster, 2001.

Clutton-Brock, Juliet. *Iraq*, Vol. LI. British School of Archaeology, 1989.

Cole, Donald P. *Nomads of the Nomads: The Al Murrah Bedouin of the Empty Quarter*. Aldine Publishing Co., Chicago, 1975.

Dickson, H.R.P. *The Arab of the Desert*. Allen & Unwin, London, 1949.

Duggan, Brian Patrick. *Saluki: The Desert Hound and the English Travelers Who Brought It to the West*. McFarland & Co. Inc., Jefferson, NC, 2009.

Gie, Daphne. *The Complete Afghan*. David & Charles, Newton Abbot, 1978.

Giudicelli, Bernard. 'Situation actuelle du Sloughi en Algérie'. Thesis presented to Université Claude Bernard, Lyon, 1975.

Goodman, Gail (ed.). *The Saluqi: Coursing Hound of the East*. Midbar Inc., Apache Junction, AZ, 1995.

Herzfeld, Ernst. *Ausgrabungen von Samarra Band III, Die Malereien von Samarra*. Verlag Dietrich Reimer, Berlin, 1927.

Houlihan, Patrick F. *The Animal World of the Pharaohs*. Thames and Hudson, London, 1996.

Lawrence, T.E. *Seven Pillars of Wisdom: A Triumph*. Cape, London, 1935.

Lloyd, Seton. *The Interval: A life in Near Eastern Archaeology.* Alden Press, Oxford, 1949.

Lovell, Mary S. *A Scandalous Life: The Biography of Jane Digby el Mazrab.* Richard Cohen Books, London, 1995.

Maclean, Fitzroy. *Eastern Approaches.* Jonathan Cape Ltd., London, 1949.

Miguil, Ali. 'Contribution à l'étude du Sloughi au Maroc'. PhD dissertation presented to Institut Agronomique et Vétérinaire Hassan II, Rabat, 1986.

Moser, Henri. *Durch Central-Asien: die Kirgisensteppe, Russisch-Turkestan, Bochara, Chiwa, das Turkmenenland und Persien.* Brockhaus, Leipzig, 1888.

Muhammad Ibn Khallaf Ibn al-Marzuban. *The Book of the Superiority of Dogs over many of Those who wear Clothes.* Tr. Smith, G. Rex and Abdel Haleem, M.A.S. Aris & Phillips, Warminster, 1978.

Munro, Alan. *Keep the Flag Flying: A Diplomatic Memoir.* Gilgamesh Publishing, London, 2012.

Parker, Heidi G. et al. 'Genetic structure of the purebred domestic dog'. *Science* 304(5674), 1160–4, 2004.

Philby, H. St John. *The Empty Quarter.* Constable & Co. Ltd., London, 1933.

Przezdziecki, Xavier. *Le Destin des Lévriers*, 1984, translated as *Our Levriers: The Past, Present and Future of All Sighthounds.* Les Amis de Xavier Przezdziecki, La Colle sur Loup, 2001.

Rice, Michael. *Swifter Than the Arrow: The Golden Hunting Hounds of Ancient Egypt.* I.B. Tauris, London, 2006.

Sackville-West, Vita. *A Passenger to Tehran.* Hogarth Press, London, 1926.

——. *Faces: Profiles of Dogs.* Doubleday, 1962.

Said, Kurban. *Ali and Nino.* Hutchison, London, 1970.

Serjeant, R.B. *South Arabian Hunt.* Luzac, London, 1976.

Sludsky, Arkady Aleksandrovich. 'The Central Asian Borzaya Taza and hunting with it' [in Russian]. Kazakh Game Hunting Biological Research Station, Alma-Ata, 1935.

Smith, G. Rex. 'The Arabian Hound, the *Salūqi* – further consideration of the word and other observations on the breed'. *Bulletin of the School of Oriental and African Studies*, Vol. XLIII Part 3, 1980, 459–65.

Thesiger, Wilfred. *Arabian Sands.* Longmans Greene, London, 1959.

Waters, Hope & David. *The Saluki in History, Art and Sport* (2nd ed.). Hoflin Publishing Ltd., Wheat Ridge, CO, 1984.

Watkins, Vera H. *Saluki: Companion of Kings.* Fenrose Ltd., 1974 (out of print).

Index

Were it not for the chase, there would be no pleasure –Anon